Inside the Security Mind

Making the Tough Decisions

ISBN 0-13-111829-3

94499

9 780131 118294

Inside the Security Mind

Making the Tough Decisions

KEVIN DAY

PRENTICE HALL
Professional Technical References
Upper Saddle River
www.phptr.com

Library of Congress Cataloging-in-Publication Data

Day, Kevin
    Inside the security mind; making the tough decisions / Kevin Day.
        p.   cm.
    Includes index.
    ISBN 0-13-111829-3
     1. Computer security. I. Title.

QA76.9.A25D39 2003
005.8--dc21   2002192976

Editorial/production supervision: *Techne Group*
Executive editor: *Mary Franz*
Manufacturing manager: *Alexis R.Heydt*
Manufacturing buyer: *Maura Zaldivar*
Cover design director: *Jerry Votta*
Art Director: *Gail Cocker-Bogusz*
Editorial assistant: *Noreen Regina*
Marketing manager: *Dan DePasquale*
Full-service production manager: *Anne Garcia*

Prentice Hall books are widely used by corporations and government agencies for training, marketing, and resale. The publisher offers discounts on this book when ordered in bulk quantities. For more information, contact Corporate Sales Department, Phone: 800-382-3419; FAX: 201- 236-7141; E-mail: corpsales@prenhall.com
Or write: Prentice Hall PTR, Corporate Sales Dept., One Lake Street, Upper Saddle River, NJ 07458.

Other company and product names mentioned herein are the trademarks or registered trademarks of their respective owners.

Printed in the United States of America

ISBN 0-13-111829-3

Pearson Education LTD.
Pearson Education Australia PTY, Limited
Pearson Education Singapore, Pte. Ltd.
Pearson Education North Asia Ltd.
Pearson Education Canada, Ltd.
Pearson Educación de Mexico, S.A. de C.V.
Pearson Education—Japan
Pearson Education Malaysia, Pte. Ltd.

To Joselhyt for her inspiration
To Michael and Sandra for their support
To Grand Master Choa for his wisdom

About Prentice Hall Professional Technical Reference

With origins reaching back to the industry's first computer science publishing program in the 1960s, and formally launched as its own imprint in 1986, Prentice Hall Professional Technical Reference (PH PTR) has developed into the leading provider of technical books in the world today. Our editors now publish over 200 books annually, authored by leaders in the fields of computing, engineering, and business.

Our roots are firmly planted in the soil that gave rise to the technical revolution. Our bookshelf contains many of the industry's computing and engineering classics: Kernighan and Ritchie's *C Programming Language*, Nemeth's *UNIX System Adminstration Handbook*, Horstmann's *Core Java*, and Johnson's *High-Speed Digital Design*.

PH PTR acknowledges its auspicious beginnings while it looks to the future for inspiration. We continue to evolve and break new ground in publishing by providing today's professionals with tomorrow's solutions.

PRENTICE
HALL
PTR

Contents

Chapter 7   Know Thy Enemy and Know Thyself   123

Prologue

In the Beginning...

It has been nine years since I first took up the sword to ward off a malicious two-headed hacker that was invading my lands. Over the past nine years I have witnessed a great deal of carnage and gore in the information security world. Securing everything from governments, Fortune 500 companies, health-care giants, medical research institutes, and even the good, old mom-and-pop shops has led me though a long maze of questioning and discovering. I have lived a cycle of life starting from the intrigued beginner, to the sworn hands-on technologist, to the enthused architect, to the senior advisor, and finally, the simple philosopher.

Like many philosophers, I cannot claim the ideas and practices in my book to be my own. They have simply been the inspiration of security related events and studies that have passed before me over the years. Eventually, the mind begins to notice things, patterns to what otherwise seems like simple madness. I began to realize what an incredible tool the recognition of these patterns presented; weapons of defense that can be wielded by everyone, not just by the security experts and the technically elite.

Here, I invite you to use these same weapons to protect your own homeland. The practices contained in this book have been proven time and again in direct combat with the enemy. The companies that have unfixed their eye from the size of their cannons and focused instead on the principles presented here have achieved security without a great deal of effort. For you see, the determining factors in a successful battle are not simply the technologies used, but the planning, strategizing, and decision making that take place before, during, and after the battle is complete.

Today, too many battles have been lost while following the commonly adopted guns and swords of information security. Too much blood has been spilled and too many retreats have been sounded in the chambers of our corporate lords. The first line of this book states, "The time has come for a different way of thinking about information security." What we are about to look into is not really "new" at all, but time honored practices of the ages, simply presented in a new and effective way.

Who Should Read this Book?

Inside the Security Mind was written in such a manner that anyone with the most basic IT knowledge will be able to read it. This was done with great care as I truly believe that everyone associated with technology within an organization should read this book. The chapters build upon constant and universally applicable rules of security that everyone should know and practice. Rather than having to spend years in study or practicing in the industry, however, the reader has only to grasp the concepts presented here. That is the goal of this book, to provide the reader with tools to think like a security expert and to correct the many flaws that currently plague the information security world. As such, I highly encourage the following people to read this book:

IT Managers. This book is designed to help the reader make good, effective, and consistent security decisions without a great deal of study. Today, security should be a concern for all IT-related managers and directors, and for many who are not directly related to IT. Even if you are not responsible for any specific security practice, it is important to protect your department, facility, or corporation from the many security and availability threats in the world. The majority of successful security attacks over the past few years could have been prevented if the local staff only had been aware of security. When the concepts contained herein are understood and practiced, you will become "security aware" without having to take a class or learn how to install a firewall. I highly encourage those in charge of any aspect of IT to read this book and recommend it to your IT employees.

Technical Gurus. As has become obvious over the years, every piece of information technology is in need of security focus. It is impossible to implement a server, router, application, VPN, or wireless extension without affecting the security of the rest of the organization. As such, anyone dealing with technology should have security awareness while performing their daily duties. This book is designed to create a high degree of such awareness and provide tools and techniques that can be applied to every type of technology, whether designing, developing, or implementing it. In the final sections, we will explore several technologies that require the most security care, and we will discuss how to safely implement them. Going far beyond this, however, the guidelines given throughout the book can and should be applied to all technologies. After reading this book, the next time you hook up a router, install a server, or bring up a new WAN link, you will know where to look for the security implications and how they should be addressed, regardless of the specific technology.

Up-and-Coming Security Practitioners. The concepts presented in this book represent the heart and soul of information security. Anyone desiring to be a security professional should become thoroughly familiar with them. So put down that firewall manual, take a break from configuring the IDS sensor, and venture to read what security is all about. This book is probably the quickest way to advance to the next level in your security abilities.

Seasoned Professional Security Practitioners. This will be a great book for building on concepts you probably already have in your head. I have found it of great use to have the concepts that are normally flitting about in the back of the mind, laid out in plain sight. Beyond this, *Inside the Security Mind* provides a great structure for you to build security practices, and is quite helpful in conveying security concepts to your managers, directors, employees, and clients.

How to Read this Book

As you have no doubt concluded, this is probably not going to be your everyday IT reading experience. The style of this book was not adopted just to be cute and friendly, but rather to set the proper mood. In a moment, you will turn to Chapter 1, and you will not find a formal textbook on information security, but a true-to-life guide on surviving in the IT industry. This book requires only that the reader proceed with an open mind and an expectation of something pleasantly different. I would not be surprised if there are sections within this book that contradict the practices you have read or seen in the past, and perhaps, at the conclusion of the book, we will all agree on why.

The book flows linearly with each concept building upon the concepts presented before it. In the beginning, we will cover The Virtues of Security, basic understandings of how security should be embraced within an organization. We will then build upon those virtues to derive The Eight Rules of Security, practical concepts that can be easily applied in just about every situation. Next, you will find higher concepts that build upon the rules, and then, finally, a plethora of practical applications where all of this information is synthesized into real-world uses.

As you can probably guess, this is not a book with which one should skip back and forth through the pages searching for a specific topic. In order to fully understand the recommendations on protecting your VPNs, for example, you must first understand the virtues, rules, and concepts that the recommendation has been built upon. As such, I would highly recommend reading *Inside the Security Mind* in its entirety, even the sections that may not seem to directly apply to your environment. Sections within this book that deal with specific technologies actually apply universally and will often yield information to help apply the same concepts elsewhere.

This brings me to my next point. When reading this book it is crucial to not get to side-tracked with any specific technologies mentioned. While we will certainly delve into specific areas to help hone in the concepts, all sections are built upon the same reasoning, understanding, and philosophy. Thus, while I am saying "a server", it is also applicable to a router, room, application, network, and employee. Our goal here is far more than simply implementing a firewall and monitoring our intrusion detection system.

Making the Tough Decisions

The main goal of this book is to arm you with the ability to make good security decisions in all situations either simple or complex. Because the human thought process is a vastly complex beast, I have attempted to isolate the major points that should always flash through the mind when making a decision. After we have journeyed through the virtues, rules, and higher practices, you will find a short chapter describing how to use this information to make a good security decision. This section is a synthesis of everything that came before it, and is a good example of how one should think with a security mind. If you follow this section with an open mind, you may find that all of your security problems follow a similar flow. You will surely notice that some of the comments I make do not apply in every situation, but the heart of the process is extremely effective in recognizing and solving security problems.

Beginning at the End

As a final thought before venturing on I believe it would be helpful to understand the ultimate purpose of this reading. So, if I may, I invite you to take a glimpse at the conclusion that it may stay in your mind during the gap between page turns.

"To date, security has been a goal unachieved by many organizations. For some, information security appears to be a large, untamable beast that they simply hope will not bite them. As we have seen, though, security is not a monster, but rather a series of interrelated core concepts surrounded by an infinite number of possibilities. By taking our eyes off the infinite possibilities and focusing on the core concepts presented in this book, security becomes a much easier matter to comprehend and deal with. Placing proper focus on daily practices allows organizations to break away from the traditional security nightmares and makes security a natural extension of everyday actions."

"When an organization makes decisions using a developed security mind, it separates itself from the struggles and costs commonly associated with information security. In this infinitely dynamic world of IT, practicing such higher principles of security is the only chance we have to defend ourselves against enemies. If organizations continue to embrace new security technologies without developing a higher understanding of security, the enemies will simply be required to develop new and more clever technologies with which to attack us. However, when organizations begin to develop a security mind, they will begin to transcend such common "thrust and parry tactics," and through these efforts, emerge from the war victorious."

Acknowledgments

To the Artists

I would like to give a special "thank you" to the primary artist, *Steve Chapman,* for perfectly capturing the state of information security in cartoon form, and to the *Chapman Family* for lending him to me. I would also like to thank *Joselhyt* for all of her artwork and for the countless hours of editing torture required to get the knights in print.

To the Peer Reviewers

I want to thank those who gave their valuable time to review the book. *Inside the Security Mind* would not be what it is without the great comments provided by *Ravi Sakaria, Vivek Shivananda, Warwick Ford,* and *Seth Leone.*

Special Thanks to:

Ravi Sakaria and the AIKO Group for the great insight, ideas, and for the long hours

Grand Master Choa Kok Sui for his wisdom and inspiration

Glenn and *Marilag Mendoza* for their energy, guidance, and example

Cynthia de Leone for her vast experience

Mario Giudice, Seth Leone, Tim Fiedorowicz, Dave Shoenfelt, Aaron Stanley, Kevin Gillan, and *Vivek Shivananda* for all their ideas, innovations, and friendship

Mary Franz and *Noreen Regina* for all of their efforts and patience

George McCafferty for his distractions, distractions, and more distractions. *"Great... moat digin'!"*

Cyndi, Casey, and Jimmy for all their support

Michael and *Sandra Day* for making it all possible

And to my wife, *Joselhyt* for all of this and everything else.

Without these people, none of this would have been possible. Thank you!

1 Introduction

THE SECURITY MIND

The time has come for a different way of thinking about information security. The continual challenges of dealing with endless hoards of malicious hackers, seas of vulnerabilities, and a seemingly limitless onslaught of exploits have quickly outdated our common point-and-click security methodologies that leave us just as exposed as yesterday. Security is not a one-dimensional process with a canned solution, but rather a relational process that requires us to adjust our everyday thinking and the thinking of those around us. If a security effort is to be successful and durable without draining vast resources from our organization, it has to be addressed not only in technology, but within the mind.

In this book, we are going to explore the essential principles of information security, which to date have been neglected throughout most of the information technology (IT) world. The methodologies contained within are the time-honored practices that the best security gurus from all ages have followed. This is not a book of new technologies, gadgets, or gismos, but rather a guide to the extremely important foundation of information security presented in a new, effective, and easy-to-comprehend way. The concepts and strategies contained within provide the core tools for you to become a security guru. Those who are already seasoned security practitioners will benefit from the unique and effective way in which these essential practices are presented.

You see, life is not as it once was. There was a time in the not-so-distant past when the only problem with technology was the technology itself. All we had to fear from our systems and networks was that a component would burn out, or that the power would not sustain the massive electrical needs of our precious systems. Technology was far too complex to be understood by most people, least of all end-users. Today, however, as our technologies have become stronger, more modular, easier to use, and more reliable, this is no longer the case. Having overcome many of the hurdles through the use of subtle and durable components, formulized development techniques, and simpler user interfaces, the world of IT has exploded in a remarkably short period of time. Yet this new modern age of information has spawned its own unique set of problems; problems that are gaining more and more public recognition every day as their disastrous effects become more obvious and costly to us all.

As time progresses, we are slowly becoming aware of a battle that is taking place within the IT world. An amazing and infinitely complex mixture of tools, intelligence, emotion, and character wages war in a struggle for resources, power, pride, ego, and survival. An entire social structure exists hidden inside a long series of wires and energy waves that surround our planet. We are witness to a new type of battlefield that is composed of infinite dimensions, with attackers and defenders on the inside, outside, above, below, and spread out around the entire world. There are no easily distinguishable battlelines or territories. There are no rules of war or formal guidelines of conduct. Castles are being constructed, armies mobilized, and great sieges are talking place day and night, unregulated by conventions of modern warfare.

These battles are far larger and have far greater implications than most people imagine. They leave a wake of destruction that is quickly obscured by numerous factors. The amount of time, attention, and money spent hacking into and defending our technologies and data could probably fund several starving nations. And here we are, the readers and the writer, with our organizations, phone lines, employees, and Internet connections, right smack in the middle of one of the most interesting wars in recent history. Are we prepared?

Serious Matters

We are all at risk. This statement is not meant to instill fear, but simply to properly represent the state of IT in our modern world. Security can no longer be a question. It can no longer be ignored, dismissed, or treated like a thorn in our side. At any given moment, an adequate amount of security is all that stands between our precious data and that wave of relentless and talented intruders striking out at our valuable resources. "Why would anyone hack us?" is no longer a defense, and, "Do we really need to secure ourselves?" is no longer a question. We are all targets. We are all vulnerable. We are all under attack, and without security, the only questions are where and when will we be struck, and just how badly will it hurt.

The Fundamental Flaw

Every hour of every day, IT security somewhere is being compromised. Every hour of every day, a company that believes itself to be secure is being hacked. A firewall is bypassed, a password is cracked, and a system is compromised. Despite the billions of dollars poured into the security industry over the years and the general increase in security awareness across the globe, most organizations are still losing their battles. Why?

There is a fundamental flaw with the approach that most organizations adopt when it comes to practicing information security. Our natural tendency is to treat information security like we do many of our other technical practices; throw a lot of money, a handful of technologies, and a lineup of gurus in for a few weeks and then wait for an ending whistle to blow and a nice pie chart to print out. Unfortunately, this is not the way security works.

Achieving Modern Security

Keeping an organization, its information, and its services secure is not simply a matter of money and technical know-how. Knowing how to configure a firewall and a UNIX Web server is NOT security. These, of course, are valuable activities to perform in the process of becoming secure, but they mean nothing if we do not first have the capacity to "think" in terms of security. To be secure, we must grasp the reasoning, philosophy, and logic that exist behind all successful security efforts. It is through this, and only through this, that security can be successfully practiced.

Security is an extremely unique field to study. It is composed of an infinite number of variables, any combination of which could make or break our networks, systems, devices, and organizations. Few technical practices can match the dynamic demands found in information security. This fact can often give one the impression that security is only achievable by experts in the field. We have all heard horror stories about companies with vast security budgets and capabilities that are compromised on a daily basis despite their efforts. Stories like these make us question not only our own security practices, but also whether or not security is even possible to achieve. Why should we go through all the pains of implementing security when even the giants cannot keep hackers from breaking down their front doors?

Security, despite its highly dynamic nature and a plethora of dramatic bad press, IS possible to achieve. It does not require an enormous amount of resources or headaches for an organization to become and remain secure. It is indeed possible to build a secure environment, whether starting from scratch or contending with legacy security issues. It simply requires that focus and attention be placed on the right areas at the correct time, and with the proper thoughts and actions to back them up.

Security should be thought of as an art; it cannot be accomplished through the old "tools and techies" model. An organization should not believe itself to be secure simply because it spends millions on security devices every year. The fact is that having an infinite budget and a large variety of security resources can often be more of a detriment than a benefit in many organizations. Organizations with vast resources at their command are very likely to try to solve security problems by implementing new security toys. I use the word "toy" because a security device, no matter how expensive or complex, is nothing more than a toy if it does not function within a greater security framework. Security cannot be handled exclusively through expensive equipment, as many of us have been led to believe. Security is not a technology; it is a thought process and a methodology. Security within our technologies is nothing until security is within our minds.

Security is achievable, and we can all become secure. Yes, it will require technical talent. Yes, it will require security tools. But to become secure, we must first understand security itself, the essential components that make it what it is, and then use this knowledge to put the proper tools and talents in place. This is how we can achieve security in the modern age of information.

What Is a Security Mind?

Unlike the mind that attempts to solve security issues by placing focus on a multitude of specific details, the security mind is a mind that focuses on what I call the fundamental virtues and rules of security. When someone attempts to focus on the dynamic details in each and every security issue, he or she will undoubtedly get lost in a never-ending pool of elements, making security impossible to achieve. When someone possesses a security mind, however, he or she looks beyond the dynamic elements in each situation and focuses on the virtues and rules, making security decisions that are clear, consistent, and effective. When you possess a security mind, your security solutions are less expensive, extremely effective, consistent, and have extended usefulness.

Security is dynamic by nature. This in turn makes the individual issues fairly complex and difficult to grasp in some situations. The virtues and rules, however, are a set of basic security principles, constant truths of security that stand at the border between good and bad decisions. Learning and practicing these rules can help us to easily and naturally develop an organization's security. This is the meaning of the security mind. This is what we will achieve through the course of this book.

WHERE DO WE START?

Because information security, in its current state, tends to attract its share of negativity and dramatic rumors, our first goal before beginning this journey is to clear our minds of the programming we have received thus far and start with a clean slate. Approaching security with a bad attitude makes it far more difficult to accomplish our goals. So, let's quickly mention a fact that people rarely discuss:

> *Security can be accomplished in any environment. It can be accomplished without monopolizing our time and resources, and without emptying our wallets. It can be accomplished without years of training and without having to know every vulnerability, threat, and countermeasure in existence. When addressed in the correct manner, security simply becomes an extension of our normal operations, and the best protective measures require the least amount of ongoing effort.*

Sound too good to be true? Practicing information security is just like practicing anything else in this world; there are good ways and bad ways of going about it. This book is designed to direct the reader to one of the good ways for practicing security. I say "one of the good ways" because there are indeed many different ways to think about and address security, and many of them are very good. This book simply chooses one of the most effective methods that is applicable to the widest variety of organizations.

Erasing the Programming Around Us

Good security practices mean nothing, of course, if no one hears, understands, or follows them. When starting, one of the most important components of mobilizing an entire organization to follow good information security practices is to vaporize the negative programming about security. From cover to cover, one of our goals in becoming secure is to convince ourselves and those around us that information security does not have to be a great burden. End-users and upper management are extremely prone to negative ideas about security since they are exposed to them day in and day out. How many companies have spent millions on security measures, only to inhibit their daily business practices? How many departments have had to switch to complex and obscure operational practices when security was introduced to the environment? This is somewhere in the minds of most individuals when they hear the word "security." The term "security" is often wrongly considered synonymous with the term "burden."

If a security practice is a great burden, then something is wrong. Security is not effective if it overburdens the end-users or overtaxes the organization's resources. Information security is far too entwined with the human and business aspects of an organization to simply focus on the technologies and policies and not their effects on everything else. Most people know this. But what most don't realize is that security, when applied properly, does not have to impair operations or business.

Knowing Ourselves

Later in this book, I will discuss some techniques for seeing ourselves through the eyes of a hacker. In the beginning, however, we really need to focus on knowing our organizations through the eyes of the owners, customers, and investors. Proper security always reflects the environment it is applied to, its assets, goals, and capabilities. *Security cannot be accomplished without first having an understanding of who we are and what we do.* We do not need a degree in business analysis, but we do need to be tuned into the company's motives and operations, more so than one may think an IT employee would.

Knowing ourselves at this level does not mean we need to search the entire complex and figure out what every switch and knob does. Our goal is far less formal and more effective. We simply need to talk to people. Here are some suggestions for anyone wanting to practice information security within their organization or within their client's organization.

I am often amazed at how many companies hire consultants to come in and "implement security," without ever going through a process to convey what it is that the organization does. This is not necessarily the fault of the organization, or even the consulting companies who have had to cater to this type of expectation over the years. Performing a business impact analysis or developing a risk model for an organization can often sound like a hustle or an attempt to bleed more money out of the client. It is very difficult to explain the need for such measures when ulterior motives are always in question. Here I will say, without a single hidden agenda, "You can't secure what you don't know about!" If an organization chooses to bring in security consulting services for any major security project, time must be spent coming to a mutual understanding of the organization. If an organization chooses to solve all its security issues using internal staff, the leaders of that staff should have a clear understanding of how the organization functions, its drivers, and its goals.

Some Important Information to Know

This is a short list, but it should cover the main information we need to get started:

1. What is the main product, focus, or drive for the organization? This will probably have multiple answers, in which case, it is a good idea to get a sense of the priorities within each answer.
2. What are the main sources of revenue for the organization?
3. What are the different departments and their main functions? How do they operate and fit together in the bigger picture?
4. What information assets are seen as the most critical to each department, and what technologies does the organization rely on?
5. Who are the customers, partners, and major vendors for the organization and how do they interact?

Where to Get This Information

The information listed above can be discovered in several different ways. This is where we put on our detective hats; only we don't need to go diving into any dumpsters for information, since there are many readily available sources for answering our questions. Remember as we go forward that the more human interaction we have, the better. Security is always an interactive process, and it is essential that we make contact with as many people in as many roles as possible. The more people we are on good terms with, the more allies we will have when fighting the security battle. Here are some good sources to find key information about your organization.

1. Read press about the organization. The media has a knack for focusing on areas that are important to an organization. You can learn a lot by reading how others perceive the organization and in what they are most interested. If the organization is public, check out press about its stock, earnings, and management goals.

2. Talk to the local IT staff. Learn about the different types of systems, and how they operate, as well as where the largest percentage of resources are allocated.

3. Hold conversations with different department managers. Ask about their operations, what they do, their priorities, and what they see as the most important function of their environment. (Be sure they know you are further expanding your knowledge, and are not doing an audit or assessment of their positions.)

4. When you have enough information and a good sense of the business, talk to the highest level executive available who is comfortable with answering your questions and has the time. In my experience, most executives are quite enthusiastic about people taking such an interest, as long as you do your studying beforehand. It is usually best to keep the conversation informal, but to have some predefined questions ready for the discussion.

Knowing We Are Ready

Take another deep breath. Having cleared our minds of negative programming and learned a little about the environment, we are now ready to move forward. The basic understanding derived from these previous few pages has already put us way ahead of the majority of information security practices going on in the world. By coming to a clearer understanding of the environment and removing some of the misnomers that negatively affect progress, we will easily overcome many of the obstacles that trip up other security practitioners. Now, let's dig a little deeper.

WHERE DOES IT END?

In contemplating the question "So where does all this end?" there is good news and bad news. The bad news is that it never ends. We will always need to think about security.

We will always need to update, modify, enhance, and grow our practices, technologies, and knowledge. We will always need to have a security staff, train our end-users, and be mindful of the evil, fang-toothed malefactors knocking at our doors.

The good news is that, if we do it right, effectively maintaining security from here until the end of time should be relatively easy and inexpensive. As has been proven time and again, companies that begin with and maintain good security practices can go hackerless for years without placing excessive resources into their security practices. Once the fundamental security concepts are known and practiced, security can be treated (for the most part) as a branch of the normal routine. As time goes on, as technology evolves, and as our ambitions and environments expand, we certainly will have to make updates, take classes, and read new books. We should never, however, need to overhaul our security infrastructure, or perform massive recovery because we were wiped out in a malicious attack.

Sunny Skies Ahead

Before we begin discussing the principles behind the security mind, it is important that we all agree on one major concept: It will never end. No matter how good our security is, it will always need to be maintained and improved. So the question is not, "When does it end?" but rather, "Where does the struggle end?"

Just as it is important to understand that security is an ongoing process, it is equally important to understand that *maintaining good security practices does not have to be an ongoing struggle*. No doubt about it, securing an organization can be difficult in the beginning. However, the horror stories we hear about companies spending endless amounts of time and effort and still getting hacked are almost all from the same source: companies that do not think with a security mind.

Don't get discouraged while reading the latest magazine article reporting that even the FBI is getting hacked. And don't let the employees, managers, or executives become pessimistic about adopting security practices. It is well within our capabilities to maintain a high level of security and go for long periods of time without being compromised. It is ultimately the organization's choice to struggle or not, to adopt good security practices or bad ones.

2 A New Look at Information Security

SECURITY AS AN ART FORM

Security is a very different world than that of networking, systems, engineering, and other related technical fields. Let's consider a few of its differences:

- The practices and specializations of information security have had a fascinating, though fairly short history.
- Security is by far the most widely discussed, argued, and debated topic in IT today.
- There are still many different opinions concerning the proper methods and procedures for evaluating, applying, and enforcing information security in home systems, companies, and governments.
- The market for security products and technical engineers with security experience has remained relatively strong, even when other technology industries have witnessed tremendous instability.
- Security is a technical practice that is more human-focused, involving creative forces on both sides of each situation.

Ever wonder why security systems and services seem to cost so much more than other services? Ever wonder why it's hard to find and retain good security engineers? Let's take a moment to explore and understand why this practice is so different and why it must be handled in a manner quite different from how we handle other technical issues.

The Youngest of the IT Practices

Information security, as a widely recognized practice, has only been known to the public for about a decade. Earlier than this, one of our first indications of how completely vulnerable our systems were came in 1988, when a little program (less than 100 lines of code) that we now refer to as the Morris Worm was released on the Internet. Taking advantage of simple security holes in specific UNIX platforms, the worm was successfully able to attack over 50,000 systems across the U.S., causing millions of dollars in damages. Here I use the term "successfully" very loosely because it is commonly believed it was not the intention of the worm's creator to do any harm at all. Regardless, it was considered the disaster of the time and it opened our eyes to the incredible insecurity of our systems, networks, and information.

Of course, this was not the first information security incident to occur, but it was certainly the one that caught the attention of the media and the world. Still, it was not until the mid-1990s that the average company considered information security as something of any value to them. And, it was still not until the late 1990s that the marketplace for information security began to explode with hundreds of organizations making new security gadgets and just about every consulting organization rushing to market their new security practices. Today, security is still very much in its youth, and as such, many of its concepts and theories have not stood the test of time nor become commonplace. Approaches to security still vary widely from organization to organization and from practitioner to practitioner. And, as if things were not difficult enough, there is still a lack of security expertise in the world.

Information security is just now reaching the stage where it has sprung legs and is making great leaps forward. All around the world, information security professionals, high-tech companies, and even some government agencies are racing forward in an attempt to keep one second ahead of the hacker community, dragging the security of the common company slowly in their wake.

Still, at any moment of any day, you can sit at your desk with a digital subscriber line (DSL) connection to the Internet and find vulnerable systems around the world within a matter of minutes or hours. Every day, new organizations are implementing one-time security measures without adopting good security practices and are left, unknowingly, with useless toys "protecting" their network. These are signs that security, though making incredible strides, has yet to truly mature beyond the boasting hype of eager vendors and hotshot consulting companies.

The Most Dynamic IT Practice

It can be easily argued that security is one of the most dynamic fields we have ever seen within IT. Several facts indicate that it will remain an extremely fast-paced and dynamic practice for the foreseeable future:

- For every security professional trying to secure something, there are about a hundred hackers out there trying to break it. With so many thousands of people from all over the world finding new ways to wreak havoc on the technology, vendors have to make hundreds of security modifications and enhancements every month.

- Every new piece of technology that is developed has some security implication. This means that every time there is a major change to any device, operating system, service, or application, there is a potential change in its security, and for every new technology that is developed, there is a security aspect to be considered. Every time a new business model intersects with technology, security must be addressed. This shows us that, no matter how fast technology moves, security practices must be able to stay one step ahead. Not only does security have to race forward with its own innovations, it must also keep pace with the growth in every other area of technology as well.

Looking at the extremely dynamic nature of information security tends to send many would-be security practitioners running for the hills. The dynamics of the industry dictate that we cannot simply follow the standard, conventional means that we use to deal with other technologies. An interesting fabrication has developed over the history of technology saying that, "The person who knows the most technical formulas and tricks is the better technologist." While this may be true in some fields, it has little relevance in the world of information security. To know every little trick is quite impossible since there can be hundreds of variations of the same attack, affecting any number of unknown vulnerabilities and every type of system in its own unique way. This makes it quite impossible to keep pace with the world of security by focusing strictly on the technical details. In fact, those individuals and organizations that choose to deal with security by focusing on the details and case-by-case issues most often make themselves quite miserable by creating unending workloads, resulting in a total lack of sleep and weekend time.

To properly assess and apply security in any environment, a global approach must be taken, transcending the millions of detailed security facts at hand. This, for many professionals and organizations, can be quite difficult to assimilate. Because it is impossible to stay secure when all eyes are on the firewall, the intrusion detection system (IDS), or the event viewer, people can be left with a very uncertain feeling about the safety of their information. To keep up with the dynamics of security, a practitioner must grow eyes in the back of his or her head and be able to think of the organization as a whole, not as a series of isolated vulnerabilities and fixes. Dealing with the dynamic nature of security is not for the faint of heart.

And About Those Humans

This may not be the most obvious of considerations, but it is one of the most powerful elements shaping the practice of security worldwide. In the history of IT, the focus has almost always been on human vs. machine. A programmer will sit in the corner and beat his or her head against the monitor for hours while trying to make the computer act in a new and improved way. A network engineer consoles into his or her router for days on end trying to change the way in which the traffic flows between devices. In both of these cases, it is a story of a human pitted against a machine in a battle of wits and determination, a classic struggle between the creative and the logical.

But the world of information security is dramatically different. Sure we have the computers and devices to contend with, but the true obstacle we are attempting to overcome is another living human being. It is no longer a battle of a human's creativity against a machine's predictable logic; it is now an *unpredictable battle between two equally creative and dynamic forces*: creativity vs. creativity! Where before the machine was the ultimate goal, here the machine functions as an extension to assist in the other creative processes taking place, much like a sword to a

Samurai. This is one of the most defining differences between the art of practicing security and the art of nearly any other IT practice.

WHAT WE KNOW ABOUT SECURITY

You will notice that throughout this book, I refer to this area of study as "the WORLD of information security." The term "world" has been used intentionally since there is a whole world found within the topic. While exploring security, we will discover fascinating subcultures of security practitioners and hackers who have propagated and spread, uninhibited by international or geographic boundaries. Continually innovative and relentless in their initiatives, their growing numbers constantly wage war with and against each other in every corner of the globe. For simplicity's sake, I will talk about these parties as the "good" and the "evil" sides of information security, the security practitioners and the hackers, respectively. There are many gray and colorful shades between the good and the bad, all of which are quite fascinating, but would simply serve to confuse the issue and distract from the focus. So for now, we will just consider them the "good guys" and the "bad guys."

The Good Guys

Simply put, WE are the good guys. By "we," I am referring to the individuals and groups of professional and amateur security practitioners working to protect the safety of IT within our own arenas. Our motivations range widely, often centering on a sense of challenge, a few noble ideals, and a desire for high compensation, benefits, and job security. Unfortunately for us, and certainly to the detriment of the security world, the desire for high compensation and profitable business tends to make the process of securing something much more expensive than the process of hacking it. Sure, security can provide a sense of nobility and truth. I rarely find security professionals who are not happy in their jobs; however, if this was the primary motivation for security professionals, then the security industry would not be the cash cow it currently is. And while a security consultant can be expensive, hackers normally work for free or even at their own expense. While popular firewalls cost many thousands of dollars, almost all hacker tools are free or extremely cheap. We will discuss this in Chapter 7, *Know Thy Enemy and Know Thyself*.

The good guys remain a strong force in the world of information security. On a global scale, however, we have only been effective in the pockets where security is practiced wisely and regularly. The majority of organizations and home users on this planet still maintain little to no security, thus providing an unending number of targets for the bad guys and a wide variety of problems for the rest of us. Government and law enforcement organizations are doing a great job with their limited funding and resources, but the budgets for information security enforcement seems far too low to be effective on a massive scale. Government institutes, in general, rely on patriotism to attract good security professionals rather than high salaries. This leaves most of the extremely talented good guys working for independent companies and not necessarily participating in the larger security community. As it stands, fighting cyber crime can be accurately compared to fighting terrorism with a bunch of neighborhood watch programs. We all have our own little neighborhoods we are watching, in case someone targets our block.

Most of the people involved in the technical world, however, seem to be in the process of becoming security-aware and are helping to make great strides in fighting this war. Beyond the tremendous growth we have seen in the average individual user, there is also a spirit of group effort in the form of non-profit organizations and semi-formal collaborations between talented security professionals. These groups work to fight crime and plan security for the sake of the whole, not just their own neighborhood. We are indeed progressing and managing to keep pace, in many respects, with the bad guys.

The Bad Guys

Vastly outnumbering the good guys, bad guys come in all shapes and sizes, from different backgrounds, levels of education, and social classes. They can be sitting across the world from us, or they could be our oldest and most trusted employees. It is important for those practicing security to have a good understanding of these individuals and groups, their resources, capabilities, and motivations. Chapter 7 is dedicated to understanding how these people think and operate; but for now, we will keep it simple.

The enemies in the world of information security are those who desire to gain access to and/or manipulate our electronic services and information against our will and without our permission. In general, the bad guys can operate with very little overhead requirements. A basic computer, an Internet connection, a phone line, and a lot of time are about all that is needed to be a successful hacker. The tools and talents can be acquired by most technically-minded people quickly and easily through hacker Web sites, forums, and chat groups.

Unfortunately, a hacker with a $1,500 budget and a few months of effort can often effectively wage war against companies with millions invested in security. It is important to understand that organizations have to spread focus across a million possible vulnerabilities, while the hacker only has to focus in on the one that was missed or not secured properly. Even worse, the average employee hacker can operate with no budget at all! We will discuss all of this in more detail later. For now, it is important to remember that the good guys are greatly outnumbered, and that while securing something can be resource-intensive, hacking into it simply requires time. For every hour spent securing something in this world, there may be thousands of hours spent trying to find a way into it.

Of course, there are many different types of hackers, each with his or her own set of motivations, resources, and each posing a different threat to an organization. There are a number of very distinct cultures that exist within the realm of the bad guys, some of which are quite fascinating and some of which are quite pathetic. The neat technical tools we saw in spy movies a few years ago comprise the stuff that professional criminals are actually using today. At the same time, the computer nerd that breaks into the mega-huge company using a shoestring and a stick of gum can also come true. Every place you look, everywhere you turn, there seems to be a bad guy. Chances are that everyone reading this book knows someone who is or has been a hacker at some point in time.

Our Abstract Battleground

Now that we have taken a peek at the two warring parties, let's take a moment to reflect on the physical reality behind the information security battlefield. All devices operate and communicate through a series of electrical pulses, mostly ones and zeros. When a person spends all of his or her time and creative effort trying to hack into a computer, he/she is simply trying to determine the correct combination of electrical pulses that will serve his/her needs. The good guys, on the other hand, spend all of their time and attention regulating the sequences of electrical pulses entering the environment to guard against attacks. Can you imagine the millions of dollars some companies spend simply to regulate the small pulses of energy coming into their information storage centers?

So next time someone asks you what your job is, you can safely say, "I work to make sure that only authorized and expected sequences of energy pulses come into contact with our information devices." This certainly does not make information security any easier to comprehend, however.

Is Anyone Winning?

There was a time in the not-too-distant past when it was extraordinarily easy to hack into a company, steal or manipulate its data, and then get out clean and easy without a trace. This could be accomplished through a simple program that could have been created in a matter of hours. Fortunately, the idea of malicious hacking was not as widespread back then as it is today.

By taking a closer look, it would appear that the world of the good guy and the world of the bad guy are synchronized. It can certainly be viewed as a symbiotic relationship, each party needing the other to exist. Through this reflecting relationship, we are all growing together. The newest form of attack is always matched by the newest form of defense, and vice versa. Any group making a great leap in technology spawns a great leap on behalf of the other party. The more agencies and governments that get involved in the battle, the more motivation there is for hackers to increase their efforts. Thus, no group seems to ever win or lose, but we all simply remain in a stalemate of thrust and parry.

This does not mean, however, that there are not losers in these battles. Unfortunately, most organizations, including software and hardware manufacturers, deal with security on a reactive basis. As the ability to hack and secure make great leaps forward, the mass population tends to wait until it feels the knifepoint of the attacker before bothering to discover it has fallen far behind in its security practices. Saying that security and hacking seem to be in a stalemate does not mean that the average organization can say the same. *While the technologies and methodologies tend to balance out, the rest of the world is still on the losing end of the battle.*

UNDERSTANDING THE FEAR FACTOR

As a general rule of thumb, fear plays a large part in the security decision-making process for most people. You may be surprised to find a section dedicated to fear in an information security book, but in reality, fear and information security go hand-in-hand. Throughout its existence, security has been primarily driven by fear: fear of unknown people lurking in the dark corners of the Internet; fear of the thousands of malicious applications that can devastate an unprepared company; fear that the computers and networks we have grown to completely rely on can be influenced by invisible forces unknown to us; fear that this could be happening anytime, anywhere, through any series of circumstances, and that we could be completely unaware of it. Open any magazine article or vendor advertisement on security and it will almost certainly begin with some fearful tale of what could happen to an organization. It is in reaction to fear that most security decisions are made today. This has had both positive and negative effects on our industry.

Positive Effects of the Fear Factor

Of course, there are some positive things we gain from this fear factor. Many organizations and their various directors would never give security a second thought if not for the fear of losing everything through a security breach. Tell the average top executive that he or she needs a firewall, and he/she will give it the same priority as ordering a new desktop computer for the sales group. But, show him/her the other organizations that have lost millions from basic security breaches and you may even be granted overnight shipping. Fear has managed to spread security through many locations that otherwise would never have created the budget or taken the effort to secure themselves. In this way, the fear factor has certainly had positive effects.

Negative Effects of Security Fears

Unfortunately, the negative effects of fear have had an even more profound effect on the course of information security within the average organization. Human fear is an emotional process that does not normally inspire the most accurate or wisest of decisions. The greatest thinkers in the world can still make bad decisions when succumbing to fear, be it on the road, in the battlefield, or in cyberspace. When we humans fear something, the automatic reaction is to push the issue away, have someone or something else take care of it, and then blindly accept the solution. Out of fear of hackers, organizations tend to run to the first vendor with a security solution and colorful slideshow. This type of re-action most often leaves them as vulnerable as they were to start with, only with an ex-pensive new toy making them feel more comfortable. Decisions made from fear often lead us to accept quick solutions that really provide no remedy to the problems at hand.

Fear of risks and threats to information lead all too often to the implementation of bad security practices. When humans fear something, the natural instinct is to run. Unfortunately, the direction in which we run is not always the wisest path to take, and may end up getting us in worse trouble than we were in originally. When inspired by fear, it is very easy for us to narrow our focus on anything that is expensive and has a security label on the front, especially when it is endorsed by known organizations and consultants. Such products may or may not help in specific situations, but have no chance of handling all security issues. Making information security decisions out of fear puts us at a much higher risk of making the wrong choices.

Marcus Ranum wrote a good article about the concepts of fear and hype in in-formation security; as of this publication, it can be read at: www.ranum.com/pubs/dark/index.html

Combating the Fear Factor

One of the goals of this book is to help the reader make wise security decisions, that are derived from logical conclusions and not from fear. Security is at its peak when all the facts are present, and rational decisions are made without any intervention from fear.

Fear has its weaknesses. Ultimately, it can be conquered through knowledge. Using the knowledge presented in this book, you will be able to combat the fear factor through the development of a security mind.

HOW TO SUCCESSFULLY IMPLEMENT AND MANAGE SECURITY

Thus far, we have been reviewing some basic information about the problems faced in the world of information security. The purpose of this book is not, however, to dwell on the problems of the world, but rather to help solve them. So now, let's store all this infor-mation in the back of our minds, breathe in some clean, fresh air, and get our hands dirty with what we came here for: solutions. How do we successfully implement and manage security? How do we work to overcome the failings of the commoner's security practic-es? It's time we begin to look at the security mind.

Yes, you too can be secure. It can it be done, and indeed it has been done time and again. Some organizations with the smallest IT budget imaginable have maintained consistently strong security practices. There have been international giants who have managed to maintain a strong level of security across their many organizations with minimal effort, impact, and cost. Of course, there have also been a fair number of Fortune 500 companies with unlimited funding and resources for security that still could not keep a cow out of their building. So what's the trick? What is the difference between the organization that is secure and the organization that becomes a hacker's playground? How do some companies seem to maintain strong security practices with minimal resources while others spend millions in defenses with no effect? It's all about focus.

Security Focus

Yes, large budgets are nice to have, and the line of security experts at the office door asking for employment is great, but these things mean nothing if an organization does not first become security–focused. It is similar to building a castle: We take a plot of land, erect some 50-foot stone walls, dig a huge moat, and pay people to sit in the towers with bows and arrows and shoot anything that swims. Having followed the manual "Securing the Castle, Step-by-Step," we are quite confident in our defensive capabilities. So, the following day, our king decides to celebrate with some games and a festival. He orders that unsightly moat to be covered up, the catapults to be filled with potted plants, and the walls to be lowered, providing easy access for the royal guests. When hiring the festival staff, he chooses to put that shady and questionable man who speaks in foreign languages and seems all too interested in where the treasure is hidden in charge of the front gate.

It is easy to see that the security problem with our kingdom has nothing to do with how high we built the walls, how deep we dug the moat, or how strong we made the gate. Our security nightmares have nothing to do with any of our new fortifications or the design of the castle. Our king simply did not maintain a security focus! And, like many organizations today, our king will not give security another thought until his enemies are washing their socks in the royal bathtub.

Following the Virtues and Rules

So what exactly should we focus on to protect ourselves from hackers? To have any hope of being secure, we must focus on a few basic underlying principles of security. Placing our focus on these principles keeps our security practices dynamic, thorough, and simple, and allows us to take a "complete" approach to addressing security issues. This brings us back to the virtues and rules of security.

When a consultant or employee is only able to grasp how to dissect and combat the newest security threat that appeared last week, that individual may be skilled, but the action is of little value in the bigger picture. If, however, someone is able to grasp the concepts, virtues, and rules of security, and prevent a threat before it is even conceived, that person has a security mind. That is the goal of this book: to develop a security mind and help prevent security issues before they are even conceived by attackers.

Security Virtues

There are four underlying virtues of security. If observed and practiced, these virtues will provide the reader with incredible tools for understanding and practicing information security. Virtues are fairly broad in scope and should guide the security practices of everyone within the environment. In the countless instances where I have seen security fall and crumble against opposing forces, it can be traced back to one of these virtues that was not known or practiced. Upholding these virtues is essential to the development of a security mind and the ability to protect ourselves from attack.

Security Rules

The security rules are the fundamental security practices that must be considered when any security decision is made. These are the actual tools, derived from the virtues, which we will use to keep ourselves safe. There are thousands of security decisions to be made in any given year, and no two are exactly alike. It is not advisable, nor indeed possible, for an individual to become an expert in the security practices of each and every information field in existence. Instead, we need to build a fundamental structure through which the best security decisions can be made with the minimal required effort. Thus, we have the development of the security rules. By walking through a logical series of steps related to the rules, we can quickly and easily ascertain the proper security solution in almost any situation. Similar to the virtues, the security rules are fundamental and will help grow the security practices of an environment through logical and dynamic processes. Unlike the virtues, however, the rules are fairly specific in their instruction and execution. If followed correctly, the rules will guide the process of building and maintaining a safe and secure environment. When the rules become incorporated in everyday thought processes, decisions will be in line with the best security practices.

3 The Four Virtues of Security

INTRODUCTION TO THE VIRTUES

Despite what seems to be the popular opinion, security does not have to be a giant burden on the finances or resources of an organization, nor does it have to torment the lives of those charged with maintaining good security practices. Most of what is considered to be "troublesome" in the area of information security can actually be handled by following the simple practices outlined in this book. The simple tricks to security are to be intelligent, thorough, and consistent while maintaining the proper focus. This is not terribly difficult to accomplish, but it does require a new way of thinking about things.

Focusing on the Virtues

Good security is all about proper focus. An incredible amount of money and energy is spent every day implementing individual security measures without ever considering how such measures fit into the overall security profile of an organization. It is imperative that organizations not fall into the trap of focusing on the flashing lights and shiny covers of the newest and most highly advertised security products. We must focus on the concepts that go beyond the technology.

Security in most environments, even large ones, can be successfully implemented and managed when the following guidelines are adopted. I call these guidelines the four virtues of security. To ensure the immediate and long-term security of an organization, the four virtues must be included in every aspect of an organization's IT practices.

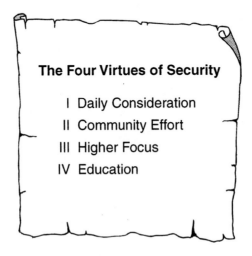

The Four Virtues of Security

I Daily Consideration

II Community Effort

III Higher Focus

IV Education

The four essential virtues of information security are:

- *Virtue I: Daily Consideration*—Security MUST be a daily consideration in every area.
- *Virtue II: Community Effort*—Security MUST be a community effort.
- *Virtue III: Higher Focus*—Security practices MUST maintain a generalized focus.
- *Virtue IV: Education*—Security practices MUST include some measure of training for everyone.

At first glance, these four virtues may seem simple and obvious, and at the risk of dispelling any great mystique surrounding this book, I will certainly agree; they *are* simple. There are enough complicated aspects of security to deal with later, but the virtues constitute the core foundation of all good security practices and must remain simple for us and our communities to contemplate, understand, and exercise. Be careful, though. This level of simplicity should not fool anyone into assuming that an environment is already in line with these ideas, or that these virtues are so simple that you can simply skip ahead to the more technical stuff. The virtues are an essential aspect of any good security practice and they have been included for a very important reason. Now, let's explore these concepts as they relate to the security mind.

THE VIRTUE OF DAILY CONSIDERATION

Making security a daily consideration solves the vast majority of security issues an organization will face. All the talent and wiz-bang technical gadgets in the world will be of little use if they are not used in conjunction with this primary virtue. As we continue through this book, I will delve into several vital concepts for building and maintaining a secure environment. These concepts will prove to be of great value, but only if they are remembered, considered, and practiced on a daily basis.

Within the Virtue of Daily Consideration is the chance for organizations to break away from the fatal patterns that are so easy to fall into. Many organizations avoid addressing security issues because they consider security to be impossible to maintain, requiring an unending cash flow while sucking up valuable time and resources. This negative image of security, however, has only been manifested through numerous organizations that have embraced a "reactive philosophy of security." We can ensure that an organization does not fall into such a trap by promoting a proactive security posture that solves the most common security issues automatically and without effort.

The Seven Steps of Doom

In my experience as a security consultant, the organizations with the most security issues are those that have not followed this virtue. Most of them are locked in a circular bind that drains money and resources while producing no results. Look at almost any company that has sunk large budgets into their security and yet are still vulnerable to attack, and this pattern will appear:

Step 1 Do something without thinking about security.

Step 2 Get hacked.

Step 3 Discover that what was done in Step 1 introduced a security flaw that allowed Step 2 to happen.

Step 4 Secure the organization against the specific attack in Step 2.

This four-step cycle is then followed by a three-step cycle:

Step 5 Wait.

Step 6 Get hacked again.

Step 7 Find out that while waiting in Step 5, another new hack was developed relating to what was done in Step 1.

How simple it all seems, and how simple it all really is. This fatal seven-step process that organizations tend to manifest creates an unending cycle of lost time, lost money, and lost sleep. This is the origin of phrases like the following: "Security is too expensive" and "Security is unachievable." This is a pattern that must be avoided at all costs. Lucky for us, we can easily avoid this vicious circle by simply adopting the proper focus and giving security its daily consideration.

The Three Steps to Success

If we do anything in security—if we could have only one goal to set for our organization that will have the most profound impact—we must simply break away from the seven-step cycle. Avoiding this infinite trap can be accomplished by slightly modifying the first three steps:

Step 1 Think about security.

Step 2 Do something (while still thinking about security).

Step 3 Continue to think about security.

In other words, we can avoid the vast majority of security issues that plague the average organization by making security a daily consideration. Understand that this simple three-step process will take a relatively small amount of time and could prevent most of the attacks that have affected organizations all over the world. To practice these three steps, we simply need to train our minds to think about security at all times. We must maintain a security focus.

Considering Security in Everything

Most security issues are not normally visible or apparent until they are exploited. This is one of those things that keeps security professionals constantly on their toes. *The most devastating security vulnerabilities are the ones that have no obvious relationship to security at all.* When we place a new Internet connection into the network, everyone is jumping and screaming about the security issues. But when a new device is installed with a tunneling capability that bypasses all security, no one thinks twice. The deadliest vulnerabilities are those that don't raise a flag until an attack.

Today, security must be considered in everything and at every moment. Simple objects added to or removed from a network can serve to bypass all the security that has been put in place. Temporarily attaching a modem to a router can bypass hundreds of thousands of dollars of perimeter security devices. We must gain control of our environment by programming this primary security virtue into our minds and the minds of everyone around us.

Practicing This Virtue

The Virtue of Daily Consideration is our only hope of building and maintaining a secure environment. Throughout the rest of this book, I will continue to describe how to make security a daily consideration within an organization, and how to use and reuse simple concepts that will keep an environment safe. For now, here are some simple steps to make security a daily consideration:

- *Make security a continual thought*—As we move forward through this book, visualize each concept as it applies in your daily environment. Think of everything your organization does and make every technical decision with the concept of security in mind. Constantly ask the question, "Could this affect the security of my organization?"
- *Encourage others to be continually mindful of security*—Spread the concept of security to the rest of the organization. Start including the word "security" in everything. Include security references on the intranet home page; have a security "thought of the day" in the weekly employee

newsletter. You can even go so far as to tape little security reminder signs in places where people look. For security to be a daily consideration, the word must be at the tip of the brain at all times, even if it is simply to laugh at the little security sign that someone hangs in the restroo*m*.

- *Formally include security in all new projects*—Add a small addendum called "Security Considerations" to any new project, proposal, or service involving technology in the environment. Those people introducing the concept, as well as those considering it or reviewing it, should be required to discuss and document any potential security side effects. If there are absolutely no security impacts, these same individuals must document this fact to indicate that they have taken security into consideration.

- *Formally include security in all new implementations*—Make it a requirement that, before any new equipment, application, service, or operating system is attached to devices and networks, it must first be approved by someone or go through some formal approval process. This approval process can be extremely fast and easy, but it must include a quick check on the Internet for security issues. You can read more on this in the *Rule of Change* section in the next chapter.

THE VIRTUE OF COMMUNITY EFFORT

In the Virtue of Community Effort, there are two communities that affect and are affected by the security practices within an environment. These are what we call the inner community, which is made up of us, our end-users, and our executives, and the public, or outer community, which consists of the IT world outside of our perimeter boundaries. Each of these communities plays a very large role in the practice of security within an organization.

The idea of security being a community effort cannot be overemphasized. It may not be obvious at first, but the majority of information security issues within systems and networks across the world come from other groups that have failed to participate in either of the security communities.

Our Role in the Inner Security Community

Security cannot be accomplished by security professionals alone. It would be quite impossible for us to widen our focus and watch for every security issue with every system, device, connection, and physical area in an entire environment. It is a fatal flaw I have seen over and over again that security administrators, managers, and chief information officer's (CIOs) desire to work independently of the "troublesome end-users." Involvement of the users is an essential component to the success of any good security practice. The end-users are our valuable allies, our eyes and ears, and indeed, our gatekeepers. Every desktop, phone line, and locked door that is put to use by an end-user is a virtual gateway into the kingdom. It is vital that these people remain on our side of the war.

One of our most important roles of a security practitioner is to *integrate the end-users into the local security practices*. We must empower them to take active roles in the maintenance of security and inspire them to be allies in our cause. I discuss this in more detail later when we discuss education. For now, I will simply express that the end-users can be our best friends or indeed our greatest enemies, depending on how we decide to deal with them, and where and when we decide to include them.

Our Role in the Outer Security Community

Many times, the organization with good security practices is compromised by a lack of security from other organizations that have ineffective or nonexistent security practices. It is nearly impossible to trace good hackers because they operate through a long, winding trail of poorly secured systems and can rarely be traced back to a hideout. Remember those movies where the FBI agents run a phone trace back to the criminal, but it must first bounce through a chain of phone calls through 20 different countries before they find out that he or she is actually calling from a phone booth on the corner? Well, this spy movie tactic is all too real in cyberspace. Most systems that are compromised are simply used to launch other attacks against other systems within other organizations. The first thing a successful hacker will commonly do is usurp a group of poorly secured and "unimportant" systems to act as his or her minions for future attacks. And guess what? Each of these poorly secured systems was administered by someone who did not participate in the outer security community, and now it's becoming *our* problem because their systems are now attacking *us*.

Our role in the outer security community is very simple: Keep ourselves safe so that others will be safe from us. It is not required that we go out of our way to ensure the safety of the rest of the world, but it is important and oftentimes motivating to understand that the security within our own environment echoes in the security of organizations across the world. Through the process of being conscious and aware of the security around us, we are much better equipped to handle the security issues within the local environment.

Practicing This Virtue

To participate in security communities, we must first start with the realization that we are not alone, nor should we be. We must be willing to give and receive information with others, inside and outside the environment. This helps to solve local issues, and at the same time, has a profound impact on all security issues everywhere. The following simple steps will greatly benefit the security of all environments:

- *Keep informed*—Everyday, have someone spend 10 minutes checking your organization's favorite security watch sites to assess if the latest security vulnerabilities and countermeasures are applicable to the environment. For even better results, have that person discuss these issues in weekly meetings. You will find a list of recommended information sources in Appendix A, *Tips on Keeping Up-to-Date.*

- *Inform others*—There will be a time when you see suspicious activities on your systems or networks coming from somewhere on the "outside." Believe it or not, information on this attack (or attempted attack) could be invaluable to the rest of the security community. For example, one of the most popular incident response Web sites posts, in real-time, the addresses from which the most attacks have been reported. It is becoming common for security administrators, first thing in the morning, to check these lists and include the addresses in their security filters. You will find a list of recommended posting locations in Appendix A as well.

  Of course, you must be intelligent about such postings as to not give away valuable or sensitive information about your own environment.

- *Keep up-to-date*—This is not to say that you should run out and install every new patch that becomes available. Rather, it is to make the point that if there is a major security issue out there, it is only a question of time before you are targeted. Be intelligent in choosing what to update, but be consistent in keeping your systems up-to-date and safe from serious security flaws. If it is not possible to patch your system, seek an alternative countermeasure. Never ignore a security problem, because vulnerabilities don't go away by themselves. It is through the simplest and most easily remedied security vulnerabilities that the most destructive and widespread attacks have spawned.

- *Inform end-users*—Informing end-users is one of the primary responsibilities of the inner community. Encourage the end-users to be "security-aware" and enlist their aid when dealing with security issues. This also includes end-user training, which is discussed in a later section.

- *Make group-based decisions*—Since security touches just about every aspect of IT, it is not wise to make important security decisions alone. Network-based decisions should include a network engineer; policy-based decisions should include the input of local executives; and end-user-based decisions should solicit input from real end-users.

BEING RESPONSIBLE FOR YOUR OWN HOUSE

Remember in 1999 when giant e-commerce sites like Yahoo, CNN, and eBAY fell victim to a hacker's work via TRN00 and TFN? This major distributed denial of service (DoS) attack left everyone wondering how we could feel safe and secure if these giants failed to be secure. The reality is that it was not the lack of security in these specific sites, but the lack of security in the general public that caused the costly damages to these sites and many others. Thousands of poorly-secured systems around the world were compromised and all commanded to attack these specific Web sites at the same time, creating a scenario almost impossible to defend. Thus, the attack was really the collective fault of thousands of organizations around the world. Good security practices require a community effort wherein everyone does their part to protect their own systems.

THE VIRTUE OF HIGHER FOCUS

One major problem with how information security is handled today is that organizations are too focused on specific details. We apply a specific patch to deal with a specific problem and then wait a week for the next version of the same problem to hit again. In the world of information security, there are thousands of vulnerabilities exploitable by tens of thousands of attacks with virtually millions of possible permutations. Placing too much focus on the exact details of a specific vulnerability, a specific attack, or an isolated security issue will only serve to distract us from taking the proper actions and developing the proper solutions. In most cases, good security cannot be practiced if one focuses on details and loses sight of the bigger picture. Security is too dynamic, and requires higher methods of thinking.

It is important when practicing security to be aware of the underlying concepts concerning the methods of attack and defense, vulnerabilities, and countermeasures. The specific details, though interesting to study, often have minimal influence in how the situation should really be managed. The ultimate guiding light in our security practices must be to adhere to the Virtue of Higher Focus, to remain focused on the higher principles of information security, which are derived from a strong understanding of the subject matter. Following good higher principles, like those discussed here, is the only way an organization can adequately maintain security in all places, at all times, and in all situations. Details of vulnerabilities should be noted and discussed, but solutions should always be driven from a higher understanding and goals.

To clarify a bit, higher practices are security practices that guide us through the details of security issues by maintaining a focus on the bigger picture. The best security solutions can easily become confused and rendered ineffective if too much focus goes into the details. Good security practices can even seem like bad practices if the higher purpose is not obvious. If we were to look too closely at the individual details of any good security policy, we could always find little exceptions that seem like harmless violations of modifications. It is dangerously easy to lose track of the grander picture and open holes in our security when we allow our senses to be bombarded with millions of little details. This greatly amplifies the need to have standard written policies that are focused on the overall good and do not allow for exceptions unless through a formal change management process.

Avoiding Details With The Townsfolk

When my sister and I were growing up, we would always barrage our parents with the famous question "Why?" To this, we would often receive a quick reply of, "Because I said so." Sure, a few times it may have been just because our parents did not know the answer, but in general, it was because the answer was something that we would not have understood or easily accepted. If they had answered our initial "Why?" you know that we would have had another more persistent "Why?" to follow it. And so the story would go unless we were given what we wanted.

The same concept applies to security practices. As we venture forth and discuss concepts of security and higher practices to end-users, administrators, and managers, they will begin to question "Why?" Even the most educated people are, in a way, similar to children. When a person desires something and is focused on getting what he or she desires, polices and procedures simply become obstacles to overcome. If what someone wants violates a general security practice, an educated person can always find arguments and justifications to make it seem okay to make the exception. Or, if they cannot find the justifications needed, they will sometimes argue that the security practice itself was bad. For lack of a better word, we will call this "innocence": focusing on a specific goal, unaware of the larger picture. It is quite easy and very common to make bad security decisions in the face of such "innocence."

Since security decisions must be based on the core principles of information security, it stands to reason that no amount of "detail arguing" should change our stance. It will be all too easy to open up that little hole that allows for a hacker to penetrate our defenses. In general, it is best to avoid such arguments when possible and defer to a written policy. If a debate over a security control has sound enough reasoning, then it should warrant changing the written policy itself. As a rule, it is important to avoid making individual exceptions to security rules.

Higher Focus Security Measures

The Virtue of Higher Focus should be adopted when implementing security measures within an organization. No security professional, tool, or policy could possibly account for millions of variations of attacks without adopting a higher focus. A properly configured firewall, for example, is only useful because it does not try to understand and defend against all forms of attacks. It is effective because it allows a handful of screened activities to take place, and then denies everything else. This "denies everything else" feature is how the firewall transcends the millions of possible attacks through the Rule of Least Privilege (discussed in the next chapter). Such higher focus should be included in as many implementations as possible within an organization.

Consider a basic automobile alarm system. There are hundreds of ways a thief can break into a car, including breaking the window, jimmying the door, cutting a hole in the roof, etc. The average car alarm, however, transcends such details by implementing higher focus mechanisms. Some, for example, say that if the door is unlocked without using a key, sound the alarm. The creators know that most thieves will end up opening the door while attempting to break in, thus this single rule helps transcend the details. One notch up, the motion alarm theory states that all of these actions cause the car to move. Thus, the motion alarm adopts a higher focus to protect the car from even more forms of attack.

Practicing This Virtue

Maintaining a higher view of security is one of the key elements in maintaining a strong security mind. The virtues and rules have been specifically designed so that higher practices can be used when handling the specific details of security. Here are some suggestions for maintaining a higher focus concerning security:

- *Learn and share the concepts behind the virtues and rules of security—* These concepts provide the foundation for almost everything we do in the world of information security. When we are able to view any situation through these concepts, we can then apply good security practices.

- *Think in terms of the bigger picture—*Avoid becoming too focused on details. Most security decisions and practices are best made when they do not focus on the individual events at hand, but on the underlying issues to which they are related. When combating the latest worm, of course we will need to apply the immediate patch to stop it from spreading. It is necessary, however, to think beyond the immediate patch and apply security to fix the underlying issue, thereby avoiding similar worms in the future.

- *Follow the practices of higher security (presented later)—*These practices will help you think of security issues and deal with them in a more universal manner. Such practices greatly enhance the ability to be proactively secure.

- *Follow the concept of the written practice (presented later)—*Put high-level security practices in a written security policy. Refer to this document for any security decision that is getting clouded with too many details and arguments. When needed, find a good political way to point to the policy and say, "Because there are strong underlying reasons enforced by our policy. Before we can do this, we must first be willing to change the policy itself."

THE VIRTUE OF EDUCATION

I address the Virtue of Education last since it reflects back on all the previous virtues. I have already introduced several areas where continual attention needs to be given in the practice of security. You may wonder how any one person can accomplish all this and still get any work done. Security, however, is not a lonely task that can be performed by a single individual. If security is to be a daily effort, a community effort, and considered in everything, then *everyone* must be involved, to some extent, in security practices. Therefore, everyone involved needs some degree of security education.

Who's Really in Charge?

Here is a good thing to think about: Every workstation attached to a network has a great influence over the security of everything else in an organization. Thus, the

security of information is literally in the hands of those using the workstation, the end-users. Wouldn't it be nice if they had a little training to go along with the extreme power they possess? I don't care how much an organization has spent in making its clients thin, centrally monitored, and centrally controlled, the end-user still has great influence through his or her workstation and local network connection. By training IT staff members, managers, executives, and all end-users on good security practices, we can transform end-users from being a security risk into actually aiding in maintaining the security of an environment.

Security training is not difficult and can be fun and interesting for the end-user. Security has the inherent perc of being an interesting topic for most people, so why not take advantage of it? No, this does not mean everyone will read the five-page essay on "How to Make a Good Password." Refer to Appendix B, *Ideas for Training*, for quick and easy training processes.

It is important to remember while implementing security that most attacks on an organization are only successful because of an uninformed or careless administrator or end-user. Most systems connected to the Internet will be lucky to go five minutes without being probed for weaknesses by someone, somewhere. This makes it far more likely that the security administrator will not be the first person to discover a vulnerability an end-user has introduced into the system. With this in mind, it is certainly worth the training effort to ensure that end-users have the knowledge and interest in maintaining the security of their workstations and the environment. Without the training and participation of the end-users, security is very difficult to achieve in any organization.

The Psychological Obstacle

The practice of training and keeping end-users updated with security information does not have to be difficult. Many organizations accomplish this with moderate budget and resources. The most common obstacle to creating an environment unified in its security practice is an artificial barrier that is drawn between IT staff and the end-users.

Tension often exists between technical and non-technical personnel. This plays a very significant role in security practices since the people making security decisions are sometimes the individuals who would rather be thrown to the lions than try to train a group of end-users (and I'm sure the feeling is mutual).

> Security is too often considered as "the IT staff vs. the end-users," which is mostly derived from the daily battles between technology-minded and non-technical employees. But truly, it is difficult enough to combat the foreign kingdoms; do we really want to isolate ourselves from the locals? The state of mind that promotes this separation has the added effect of making the IT professional unwilling to teach, and the non-IT staff uninspired to learn.

We must always remind ourselves and those around us of one vital concept: Security is of great importance and it cannot be done alone! There is no technological solution for security that cannot be undone by a group of untrained, uninformed, or uncooperative end-users. A good security professional is one who is able to perform his or her duties while maintaining contact and a good relationship with the actual technology users.

Practicing This Virtue

Practicing this virtue does not mean we need to send all the end-users to get certified in security. Nor does it mean that we need to go to every desktop and show each person how to properly secure his or her computer. *We simply need to make the end-users aware of security.* Users need to understand that security is a very serious matter, and that the only way to keep the organization secure is to have everyone be responsible for his or her own part. Some important guidelines to stress to end-users include:

- *Good software installation practices*—Employees must know when it is not proper to install or run an application (from email, from the Web, etc.). It is great to have a policy, but make sure the end-users know "why" this is important or they will never follow it.

- *Good awareness practice*—End-users should be aware of activities concerning them and their systems, and should report anything suspicious to greatly increase security. Let them know that they are far more likely to be a witness to a hacker's activities than an administrator, which makes them a vital element in the practice of security.

- *Good Web-browsing practices*—Users should know where not to go, what information is and is not safe to give over the Web, and they should understand basic browser security terminology and practices (plugins, cookies, scripts, etc.).

- *Good confidentiality practices*—It is important that everyone knows what is confidential and not confidential within the organization. Confidential information of any kind should never be given out, emailed, or transmitted outside the local network without following company security procedures.

It should be stressed that security measures protect everyone in the company. When anyone bypasses these procedures, it may allow a hacker access into the environment and compromise the safety of everyone's information. Here are some interesting ways to introduce end-users to these concepts:

- *Continually present security concepts to employees*—Provide security information and stories in regular employee publications. Such writings should include an interesting title with a short, interesting story or anecdote about security (use those old and trusted media techniques to your advantage). As an example, you could write "New Worm Devastates U.S.-based Organizations," followed by a quick story, and ending with "How This Affects Us and What YOU Can Do." Or, if the occasion calls for it, simply cut and paste a bit of interesting news from a more formal publication, or from the Internet.

- *Provide in-house education*—If possible, give periodic classes/lectures (auditorium-style is fine) with a projector and some colorful pictures. Don't call the class "How to Secure Your Desktop"; instead, call the class something interesting like "How to Combat Hackers and Spies." Pull people in for 30 minutes after lunch or during a coffee break and give 15 minutes of interesting hacker stories mixed with 15 minutes of practical security measures. Remember:

  a. Security is an interesting topic to most people, so use this to your advantage. Don't give a lecture on password policies; give a presentation on how a hacker cracks passwords and how to beat him or her at the game!

   b. People are much more likely to follow a particular practice if they
   have some real-world reference, like a good hacker story to go
   with it.

- *Provide security reminders across the entire organization*—Put a security
  topic-of-the-day on the intranet site, email it to all the end-users, or have
  it appear on users' desktops at login. Topics should change every day or
  every week, and be only a few lines long.

- *Learn from the mistakes of others*—Avoid the common pitfalls that result in the loss of the end-user's attention and make him or her not care
  about security:
   a. Never hand an end-user a security policy or employee agreement
   and expect him/her to read it or retain any of the information.
   b. Never give boring, mandatory lectures on proper security practices.
   c. Never try to avoid educating users by enforcing drastic policies
   that deny end-users the ability to be productive.

USING THESE VIRTUES

If we keep these virtues in mind as we go through our day and continually reference
them in our practices, the process of securing ourselves will be vastly simplified and
infinitely less expensive. Throughout the rest of this book, I will continually refer
back to these virtues as the core of our practice. In the next chapter, we will begin
diving into more detail as we discuss the actual rules of security, which are also
based on the virtues.

4 The Eight Rules of Security (Components of All Security Decisions)

INTRODUCTION TO THE RULES

Frequently, there are so many interwoven elements surrounding a given situation that the best security solution becomes obscured. This causes many organizations to make bad security decisions on a regular basis. Effective security decisions must be consistent and based on sound reasoning that balances both the immediate and long-term impacts. A decision made about one security issue should be in line with previous decisions and with those decisions that will be made in the future. Making ad hoc decisions will eventually lead to flawed security practices. Thus, security is best approached as a series of rules based on the fundamental virtues we just discussed.

Making security decisions from a standard series of logical, constant, and universal rules is a common practice among good security professionals. Often unaware of it, the best security professionals simply follow a similar series of logical security rules over and over again. Therefore, it is reasonable to conclude that everyone can make good security decisions if they simply learn to follow similar essential rules. The eight essential rules of security are:

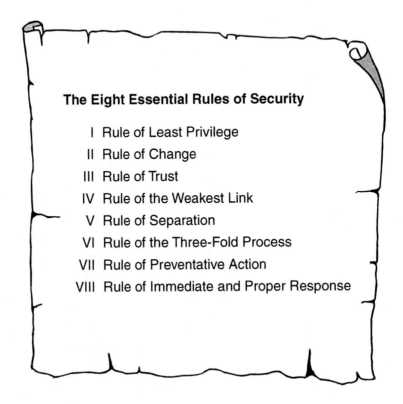

The Eight Essential Rules of Security

    I Rule of Least Privilege

    II Rule of Change

    III Rule of Trust

    IV Rule of the Weakest Link

    V Rule of Separation

    VI Rule of the Three-Fold Process

    VII Rule of Preventative Action

    VIII Rule of Immediate and Proper Response

In a moment, we will begin a walk through the eight essential rules of security. Understanding and applying these rules will build a foundation for creating strong and formal practices through which we can make intelligent and consistent decisions. Remember while reading this section that each rule, though specific in its construct, needs to be thought of as universal in its application. The reader will, of course, quickly think of specific applications to each rule within the context of a specific situation. However, it is when we are able to retain these key concepts in our minds for all security decisions, even if they do not seem obviously applicable, that we will be ready to deal with our real security challenges. The examples I give for each rule are intended to be just that, examples. Keep in mind that when an example is given using a server, that same rule also applies to securing a physical room, writing a policy, developing an application, or any number of real-world events.

RULE OF LEAST PRIVILEGE

The Rule of Least Privilege is the most fundamental and well known of the security rules. If this rule is not practiced, the peasants will soon be using the throne room as the privy and the treasure room as their own personal piggy bank. The Rule of Least Privilege is that simple. So, whether someone is new to information security or is spending their days contemplating the Clark-Wilson and Bell-LaPadula access control models, this essential rule is what it all comes down to.

Concept

Allow only as much access as is required to do the job, nothing more. In addition, allow only as much access as an individual, group, or subject is capable of being securely responsible for. In any and all situations, it is best to start with the idea that nothing is allowed and work from there. This is the one and only way in which we can be sure we know who has access to what, and why.

Subjects, Objects, Access, and Contexts

To work with the Rule of Least Privilege, we must first understand the components involved. There are numerous access control models that deal with privilege in different ways, but they all use similar components. The following list covers some standard terms when dealing with access control:

- *Subject*—The person, place, or thing gaining access
- *Object*—The person, place, or thing the subject is gaining access to
- *Access*—The level or degree of access given to the subject
- *Context*—The situation or circumstances surrounding the access

Table 4.1 shows some examples:

Table 4.1   Sample Components of Access Control

Subject	Object	Access	Context
Regular employees	A physical system	Read	During off-peak hours
John the janitor	A network address	Modify	
Systems across the Internet	Normal data	Execute	From the local computer without supervision
	Sensitive data	Physically touch	
Unsecured networks	An application	Physically see	Via an Internet-based VPN
Locations outside the country			Through a secured relay

Whether installing a firewall, building a new network connection, or developing an application, we must always reflect on this primary rule. Given a situation, we deny all possible access, and then, as required, we define exactly who needs access to what, and how.

Natural Tendencies

Unfortunately for security, the natural human tendency is to simply put objects "out there," without any restrictions, and then try to secure them. Thus, our most common methods of security are derived from a long series of post-implementation controls such as, "Let's block this... and that.... oh, and this as well." However, taking into consideration the billions of "thises" and "thats" possible in the information arena ultimately leads to an insane level of complexity that quickly becomes unmanageable.

EXAMPLE OF SECURITY CONSIDERATIONS BASED ON SUBJECT, OBJECT, ACTION, AND CONTEXT USING THE RULE OF LEAST PRIVILEGE

- System administrators are allowed to access Application X to add, delete, and modify accounts from within the LAN between the hours of 8 a.m. and 6 p.m.
- End-users are allowed to access their own account information for reading. This can occur anytime and from any external location.
- No other access is allowed into this application until formal amendments are made to this rule set.

Ever notice that when account administration is performed, the administrator is not allowed to see the end-user's password? One may wonder what the point of this is when the administrator has full access to that account, or could simply change the password to gain access. The truth is that the administrator never needs to know the end-user's password to perform his or her duties, and by denying all such unnecessary privileges, we enhance the security of the environment. In this case, the Rule of Least Privilege can protect the end-user's password in case it is shared among other systems, and it also forces the administrator to take extended actions (which will be logged) when gaining access to an end-user's account. There are actually numerous reasons for denying such actions that may not be immediately obvious. By following the Rule of Least Privilege, however, we solve the problem without having to account for all of these details.

Consider this scenario: We just put a new Payroll server online in our financial network. After getting it running and tested, we then take a look at security and begin to decide how we will protect it. Here, we attempt to ponder all the things we don't want to happen to this server:

- No one should have access to administer the system over the Internet since the Internet is impossible to secure.
- New employees should not have access to modify sensitive data since they may destroy valuable information.

- Accessing the system via Telnet is really not secure, so we should re-move that capability.
- The janitor who comes in at night should not have access to play video games on the system.

If we take even a simple situation with five employees, five systems, five networks, and five physical locations, we will come up with a list of a few thousand circumstances, and we will still be missing vital security holes. This problem can only be remedied through the Rule of Least Privilege, defaulting to no access and then specifying what is allowed. Lawyers follow this practice, as do casinos, the military, and now information security personnel.

> Have you ever been to a casino? If you ever wanted to learn about the Rule of Least Privilege, Las Vegas is the place to go. Casinos are built from an initial foundation that "nothing is allowed," which is later eased to allow only the most controlled of actions. A casino will allow its customers to walk all over its front end. The moment, however, a customer attempts to step over the line, the Rule of Least Privilege steps in, and there are no excuses and no exceptions that will allow someone beyond that access control point!

How Far Is too Far?

Most successful attacks are based on exploits that take advantage of seemingly inno-cent access. No one could ever possibly predetermine all the ways someone could hack into an object. Thus, the Rule of Least Privilege can be taken to far extremes be-fore ever being considered obsessive or overprotective. For instance, do employees re-ally need to ping systems on the Internet? We may not consider this a risk, but in reality, some hacker tunneling protocols can be established using the protocol Ping belongs to. By simply allowing outbound pings from our internal systems, we are tak-ing on an unnecessary risk that could lead to an exposure. Following our Rule of Least Privilege, the relevant access restrictions regarding ping should be as follows:

- Our firewall blocks all pings to anyone.
- Administrators of our network will need to be able to ping the out-side for testing, and we would incur a high cost in productivity if they could not, so ping is allowed from administrators to the outside.

- No one else has a real need for ping, and thus it will not be enabled for anyone else until there is a practical business need.

By the nature of the rule, restrictions can never be taken too far. If the rule ever causes a conflict, then the rule is not being used correctly. For example, if so many restrictions are placed on an employee that he or she can no longer be productive, then we are obviously not following the Rule of Least Privilege. If an employee cannot perform his/her job without access, then the Rule of Least Privilege will say that such access should be granted. Just keep in mind that those things that are required to keep employees productive, customers happy, and business flowing are the very things that are considered "essential" and should be allowed to take place. Everything else should be blocked until such a time as they become required.

> While writing this book, I often sent encrypted backup copies to a partner of mine in California. I never, however, told him the key that could unlock the encrypted files. This was not a matter of trust, nor could I imagine that he would do anything to harm the work. There was simply no need for him to know the secret key or access the information, and thus this process was subjected to the Rule of Least Privilege.

Practicing This Rule

This rule should be applied to everything needing security. The degree to which the rule is enforced should only be moderated as to not create an excessive burden on devices, employees, administrators, and customers. By "excessive," I mean any measure that causes more harm than good. But be careful with how "excessive" is defined, and always compare it against the idea of being hacked (I will address evaluating risk later in Chapter 8, *Practical Security Assessments*).

The Rule of Least Privilege should be taken into consideration when any decision is made to introduce a new device, service, application, network, or access point in an environment, or when making any change to the environment. This rule is one of our only defenses against hidden security vulnerabilities that are not normally discovered until exploited. Thus, the more restrictive we can be in allowing access to objects, the less likely we will find ourselves on the receiving end of an attack. Here are some practical tips to help apply this rule:

- **Create all security policies from a stance of the Rule of Least Privilege**—When considering access to different objects, write down exactly what is allowed and finish by stating that all other forms of access not explicitly listed are in violation of the policy.

- **Always begin by denying everything**—Applications, databases (DBs), network devices, and all other object access points should start from the point that nothing is allowed. Once everything is denied, authorized access should then be specified taking into consideration the subject, context of access, and different levels of privilege. Trying to program openly and then blocking out vulnerable actions later can be a very dangerous practice.
- **Always include the Rule of Least Privilege in all of the following security practices:**
  - Written policies
  - Rules for firewalls, proxies, router controls, and all other network-based controls
  - Server implementation, hardening, administration, and all other system-based controls
  - Local workstation implementation and end-user access privileges
  - Development or implementation of new applications, services, and DBs
  - Physical access to sensitive areas and devices

Five Steps for Applying the Rule of Least Privilege in Any Situation

Here is a quick method to use to apply the Rule of Least Privilege in a security decision. Creating a one-page document with all the following information will be extremely helpful for understanding and reflecting back on your decision in the future. As always, the steps below are a guideline; be sure to keep an open view and embrace the concepts behind the steps given:

1. Start by writing, programming, placing, or configuring controls to allow NO ACCESS.
2. Classify the objects (the items to which we are gaining access), the subjects (the people or things gaining access to them), the access in consideration, and the context for access (over a network, from a secure system, etc.). Remember that a subject can be a person, a group of people, an application, or any other thing that needs access to the object.
3. Determine if the subject really needs access to the object, under what circumstances, through which means, and how important it is that it

gains such access. Consider whether or not the subject has a strong need and a high enough level of responsibility to access the object. Focus attention on the following details:

- *Required access (Does the subject need it?)*—What level of access is required in the subject's role? Only this level of access should be assigned.
- *Access responsibility (Can the subject handle it?)*—Is the subject trusted enough to handle the access?

  Does the subject have enough security itself?

  If the subject is a person, has he or she been trained and screened, and has he or she signed the proper legal agreements?
- *Access context (Is the context safe?)*—Under what context is this access safe to take place?

  Can we trust the location, the system, and the time frame for the access?

4. Using the information gained through this process, we are now better armed to make a sound security decision. Even if the decision is to allow for unlimited access to a critical resource, we have at least gone through a formal consideration process and weighed the factors, and we are not naive to the potential issues.

5. Document the level of access that is to be granted so that a record exists and so that similar situations can be addressed without having to go though this process again.

RULE OF CHANGE

For any organization to remain dynamic and competitive, it must be able to adapt and change with the world around it. For IT professionals, this means a continual flux of upgrading, enhancing, and replacing the technology. This presents several challenges to information security practices.

Concept

The Rule of Change states that *change must be managed, coordinated, and considered for possible security implications*. Any change within an environment carries with it some form of risk. Installing a new Linux system could introduce a security hole; patching a Windows 2000 server could cause a working application to crash; and, making a change to a firewall could block email from flowing to customers. To make matters worse, every change is prone to having different effects based on the current environment. If experience tells us anything, it's that Patch X working great at home does not mean that Patch X will work great on our critical server!

A great many changes are occurring in a technical environment at any given time: new applications are being installed, routing paths are being modified, software and operating systems are being updated and upgraded. You name it, and it's changing. Every changing component carries the risk of affecting the environment in terms of security, integrity, and availability; and most of the time, this risk is not obvious.

A significant contributing factor to down time in corporate environments is the lack of coordination among system administrators, network administrators, security administrators, and end-users as changes are taking place. Likewise, a great number of security vulnerabilities that appear within the average organization come from unmanaged changes. Everyone is a culprit: the IT administrator installing a new application, the desktop user plugging in the phone line to a new laptop, and the new intern installing video games to play during lunch. It is truly difficult for a human to sit in front of a dynamic device like a computer and resist making some form of major change. Most of these changes seem simple enough, and it is often hard to imagine the global impacts they can have. But changes, if not managed correctly, will eventually become loose bricks in the castle wall. Thus, managing change is key to the security of any organization.

The Guinea Pig Phenomena of Change

Changes should only occur after they have been proven to be safe. Software companies, especially the larger ones, are notorious for releasing products with more things broken than working. Partly credited to the lack of adequate testing requirements and closed source code issues, and partly credited to the extreme difficulty in testing abstract cases, new technical developments are inevitably "buggy." The human mind's desire for newer and better things, combined with our general lack of patience and caution, gives us the impulse to run out and get new products hot off the shelf. I call this the guinea pig phenomena: thousands of people rushing out to get a product, basically paying to be the ultimate testers for the development company.

Introducing any new software or hardware product into an environment comes with some degree of risk. Not only could the new product be unstable, but it could affect the stability of the software, systems, and networks around it. It is important to be aware of this fact before implementing any new objects in your environment.

Issues with Diversity in Change

Changes should be consistent and not introduce a great deal of diversity. Within an organization, the more diverse the technologies, the more difficult it will be to maintain security. If all systems within the organization are either Compaq or Dell, all the routers are Lucent, and all the systems are Windows 2000 or Solaris 2.7, then it will not be difficult to keep up with the various issues and vulnerabilities associated with these products. If, however, managers are allowed to purchase their own equipment, the environment will become very diverse in its technologies. It may prove to be impossible to keep up with the various security patches, hot-fixes, and other issues when such a wide variety of technology is deployed.

Practicing This Rule

Two key words every security manager must know are "change management." Without some form of change management or change control, an organization will be plagued with down time, security breaches, and general confusion. A significant change in any part of a network constitutes a significant change in the network as a whole. Multiple changes at the same time can cause unpredictable issues, and can make troubleshooting impossible. Unauthorized or unreported changes in an environment can bypass all security measures and leave the environment open to the most basic of hackers.

Without change management, there is little hope to maintain security within an organization. *There is no security measure that cannot be undone by someone making an unauthorized and unreported change to a server, network, or workstation within the environment.* Here are some good guidelines for following the Rule of Change within your organization:

- **Implement change control**—It is essential that organizations implement some form of change control/change management system. I will cover a sample change management process at the end of this section.
- **Make the process efficient**—The success of a change management process is heavily weighted on its ability to function without becoming an impediment. The primary goal of the process should be to document and coordinate changes. If the process is made too cumbersome, no one will follow it. Sometimes, the change management process can be as simple as an assistant compiling all proposed changes into a list reviewed by a good administrator capable of spotting major issues and changes that should not be made together.

- **Apply the process universally**—Nothing should be installed, patched, or significantly modified on a server or device without first following the change management process. In some cases, permission may not even be required and simple documentation of the steps taken might suffice. In such cases, it is simply important that the change management process was observed.

- **Scrutinize security changes**—Changes, upgrades, or modifications to any security filter must also go through the change management process. Decisions should not be left to the technical administrators alone, but rather, they should be made as a group.

- **Control desktop changes as well**—A list of tested and approved applications for desktops should be included in the desktop policy. Any new applications to be installed should first be approved by management and included in this list.

- **Remove the guinea pig phenomena**—As a general rule, do not deploy a product until it has been tested by the first wave of users. Go so far as to make this a written policy: "No new product may be installed within the environment unless it has been distributed in its final form for at least 4–6 months, or unless permission has been granted from a higher source." This should include new operating systems, new applications, and new devices that attach to the network.

- **Standardize on a handful of technologies**—By no means should you lock yourself into one particular vendor or any specific technology; however, it is important to have some limit in the diversity of your environment. This will greatly reduce the number of potential issues and vulnerabilities, while enhancing the organization's ability to keep up with security updates and fixes.

Concerning New Updates

Avoiding the guinea pig phenomena with new products is easy enough; however, sometimes we find ourselves in a tight position regarding new updates. When a new patch is released to fix an annoying problem, we want to install it right away. This begs the question: "Should we install a new patch in light of the risk of change?" A good measurement is to imagine the cost of having to reinstall the entire application and troubleshoot for hours before determining if the patch is worth it. Remember that it is very common for development companies to patch their patches because of errors and incompatibilities. New patches introduce new bugs that need to be patched again until everything functions correctly.

Concerning New Security Updates

Security patches are often the most difficult objects to deal with. There is a direct need for the patch, but otherwise, the system is running fine. We don't want to take a chance of hurting a functional system with a new patch, but at the same time, we do not want to be vulnerable! Again, the decision can be very logical if we consider the nature of the patch and the potential risk of an issue. It is important to understand the extent of the vulnerability being patched and compare that against the cost of disaster (if the system was affected by the patch and had to be rebuilt).

Always remember: For a vulnerability that goes unpatched, it is simply a matter of time before that vulnerability is exploited. Security patches should always be installed unless the risk of applying the patch is higher than the risk of being compromised.

Reflecting on the Rule of Least Privilege

The Rule of Least Privilege says if access is not required or access cannot be handled properly, access should be denied. This holds very true with end-users and administrators making changes within the environment. No group should be given access to make changes if they are not qualified to make them. The word "group" is used here specifically because this must be enforced even when we have some individual end-users who are quite capable of making intelligent system changes.

> Professionals are certainly no exception to this rule. Specifically, we should watch what we install and where we install it. If many changes are required, consider building a test network unattached to the main network. Also refer to the discussion on limiting the use of administrator and root accounts later on in Chapter 11, *The Rules in Practice*.

Six Steps for Implementing a Basic Change Management Process

Here, I have provided a basic change management process. This process is just a guideline to get started. Keep in mind that a change management process should be tailored to the needs of an organization.

1. Write a policy to designate a change management process and the types of changes that fall under it. The rules in this policy should be made mandatory and readily enforced for all engineers and managers.

2. Make a standard schedule of events for common changes and activities that affect the environment:

> Every 11:00 p.m.: Start system backups for all networks
>
> Every 2:00 a.m.: Download latest antivirus update
>
> Tuesday 5:00 a.m.: Perform standard security scan

3. Provide a classification for all uncommon types of changes, summarizing the risks they pose to the environment. This list should be tailored to the specific needs of the organization. Here is an example:

> Level 1: Cosmetic change to a server, router, WAN, or other device
>
> Level 2: Functional change to a normal server, router, WAN, or other device
>
> Level 3: Functional change to a critical server, router, WAN, or other device, or change that affects multiple devices

4. Provide a classification for all types of changes being made using a scale of criticality. The assigned value should designate how urgent a change is.

> Normal: These are the average IT changes that could wait several days to be performed. Most changes fall into this category.
>
> High: These are urgent changes that should be performed within 24 hours. Changes like this include patches, updates, and configuration changes that would be highly beneficial to the organization if performed quickly.
>
> Critical: These are extremely urgent changes that should be performed immediately on approval. This category covers urgent security patches and updates that are required to avoid pending issues.

5. An approval system should be put in place by which engineers and managers must announce changes they plan to make. For changes of a significant level, approval must be received from the individual or group in charge of coordinating changes. At a minimum, the following information should be submitted for approval:

- Basic details of the change being made
- The levels of risk and criticality for the type of change
- A scheduled time and date for the change to occur
- Contact information for the individual making the change and the individual who approved the change

6. An updated list of approved changes should be made available to engineers and managers. If there is ever an issue during normal daily activities, this list should be reviewed to see if any scheduled changes could be at fault. Suspicious events should also be compared to this list to see if there is any correlation.

 RULE OF TRUST

A good security practitioner of the Rule of Trust is one who is a friend to everyone, but really trusts no one. Since saying we don't trust someone or something often has negative overtones, let's be more politically correct and simply say, "Anything can happen."

Sure, Mel has been a faithful employee for 20 years and helps to find orphaned kittens new homes during the winter holidays. This does not mean we should give him the combination to our safe, or let him enter the computer room without signing in with security. The fact is that *anything can and will happen.* Mel could suffer a breakdown and decide to erase all our customer data. Mel may also be harboring a secret grudge against the manager of Human Resources because the guy hates cats. The truth is, you just never know.

Concept

Understand the full effects before extending trust to anyone or anything, and only trust that which is required (Rule of Least Privilege). Understand that "trust" is an extremely strong word and can have drastic effects on an organization. In security, giving someone or something complete trust means that we are putting a lot of power in their hands. The moment someone is "trusted," he or she has the amazing power to get away with anything. If no one is checking up on him/her, then the rules can't really apply. This is a very dangerous situation.

Security policies should be made with the idea of layered trust. To perform a job function, the company must have some level of trust in each employee. This level of trust, however, should be different based on the individual person and role. In correspondence with the Rule of Least Privilege, it must be reinforced that no one should get access unless that person needs it and can handle it. Feelings of personal trust, friendliness, and lack of suspicion should never affect basic security practices. All individuals and groups should be treated equally according to the Rule of Least Privilege.

While performing security audits, I have noticed that the majority of my clients' employees suffer from an overwhelming sense of trust. Walk into a server room unannounced with a nice suit and most people will trust you and point you to the nearest network jack. Being secure means being suspicious and asking questions. A hacker rarely announces himself/herself or presents a hacker business card. Don't be unfriendly or make any enemies, but at the same time, don't let anyone go unchecked.

We need to be especially careful when trusting our partners, vendors, and any other entity that harbors systems, networks, and physical areas outside of our immediate control. Sure, it may be a giant company with great security, but unless we control who touches their system, and unless we are in direct control of hiring and firing their personnel, we really don't know who we are dealing with. Their best employee could let his/her son use a workstation to do homework and, next thing we know, all the e-commerce servers are hosting the latest version of Quake.

Practicing This Rule

To practice this rule within your organization, simply remember that anyone can be the enemy, even you. This is not intended to incite paranoia, but honestly, the best hackers do not dress in torn-up jeans and wear anti-government slogans on their pizza-stained t-shirts. Humans are very complicated beings with very complex minds; knowing everyone's motives and how they would react in any situation is beyond our capabilities. So always remember:

- **Trust nothing outside of your immediate control**—Anything that is not in the immediate control of the organization, its policies, and its security mechanisms should be treated with a lesser degree of trust. This includes large vendors, partners, consulting organizations, etc.

- **Look at all the angles before extending trust**—Before extending trust to anyone or anything, first consider everything to which it has extended trust. Remember, if you trust Company A, and they trust Company B, you are essentially trusting both A and B! (I will discuss in the section on *Understanding Relational Security* in the next chapter.)

- **Make policies apply beyond all levels of trust**—To be effective, security policies must apply to everyone, even the people who write them. Trusted individuals and entities should not be allowed to break policy.

- **Maintain an accurate perception**—When a rule is broken, but it is unknown as to who broke the rule, do not eliminate any possibilities, regardless of trust.

Seven Key Considerations Before Extending Trust to Any Object or Entity

1. Is this object within your direct control?
2. Is this object required to conform to your security policies?
3. Is the security of this object properly maintained and monitored?
4. Is your organization allowed to monitor and review the object's logs?
5. Is your organization allowed to perform a vulnerability test on the object and its environment?
6. Does this object have a history of security issues or failures?
7. How many other entities have access to this object?

IV RULE OF THE WEAKEST LINK

Everyone knows the concept of the weakest link, and that any chain is only as strong as that stick of chewing gum binding its middle links. This old cliche has never been so true as when it is applied to technical security practices. Hackers are not going to bother running a complex, time-intensive, brute-force attack against our new, cool, triple-hashed password file if they can simply walk into the assistant's office and find the password written on a desk. Most organizations have a heavy mix of strong and weak security measures, which is often the fatal mistake that grants an eager attacker access to systems and data. The Rule of the Weakest Link is: A security practice is only as strong as its weakest control!

Concept

Contemplating the weakest link requires some consideration of the security practice as a whole. We must be able to contemplate an organization not in its individual pieces, but as one large entity with a related series of defenses, and make decisions from this perspective. If, for instance, we spend 90% of our time, attention, and budget putting a firewall in place and then allocate no time or resources to the security of a new dial-up server, the firewall is worth nothing. If we spend $50,000 on a front door, $20,000 on a back door, and $500 on a side door, the entire enterprise security will be worth $500, even though we are still left with a $70,500 bill!

The tendency in many organizations is to place a lot of attention on the most common security controls, while the not so obvious controls receive little or no attention at all. Frequently, so much attention is focused on an organization's Internet connection that the staff becomes oblivious to the numerous security holes in its internal environment. Here, the firewall becomes the $50,000 front door, while the other entrances are protected by the $500 special.

Practicing This Rule

To apply the Rule of the Weakest Link, one must think and act with a global mind set. *Each security decision must reflect the strength of other security choices made.* We must be continually aware of the environment and always be able to identify the weakest links within the infrastructure. Any "weak links" in the security chain must be given some amount of attention, even if it is to simply say, "We acknowledge this weakness and are going to do nothing about it." Good practices to follow for this rule include:

- **Continually search for the "weakest link"**—Perform regular audits and risk assessments of your entire environment (as discussed later in Chapter 8). Be sure to keep abreast of new projects, initiatives, and changes within the environment. Remember, the weakest link is a moving target and can hide quite well inside of even the most successful projects.

- **Document where security weaknesses exist**—Wherever the weakest links are in the environment, it is important to acknowledge them. They should be discussed and documented with appropriate staff members. Even if there is nothing that can be done about them, simply knowing where they are is invaluable to the security of the organization. *Hiding the weakest links from the organization is always a very bad idea.*

- **Avoid introducing new weak links**—Have strong policies governing changes within the environment, especially where new methods of access, new applications, and new methods of data storage and management are concerned. Try to minimize the number of weaknesses introduced into the environment. Follow the Rule of Change discussed earlier.

Remove the Most Common "Weakest Links"

The following is a list of the most common weak links that I have seen expose organizations to attack. Another good vulnerabilities list was compiled by the FBI and can be found at: www.sans.org/top20.htm

- *Default installations*—This includes servers, devices, and applications installed with default installations, without any security applied, or without any default services turned off. A high percentage of products come with features enabled by default, which will introduce vulnerabilities in the environment.

- *Bad passwords by end-users and administrators*—The security of an object with 100 great passwords and 2 lousy passwords is only as good as the 2 bad passwords. It is very common to find bad passwords protecting otherwise secure objects.

- *Active modems attached to desktops, servers, and routers*—Modems are not always recognized for the incredible security hazard they are. Modems often come pre-installed in computers and are used by users wishing to bypass corporate Internet restrictions, dial in from home, or simply do not know any better and do not follow company policies. Modems are commonly exploited to attack an otherwise secure organization.

- *Neglect of logging and monitoring*—When objects go unmonitored, it is nearly impossible to know if they have been compromised or not. I have seen many situations where the firewall and IDS report suspicious activities, but no one is assigned to monitor the logs. Such organizations are unable to react to attacks and prevent future attacks.

- *Unsecured backup/redundancy connections*—Redundant Internet connections, backup dial-in access, and other emergency wide area network (WAN) links often have far less security applied than main connections, thus exposing an organization to attacks.

- *Temporary servers, workstations, and other devices*—Such objects are usually not secured and left online for far longer than originally expected, thus leaving their vulnerabilities exposed.

- *Neglected backups and untested backups*—Most organizations never seem to test their backups. Unfortunately, backup media can be really tricky to restore and are prone to error. This exposes many organizations to the threat of data loss. It is bad enough to have a server failure and suffer through downtime. Imagine, however, how it would be to discover that a backup device was configured improperly and critical data cannot be restored!

- *Unauthorized applications*—End-users and administrators tend to install new applications on their systems without concern for security. Complicated applications often leave a system vulnerable to attack. Some applications even contain back doors or are infected with a virus.

- *Outdated antivirus software*—Most organizations install antivirus software on the majority of their systems. The main problem seems to be keeping all the systems current. I often see viruses and worms break out in organizations that have small pockets of systems with no updated antivirus software.

RULE OF SEPARATION

The Rule of Separation states that to secure something, it must be separated from the dangers and threats of the world around it. In accordance with the Rule of Least Privilege, we should only bestow access to our treasure room on those who really require such access. Consider, however, if we also had a library in the middle of our treasure room, and had to allow students to come in to study. We don't want the students to have access to the gold, but we can't deny them access to the books!

Often, our treasure rooms are not so cut and dried as to say, "The gold is inside and the thieves are outside," just as the protective barriers we build do not always exist at the perimeter of our networks. Many times, it is important to separate different internal objects to avoid introducing unnecessary exposure.

Concept

It is commonly known that the more "tasks" a device must perform, the more issues it is likely to have. It is ill-advised for any company to have 10 applications running on one system due to the likely chance that these applications have not been designed or tested to share the hosting server with other applications. It is also commonly known that the more subjects that have access to an object, the higher the chance that the object will have an exposure. By not practicing the Rule of Separation, an organization multiplies its exposures and, at the same time, reduces the overall level of security for each object.

Multiplying Exposures

The strengths and weaknesses of any particular object can usually be related to the tasks that object performs. The more something does, the more complicated it has to be, and thus, the more potential security weaknesses it will have. Every service running on a device has some degree of programming errors, incompatibilities, and vulnerabilities. Running multiple services on a single device not only combines existing vulnerabilities, but can also introduce new ones. Thus, if an email service has three vulnerabilities and a Web service has two, running them both together may even surpass five vulnerabilities. When services are combined, each service adopts the weaknesses of the other services running with it. Some services are less stable than others, and some have more vulnerabilities than others. When we combine services, we compound these negative attributes.

Reducing the Level of Security

Each service also has its own unique sensitivity considerations. One service may not be important to our organization, while another service may be vital. Similarly, some services deal with meaningless data, while others store and process sensitive transactions. By combining services together on a single server, we are essentially combining the different levels of sensitivity along with the different levels of security. An FTP service may not be vital to an organization, and thus the application may not include a great deal of security. The email server, however, may be vital to the organization and its applications may be highly secured. By combining these two applications on a single system, they are essentially placing the weak security controls of the FTP services into an otherwise secure, critical email server.

Example of Reduced Security Through Shared Services • As seen in Table 4.2, System X runs three applications: email, Web, and FTP. Each service has its own level of security and its own vulnerabilities. Each also hosts a different set of data with different levels of sensitivity. Thinking back to our Rule of the Weakest Link, imagine what we have done to the security of this system. We have combined the worst of the vulnerabilities with the most sensitive of data! If any one of these applications is compromised, all data from all applications could easily be exposed.

Table 4.2 Reducation of Security via Shared Services

Service	Sensitivity of Data	Security of Application	Number of Vulnerabilities
Email server	Extremely sensitive information	Highly-secured email host	2 security vulnerabilities/year
Web server	Somewhat sensitive data	Medium security, Web-hosting software	2 security vulnerabilities/year
FTP	Nonessential information	Minimum security applied to application	3 security vulnerabilities/year
All services	**Extremely sensitive information**	**Minimum security**	**7 security vulnerabilities/year**

Practicing Separation

The application of this rule does not require us to place every single service on its own bulletproof device, locked in an airtight chamber. If we follow these guidelines, we should be able to make practical and secure decisions without great expense:

- **Isolate important services and data**—The more critical a service is or the more sensitive its data, the more important it is that it be isolated.

- **Isolate services that are more prone to attack**—Services that commonly have "known vulnerabilities" and "new security patches" should be separated from more secure and stable systems.

- **Isolate all security services**—Security devices should never have multiple services on them unless absolutely required. The best practice is to make the firewall only a firewall and put extra services like authentication, mail relay, and virus checking on other systems. If this is not possible, at least limit the firewall's services to those developed by the same manufacturer (that is, don't install a Checkpoint firewall with a third-party domain name server (DNS) relay on it).

- **Only group services based on common security factors**—When services are grouped together, it is best if they are of similar risk levels and a similar level of security should be applied to each service.

- **Understand exactly what is being grouped together**—If a service is to be run on the same system as another service, it is well worth it to take the time to research the applications and how well they interact with each other.

Six Sample Considerations to Determine if a Service Should Be Isolated

Table 4.3 is an example scoring system to show the thought process one might go through when deciding to share services. Take a specific object and review each consideration on the left. Select the best answer on the right and add the points together. Then, compare the score to the recommendation at the bottom of the chart.

RULE OF THE THREE-FOLD PROCESS

Security is an exciting field to work in and many organizations have employees eagerly lined up to volunteer for their new security initiatives. The tendency, however, is to

Table 4.3 Basic scoring system for Isolating Services

Consideration	0 Points	1 Point	2 Points	3 Points
What would be the cost if this service stopped running?	No cost	Low cost	Medium cost	High cost
What would be the cost if the data related to this service was compromised or corrupted?	No cost	Low cost	Medium cost	High cost
What would be the cost of isolating this service?	High cost	Medium cost	Low cost	No cost
How complicated is the application running this service?	Simple	Complex/ Unknown	Very complex	-
Was this service developed to work with the other services in question?	Yes	-	No	-
How many vulnerabilities have been discovered for this service, or how many patches were released in the past year?	0	>1	>3	>5
Total Score				

—Results—

A score of 0–4	May indicate a situation where it can be shared with other services of an equal score.
A score of 5 or more	May indicate a situation where isolating the service from others is best.

rush to market to purchase the next great firewall and a host of other security devices and then spend a month getting the devices to work, tweaking them, tuning them, playing around, and then sitting back and enjoying the security of these new-found toys. Unfortunately, it is easy to get over-excited only about the implementation of security, after which the magic tends to die. Think back and try to recall the last time you heard someone say, "I just can't wait until we get to apply a new signature and perform administrative tasks on our IDS."

It is vital for every organization to understand that *security does not stop with implementation.* Thousands of security systems around the world are compromised because the process stopped after implementation. According to the Rule of the

Three-Fold Process, all security measures must be thought of as a three-fold process, including implementation, monitoring, and maintenance:

- *Implementation*—The first task is that of design and implementation. This is where we perform our analysis, design a solution, purchase the tools, build it, test it, and cut it over to production. By far, the majority of security consultants and security staff I have interviewed for projects think only to this point and no further.

- *Monitoring*—This second task of security is just as important as implementation. There is no such thing as fully automated security; all countermeasures require some human intervention. An implemented security device is like a locked room; you may have been sold a big door and a loud alarm, but when the alarm goes off and no one is there to hear it, does it make a sound? No.

  Monitoring is a key to success in all security solutions. Almost all security devices, firewalls, IDSs, authentication engines, and OS lockdown tools have two jobs to do: they stop patterns they have been programmed to recognize and they report activities that may be of interest. Since a security device can only be programmed with so many automated patterns to watch for, it is vital that a human with active intelligence be present and alert to catch all the things a simple logic firewall cannot. *Security requires thinking, not just computing.*

> It is far too often that I walk into a client to perform an audit and find that they have absolutely no logging enabled on their security devices. I have seen numerous clients with passive IDSs (the only purpose of these systems is to log suspicious activity), and yet there is no one assigned to review the logs or monitor the activities. It is not difficult to understand that such systems are literally expensive paperweights, serving no purpose but to take up space. Such systems are usually sold directly by vendors who claim, "It is easy to use and practically runs itself." Just remember that your car runs itself, but someone still has to be there to drive it!

- *Maintenance*—On average, any security devices left without updates for an extended period of time will fail to recognize or catch new attacks, and will themselves become vulnerable. "Code Red," for example, infested many firewalls and security devices that had unpatched Web services enabled. It is important to understand that security is only good on its own for a very short period of time. Plan that with any implementation, you will need to spend a small amount of time each week maintaining the systems. You will need to do this throughout the entire lifetime of any device.

Ever wonder in amazement why you buy a cool new security tool for $5,000, only to find out that the maintenance to support it is $5,001 every year? Yes, it's a crime, I know. But just like buying a car, it is important to be careful of the hidden costs. Vendors know that a security product without updates will be useless in a year. Be sure to subscribe to maintenance and consider these costs up front.

Practicing This Rule

This rule ties in directly with the virtue of daily consideration. From the moment we secure anything within our environment, we could start a timer, and every second after, the object will become less and less secure. Thus, it is vital to make the Rule of the Three-Fold Process part of our daily lives for every technology we work with. Here are some guidelines:

- **Consider the Rule of the Three-Fold Process from the beginning**—Before any implementation occurs, take into consideration the requirements for monitoring and maintaining the devices. Budget this into the price up-front and be sure to reserve resources for these processes. Consider contracts for updates to your security devices as a "must," and include the cost before making any purchasing decision. This is especially true for firewalls, IDSs, virus scanners, and host-based security mechanisms.

- **Be sure logging and maintenance controls are understood**—If your security devices are installed by consultants or other parties, make sure you fully understand the system and how to monitor and maintain it before they leave the premises.

- **Keep up-to-date**—Make it a point to check for updates often and review the log files at least once a day. Always remember that any device left unmonitored and any device that is not properly maintained will eventually be compromised. Include status reports for all security devices and applications in your regular meetings. Status reports should point out new updates and new vulnerabilities, as well as suspicious log entries.

RULE OF PREVENTATIVE ACTION (PROACTIVE SECURITY)

The Rule of Preventative Action is: *Security can only be successful if it is accomplished through a proactive approach.* This is another vital separator between those organizations that have had no major security issues and those that are continually plagued with hackers and "mysteriously" malfunctioning systems.

We, as humans, have a strong tendency to lean toward a reactive response in most situations. Often, we consider proactive measures to be quite time-consuming and distracting from our real work. Somehow, patching the roof seems like so much more work when it is not raining outside. Likewise, checking for new security patches seems quite wasteful until our critical email server is compromised from a well-known exploit.

It is important to recognize that resistance to proactive measures comes from several sources, including users and management. In many organizations, adopting a proactive response to security is met with the following responses:

- *Management* resists proactive measures since the results of a response cannot be easily seen or weighed. How can there be justification without any visible proof of effectiveness?
- *The user community* tends to treat proactive measures with great skepticism, often considering them over cautious and too much of a burden. Why should they change their ways when there is no proof that it makes a difference?

The main social dilemma here is that placing added security controls where there appears to be no security issues is scrutinized, while the reactive response of kicking a hacker out of a network is considered a glorious triumph. To be a good security professional, and to overcome many obstacles of security, we must always be proactive, despite our human programming. Without taking proactive measures, an organization has little hope of remaining secure.

Practicing This Rule

To apply this rule and maintain the security of an infrastructure, proactive security measures must become the focus. In accordance with the virtues, security must be considered in every decision. Before an action is taken, security implications must be accounted for. It should be a daily routine for an organization to check for new vulnerabilities and exploits, apply patches, and otherwise participate in the security community. Here are some good practices to start with:

- **Keep aware of current security issues**—Make a list of two or three good security maintenance sites and visit them on a scheduled basis to stay aware of new security vulnerabilities and measures. (Some suggested resources are included in Appendix A, *Tips on Keeping Up-to-Date*.)

- **Perform regular tests on security devices**—Try to find security holes before a hacker does. Regularly run vulnerability scanners and other tools to search for vulnerabilities and weaknesses.

- **Don't stop with just the common issues**—Practice making security a consideration in everything and find vulnerabilities before they happen.

- **Maintain a strong three-fold process policy:**
    - Make a list of operating systems and critical applications and check for security patches regularly, at least twice a week. Apply every applicable security patch that can be safely applied (see the Rule of Change).
    - Update antivirus software every time a new definition is available.

 # VIII RULE OF IMMEDIATE AND PROPER RESPONSE

Every organization will eventually be attacked. This includes my organization, their organization, and most likely, your organization as well. *The steps we take after an attack has occurred are just as important as the steps we took to prevent the attack.* Whether an attack was a success or failure, there should be an organized response to investigate the details, analyze pending risks, and plan future steps.

This section is not going to cover how to develop an incident response plan, since incident response is a whole subject of its own and there are several good books available (you will find a list of recommended books in Appendix D: *Recommended Reading*). We will, however, discuss the Rule of Immediate and Proper Response as it is related to IT security. Many organizations get themselves into trouble when they are caught with an intruder and have no idea how to react. Reacting poorly to an intrusion can potentially do more harm than the hacker did in the first place. It is thus important to consider the Rule of Immediate and Proper Response long before a response is needed.

Reacting Quickly

Incident response is a very time-sensitive task requiring good, proactive planning. Preparations must be made ahead of time so as to have the right tools, skills, and processes in place for conducting a proper response. Every organization should have some form of written incident response plan detailing how to react during an attack situation. Small or large, this plan should provide a clear and repeatable process, void of the panic and confusion that is likely to be experienced during an incident.

Reacting Properly

After spending several consecutive weeks applying patches and reviewing un-eventful security logs, we have a tendency to jump at anything that looks remote-ly interesting in our logs. A small ripple can seem like a tidal wave if the pool of water has been sitting still for long enough. Things have a tendency to get out of hand almost instantaneously when the right series of alarms are triggered. Key phrases to remember and share with your organization are:

- "Don't panic or get excited."
- "Be discrete."
- "Follow the process."

Keeping a suspected attack confidential at the beginning of an investigation is crucial. Even the slightest mention of a potential attack overheard by staff members can seem interesting enough to share with friends and co-workers. In a few cases, I have witnessed small system glitches publicized as major security breaches when someone overheard a security professional saying, "Well, it could be an attack."

Attacks have the tendency to get security professionals quite excited as well; after all, this is what we are there for. With spines tingling, it is very easy to overreact before the full details are known. Sometimes, we are even tempted to take steps that are far worse than the attack, or take steps that destroy valuable evidence. We don't want to pull the plug on a critical system if we simply "think" there was an attack. In such cases, it is easy to become our organization's worst enemy! This again emphasizes the importance of following a written, methodical response process.

To react properly to an incident, follow the predefined incident response plan, which was written during a calmer state of mind. Normally, this plan will dictate which managers and security staff members need to be informed of potential incidents. It is then up to the supervisor in charge to pass the information along. This plan will outline what steps should and should not be taken, and what can and cannot be done without first getting authorization from a higher source.

Documentation

For every incident and response that occurs, there should be documentation detailing the reaction and results, plus what the organization learned. Even small incidents should at least have a three-line write-up for the weekly meeting that later gets stored with other historical records. This document will help enhance security awareness, improve on responses, and assist in recognizing patterns of attacks against the organization. Additionally, if there ever is a need to go to court, it can assist in creating a chain of evidence.

Turning an Attack to Your Advantage

Earlier in this book, I discussed the difficulties involved with security brought on by the fact that security is intangible, invisible, and if done correctly, not even noticeable. This can make it difficult to gain funding and approval on many security projects. However, when an attack is successfully detected and/or prevented, the information can be an invaluable incentive for increased attention and funding.

There are many instances of organizations having to squeeze out every nickel for the security budget. But then, after a security engineer successfully detects a worm, virus, or an active hacker crawling around inside the organization's network, future funding begins to pour in. Even though it is still invisible, events such as these can become tangible when we draw simple relations to the real world: "This hacker had penetrated System X, from where he/she could have gained access to read, modify, or destroy our financial records. But, we successfully detected the attack and rid ourselves of this risk."

Of course, these issues can be extremely sensitive and require tact in the delivery, so use discretion on a case-by-case basis. Take advantage of any opportunity to gain from a security violation.

Practicing This Rule

Incident response is a very big topic and I suggest buying a good book on the matter or taking a good training course. As far as the Rule of Immediate and Proper Response is concerned, here are a few steps to follow:

- **Develop a good incident response plan**—This does not have to be long or filled with painstaking details, but it must remain constant in its processes. There are a few good books on incident response outlined in Appendix D.
- **Have a very clear and widely known chain of command in such issues**—Anyone thinking they see a security issue should report it to X. X then must report to Y, Y to Z, and so on.
- **React quickly**—Immediate action should be taken with any incident when there is reasonable evidence that there truly is an incident.
- **Make sure everyone sticks to the plan**—During the response, an incident response plan should be followed to avoid making mistakes or panicking.
- **Follow up on the incident**—At the end of the response, the actions taken should be documented and discussed with appropriate members of the organization.

INCORPORATING THE RULES

We just finished covering the eight essential rules of security. These rules can be a valuable tool when making a security decision, assessment, or when contemplating any security issue. With all rules, I have made suggestions as to how you might incorporate them into your own organization. We can look back to these rules regularly as they can provide clarity in otherwise confusing security issues. So, let's quickly review the rules we just discussed by studying Table 4.4.

Putting the Rules in Writing

The rules practiced within an organization should be written and published. Even if it seems like no one reads them, it still remains true that each rule will not be effective unless it is incorporated into a security policy. One of the powers of the written word is that it provides constancy and authority to the idea being written. If, for instance, there is a

Table 4.4 Overview of the Eight Rules of Security

Rule	Action
Rule of Least Privilege	Allow only as much access as is required to do the job, nothing more. In addition, allow only as much access as an individual, group, or object is capable of being securely responsible for. In any and all situations, it is best to start with the idea that nothing is allowed and work from there.
Rule of Change	Changes within an organization very often bring about new risks and vulnerabilities. To remain secure, one must be aware of changes going on within the environment. Changes should be well-coordinated and we should make sure we do not succumb to the guinea pig phenomenon.
Rule of Trust	When an organization trusts someone or something, that organization takes on some degree of risk. Trusting any subject means we are also trusting anyone and anything that has access to that subject, thus establishing a chain of trust. We should always be conscious of whom we are trusting and the risks related to that trust.
Rule of the Weakest Link	An organization's security is only as strong as its weakest link. It is important to plan your security as a whole and avoid building up strong front doors while leaving weak back doors.
Rule of Separation	To maintain a high level of security, it is important to separate objects to different security levels and apply different access rules to them. It is also important to perform security verification at all levels, making sure that even security administrators are monitored.
Rule of the Three-Fold Process	Every security project has three processes: implementation, maintenance, and monitoring. All security implementations should include the other two processes in the projected budget. If any one of these three processes is missing, then the security gained will be minimal, if any is gained at all.

Table 4.4   Overview of the Eight Rules of Security *(Continued)*

Rule	Action
Rule of Preventative Action	Reactive policies and processes can't be allowed to drive security responses. The main goal is not to rid an environment of an attack, but to prevent the attack from ever happening. An organization must be focused on dealing with security issues before they manifest, not after.
Rule of Immediate and Proper Response	Every organization should have an organized plan on how to respond during an incident. This plan should be clear, concise, and updated regularly. Everyone should be familiar with his or her part in the plan.

violation of the security policy leading to some argument or confusion, the strongest aid we can have is a written and approved paper exactly stating the policy. *Until it is written, we have little power or authority to enforce the rules within the environment.*

Decision-Making with the Rules

Each rule can be looked at as a component of a security decision. By simply walking through the rules from start to finish and asking if the matter at hand relates to any of them, the security process is automatically taking place. I will address more of this in the coming chapters with an overview on how we can make just about any security decision by simply following the rules and virtues. By making sure each rule is included in the decision-making process, we can avoid most of the confusion and error commonly found in the security decision-making process.

Thinking with the Rules

Each security rule exists in a symbiotic relationship with the other rules. Using the rules by themselves is a good general guide, but when all the rules are known well and practiced regularly within an environment, they form powerful relationships among each other and are much more effective. They help to form a security consciousness that will keep an environment safe in just about every situation.

5 Developing a Higher Security Mind

THE ART OF HIGHER SECURITY

Earlier I discussed the Virtue of Higher Focus as a fundamental security concept. With hundreds of thousands of hackers using hundreds of thousands of tools to exploit hundreds of thousands of vulnerabilities, there is little hope of addressing every possible security issue directly. Thus, it is important to approach security from a "higher" view.

If a new worm broke out, putting the Internet on high alert for contamination, it would, of course, be necessary to take a specific action, apply a specific patch, close a specific port on the firewall, or add a specific signature to all IDS devices. This is not contradicting the Virtue of Higher Focus. However, if we took specific actions that prevented only this worm and not the 100 similar worms soon to be developed, we would be in violation of this virtue.

The Virtue of Higher Focus represents the way in which we must think about security in our everyday lives. Addressing security in a higher manner helps us deal with two common security problems:

- It is impossible to secure ourselves by applying unique security measures for every vulnerability in existence.
- By thinking in terms of specific vulnerabilities and exploits, we are only able to react to security issues rather than deal with them proactively.

The question is, then, how do we deal with higher security? How do we work to keep ourselves safe when hundreds of new exploits are developed every month? The answer to these questions comes with some time-honored security practices, best practices that have been used for thousands of years. In this chapter, I will review several of the key security tools that will keep an organization safe, despite the highly dynamic nature of information warfare. All of the following practices help to generalize security practices and further develop security minds. These practices include:

- Thinking in zones
- Creating chokepoints
- Layering security
- Understanding relational security
- Understanding secretless security
- Dividing responsibilities
- Failing securely

THINKING IN ZONES

Zoning is a process that is essential for making any security decision. Briefly, zoning is the process by which we define and isolate different subjects and objects based on their unique security requirements. Again, I use the standard terms "subjects" and "objects" because we could really be talking about anything. Zoning is most commonly thought of as a network-based solution, but truly, the concept of zoning is fundamental to all security decisions. A store pharmacy could, for instance, be classified into three zones, or three separate places where security is treated in a different manner. There is the front counter, where the customer requests the drugs and provides payment; there is the technician, who relays the request to the lab in back and returns with the drugs; and then there is the actual pharmacist, who fills prescriptions. Each of these areas has its own unique risks, vulnerabilities, and security needs that define its zones. Imagine if we simply let the customers directly into the back room to fill their own prescriptions!

In this section, we will discuss several different zoning scenarios that are possible and the advantages each has to offer. We will then work to apply the zoning process by defining subjects and objects and determining which zoning scenario fits best. Almost every security decision, technical or non-technical, involves zones, so while going through each zoning scenario, be sure to keep an open mind for how these concepts can be applied. Remember that zoning is not a network-specific concept, and that zones should be created for applications, physical areas, and even for employee interactions as a defense against social engineering.

Defining a Zone

The term "security zone" is thrown around a lot in the security world; it is used for everything from application design to security camera placement. So, how do we define a zone?

A zone is a logical grouping of resources that have a similar security profile. That is to say, it is a grouping of objects that have similar risks, trust levels, exposures, policies, or security needs. A client's computers connecting from across the Internet, for example, have a different level of security and trust than an internal DB server. Similarly, a local mail server that accepts mail directly from the Internet has a different level of exposure than an internal mail server. Thus, the two would be considered to be in two different zones.

Though there can be numerous zones within any situation, the most common scenarios involve the three zones shown in Table 5.1 the trusted (or internal) zone, the untrusted (or external) zone, and the semi-trusted zone (or DMZ). These three zones can apply to almost anything, including networking and application programming, as well as designing physical security layouts.

Table 5.1   Zone Definitions

Zone	Description	Examples
Trusted	The trusted zone is where the organization's most valuable and sensitive resources exist. This zone is under our control and governed by our policies.	*Network:* Internal servers and workstations *Application:* Trusted pieces of application code *Physical:* Server rooms
Semi-Trusted	The semi-trusted zone (or DMZ) is for resources that have some degree of direct exposure. This zone is still under our control and governed by our policies, but is somehow exposed or more vulnerable than a trusted zone.	*Network:* Externally accessible Web, mail, and DNS servers *Application:* Front-end code or untrusted third-party code *Physical:* Lobbies and waiting rooms
Untrusted	The untrusted zone is the area where we have no direct control and which is not governed by our policies.	*Network:* The Internet and dial-up phone lines *Application:* End-users or external devices *Physical:* Everything outside the building

Separating Zones

Having a security vulnerability or exposure is similar to having the common cold. If one object has it, all other objects near it are likely to be exposed. To protect valuable resources, we must be able to maintain high levels of security by protecting resources from zones of lesser security control. "Zoning" is the process by which we group similar objects into proper zones and separate them from other zones for added protection. The separation mechanism could be as simple as a firewall, a security control applet, or a locked door. The goal is to have some degree of control over what happens between the different zones.

Communication Between Zones

While separating zones is all well and good for security, it would not be practical to completely isolate all zones from each other and never allow them to communicate. Just because the Internet is untrusted does not mean we should simply cut off all internal access to it. However, allowing communication between zones can be extremely dangerous if the proper security measures are not taken. Fortunately, there are several conventions to safely allow access to take place between different security zones. Each convention has its own advantages and level of exposure to consider, but almost every situation can find a security solution in one of these zoning conventions.

In the following section, we will be looking at these zoning conventions. We will look at the different zoning possibilities and the levels of exposure associated with each, as shown in Figure 5.1. We will start with the least secure and least desirable scenario and progress to the most secure and desirable scenario. Each added level of security has its potential drawbacks in flexibility and functionality, so it is important to adopt the practice that provides the least exposure without making any harmful sacrifice in usefulness.

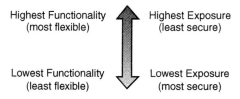

Highest Functionality (most flexible) Highest Exposure (least secure)

Lowest Functionality (least flexible) Lowest Exposure (most secure)

Figure 5.1 As zoning functionality increases, exposure increases.

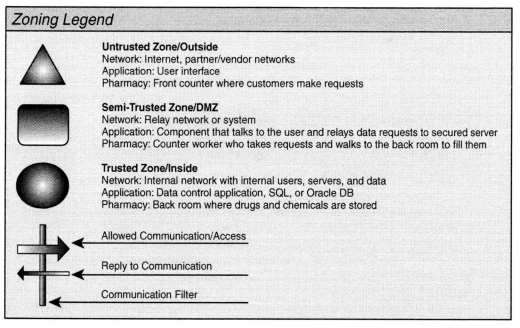

Figure 5.2 This section includes several diagrams; this legend will help us talk about them.

Inbound Communications/Access

When we think about access security and zones, we normally think about inbound communications. These are the communications where something in an untrusted zone needs to talk to something in a trusted zone. A common example of this would be customers on the Internet accessing a page on a corporate Web server.

The inbound access zoning scenarios we will discuss include:

- *High exposure*—Direct inbound access/communication
- *Medium exposure*—Relayed inbound access/communication
- *Medium–low exposure*—Indirect inbound access/communication
- *Low exposure*—Inbound traffic to an isolated DMZ

High Exposure: Direct Inbound Access/Communication

The situation depicted in Figure 5.3 is the most exposed and the most unsecure of the zoning scenarios. Here, an untrusted subject is allowed to make direct contact with a trusted object. In a casino, this would be similar to allowing the customers direct access to the vault, with perhaps one or two guards restricting this access. The trusted object is exposed to attacks from the untrusted zone. If an attack is successful, critical information and services on the trusted object will be compromised.

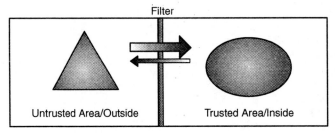

Figure 5.3 High exposure: direct inbound access/communication.

Medium Exposure: Relayed Inbound Access/Communication

In the scenario in Figure 5.4, we introduce a middle relay into the mix. A relay is responsible for negotiating communications with an external untrusted party, making

Here it is important to point out that, despite the fact that there is a filtering mechanism in place, communication is still taking place "directly." While a firewall or filtering code may exist between the two zones, it is only acting as a security bridge between the communicating parties. The actual channel of communication is directly connecting the two parties, exposing the trusted party to attack. A successful attack could compromise any system hosting sensitive data.

sure they are acceptable, and then passing them on to the receiver in the trusted area. The filters in this situation limit the access from the untrusted area into the relay, which allows the relay to remain dynamic, and communicate with many parties with some level of protection. This would be similar to having casino customers request their money from the vault and using trusted employees to actually collect the cash.

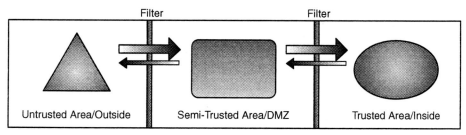

Figure 5.4 *Medium exposure: relayed inbound access/communication.*

Here, the relay is exposed to attack from the untrusted area. The relay is, however, dedicated to its task and is not running extra code, applications, services, or other things that would expose it to many attacks. The communication between the relay and the internal object is also extremely restricted. Unlike the channel to the untrusted zone, the channel between the relay and the trusted zone is highly restrictive and communications must conform to a strict set of expectations. Thus, if the relay is compromised, the chances of being able to use the relay to attack the system in the internal zone are greatly reduced.

This scenario is one of the most commonly adopted for securing an email or DNS server, authentication and data access application models, and other services or functions that require real-time access to systems, applications, or services in a trusted area.

Medium–Low Exposure: Indirect Inbound Access/Communication

We make another major improvement in our relay scenario when we can treat the relay as a mechanism that listens to everyone and talks to no one (see Figure 5.5). More accurately, the relay receives requests and updates from parties on the trusted and untrusted sides, but initiates no requests of its own. Thus, the relay has no direct access to any resources in the trusted zone. This would be similar to having security personnel supply the casino cashiers with funding from the vault, rather than letting the cashiers get funds directly.

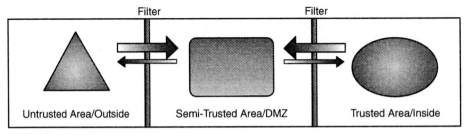

Figure 5.5 Medium–low exposure: indirect inbound access/communication.

A common example for this scenario is a Web server or application that replicates data from an internal source on a regular basis. The Web server may be designed to request information from customers over the Internet. When a customer enters the information, it is not directly relayed to the internal system, but rather, it is stored in a temporary location until the internal system performs a scheduled polling. This allows for customers on the Internet to update their information without exposing the internal data system to the untrusted Internet, or to the semi-trusted Web server.

Low Exposure: Inbound Traffic to an Isolated DMZ

Figure 5.6 shows the most secure approach that can be taken when hosting a service accessible from an untrusted zone. In this scenario, the semi-trusted application or server functions independently of the trusted zone. It services requests from the untrusted area without risk of compromising trusted zones. This would be similar to having the casino cashier only give out chips, with no access to the vault at all.

As might be expected, our most secure solution is also the least functional. While it provides the most secure approach to hosting services and applications, it can only be

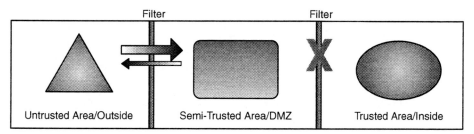

Figure 5.6 Low exposure: inbound traffic to an isolated DMZ.

used in limited situations where data updates and requests are not required to or from a trusted area. The classic use for this scenario is in an external Web server that requires no data to be polled or pushed from an inside network. Updates for Web pages are copied to a CD-ROM and installed manually on the server. If there is any statistical information on the Web server, it is copied manually via diskette and not through the network. This scenario is highly recommended for systems and applications that do not require heavy maintenance or dynamic data.

Outbound Communications/Access

Outbound communications and access are often thought of as being safe and secure. In networking, for example, many organizations put up firewalls with a simple ruleset that states: "Everything is allowed outbound; nothing is allowed inbound." In fact, there are even professional firewall devices from prominent network companies that use this as the default configuration, encouraging their customers to worry only about inbound communications.

It is true that outbound communications are less often exploited than inbound communications. This is only true, however, because hacking into a system through its outbound access does not present quite as many easy opportunities to strike. Hacking a system making outbound calls is still however quite common in the security world and is just as deadly as hacking an object accepting inbound calls.

In most forms of access, there must be data transferred in both directions. To browse a Web server, for instance, that server must send pictures, text, files, and even scripts. Sometimes this communication is obvious; sometimes it is transparent and hidden by other tools. Most modern firewalls, for example, automatically open a port for an untrusted party to send data back to a requesting client. This data can be loaded with malicious scripts, files, and miniature applications that can be used to hack a system or network.

The NIMDA worm, for example, infects Web servers and then infects the PCs of those clients browsing the server's pages. Those PCs would then spread the worm to internal systems and servers via numerous other methods. A normal network firewall would be unable to detect or prevent such activities, even if the firewall strictly forbade access from untrusted to trusted systems. Since the client is the one requesting the access and opening the channel, NIMDA simply rides back on the existing communication.

The outbound access zoning scenarios we will discuss include:

- *Medium exposure*—Direct outbound access/communications
- *Low exposure*—Relayed outbound access/communications

Medium Exposure: Direct Outbound Access/Communications

In the scenario shown in Figure 5.7, an internal system is communicating with an external system in an untrusted area. For instance, in a networking example, internal users would communicate (through an open firewall) to systems on the Internet for Web browsing or chatting.

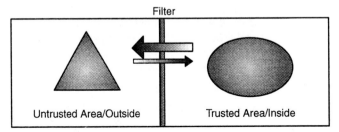

Filter

Untrusted Area/Outside   Trusted Area/Inside

Figure 5.7 Medium exposure: direct outbound access/communications.

There are two primary concerns when considering this form of direct outbound access, be it via networks, applications, or physical means:

- *Possible exposure in the return path*—In almost all cases where outbound access is required, a small gap must be made in security to allow for the untrusted party to reply. When we open our front door to talk to a person outside, there is always the chance that the individual will attempt to force his or her way into our protected area. If we make a network communication with a partner, there is always the chance that the second half of the communication will contain an exploit or virus.

- *Increased chance of exposure from internal parties*—When direct outbound access is allowed with external parties, there is a much greater chance for an exposure to occur from the inside. If, for example, a bit of malicious code is launched within an internal application, it can open a communication channel to untrusted areas, allowing for remote control. For example, a back door on a computer can initiate a tunneled communication to an external party to allow it to hack into the trusted network.

Low Exposure: Relayed Outbound Access/ Communication

To allow access from a trusted area into an untrusted area without being openly exposed requires a relay between the subject and object. Similar to the inbound relay scenario, the relaying system or application component must be a dedicated device or code that is responsible for communicating with the external server on our behalf. A classic example of this process would be a network proxy server (application firewall) that relays all Web requests to the Internet for us.

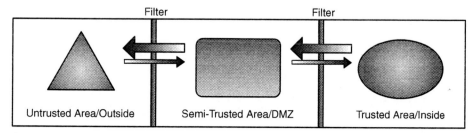

Figure 5.8 Low exposure: relayed outbound access/communications.

The system or application performing the relay services accepts numerous requests and replies from both trusted and untrusted networks. The relay limits its own communications to the internal systems in such a way that it will only pass on normal data and will strip any unexpected, extraneous, or unauthorized data. This process helps to protect all systems, and focuses more security attention on the relay instead of the internal object.

Applying the Zoning Concepts

To apply these zoning concepts in our decision-making process, we must learn to quickly recognize where different levels of security are needed. The following six-step procedure can help in this process:

Six-Step Zoning Process

1. Identify any instance where an untrusted or less trusted object comes into contact with a trusted, valuable, or more sensitive object.

2. Determine the direction of communication that is required. Ask yourself, "Is it possible to use an outbound model, or does the communication need to be initiated by an untrusted object?"

3. Determine where it would be possible to separate the trusted object into two components: one that handles the sensitive data and the other that acts as a relay or middle entity in the transaction.

4. Decide what forms of communication need to take place between the outside, middle, and inside, and which zoning model to apply. Work through them in this order:

    a. Can you effectively and efficiently use the low-exposure models?

    b. If not, can you use the middle–low- or low-exposure models?

    c. If neither model can be used, does the value of the communication and its potential risk make the high-exposure model an acceptable solution?

5. In the model that is chosen, place as many security controls between each of the components as is reasonably possible.

6. Document the reasoning, supporting data, and conclusion in this decision-making process. Keep this document for reference and to simplify the decision-making process for similar situations in the future.

Example of the Zoning Process

A baked goods engineering division has an existing server within its internal infrastructure that keeps the recipes for various types of bread. This information is kept in a secure DB on an internal network. A new initiative has been made to allow for partner bread-baking companies to access specific entries in the ever-changing DB. The board of directors has requested access to designated recipes for partner companies with a valid login and password through a secure Web browser.

Step 1   In this situation, the trusted/sensitive and untrusted objects are obvious:

Trusted/Sensitive object: Recipe data

Untrusted object: Bread-baking partners

Step 2   Since the bread-baking partners are going to be accessing the data as they need it and will be using a standard Web browser, we must allow them to initiate requests for information. The communications will be inbound (their Web browsers will be coming into the network to access the recipes).

Step 3   The recipes are stored in an Oracle DB; a standard bread-bakers application is being used to access the information. For external partners, we will need to create a Web server to act as the front-end. The Web server will be in a semi-secure part of the network and will get its data from the Oracle server, which will remain safely in the internal network.

Step 4   In considering the different exposure models, the low-exposure model would make it nearly impossible to handle real-time requests. By the nature of the project, partners will be accessing the data in real-time, and thus we must be able to relay the request at the same time that it is made. As such, the medium-exposure model, where the Web server will authenticate a user and then pass the request for information back to the Oracle DB, is a better choice. The Web server is the middle entity, so if it comes under attack, it does not directly contain any sensitive data.

Step 5   The Web server is on an isolated network protected by a firewall and IDS devices. The firewall allows only Web (Hypertext Transfer Protocol [HTTP] and Secure Hypertext Transfer Protocol [HTTPS]) traffic to flow from the partners into this Web server. The Web server must then pass through the firewall again to access the internal Oracle server. This communication is limited to a very strict and defined set of DB calls that allow access only to required types of information. Thus, if someone manages to attack the Web server, there should be no effect on the critical DB server.

Step 6   Document the decisions made with each step and place them in our "Security Decisions" folder for future reference.

CREATING CHOKEPOINTS

Chokepoints have been the key to security practices since the dawn of warfare. A chokepoint is a tight area wherein all inbound and outbound access is forced to traverse. Kings of old have understood that funneling enemies through a tight doorway makes it much easier to rain down fiery oils on them. Likewise, it is much easier to keep a thief out of a network when the network has only one gate leading in and out. In information security, chokepoints offer many advantages, including:

- *Security focus*—A chokepoint focuses our attention and resources on one area of control. This greatly enhances security while reducing the ultimate taxation on our resources.

- *Ease of monitoring*—Chokepoints greatly enhance our ability to monitor access and watch for intrusions. It is much easier to see enemies entering the castle when there is only one place to look.

- *Ease of control*—Chokepoints allow for a stronger breed of security control. It is much easier to implement good security mechanisms when only dealing with a limited space.

- *Cost reduction*—By filtering all access though one point, we will only need to implement one control device as opposed to implementing a separate control for every object. This reduces the time and materials required for the implementation and maintenance of security measures.

- *Exposure reduction*—By focusing on one or two areas of access, we introduce fewer opportunities for error and exposure than if we enforce security controls in multiple areas.

Chokepoints are a key element in maintaining a higher security practice. Creating chokepoints greatly reduces the infinite number of possible attacks that can take place, and thus are some of the best tools to use in information security.

Network Chokepoints

Network security uses chokepoints all the time. Rather than having all desktops dial into the Internet, it is common to consolidate traffic through a single controlled access point. Such chokepoints enable a high level of control on transactions between internal trusted networks and the outside world. Without such a chokepoint, higher levels of security would be needed at all entry points, making security much more difficult and expensive.

Every entry point from an external network into an internal network should be consolidated through one or more protected areas. Policies and practices in this respect should be focused on two things:

1. Securing chokepoints via filtering and monitoring
2. Ensuring that all traffic flows though chokepoints and that no new entry points are introduced

Common forms of traffic to force through a chokepoint include:

- Internet connections, including inbound and outbound access
- Vendor, partner, and customer WAN connections
- Virtual private network (VPN) and dial-in access points
- Wireless networking access points

Application Chokepoints

Chokepoints are important in both applications and services. User access into an application should be controlled by a module that filters and monitors activities. Rather than allowing a user to jump from service to service and having to enforce security on each, we should place the majority of the security focus on a single point.

If we take, for example, the Microsoft Windows 2000 operating system (or indeed, many other operating systems), we see that each workstation and server belongs to a larger domain that controls authorization, monitoring, and other aspects of security. Each user or group of users belongs to a specific domain. This scenario allows us to make the domain controller an application chokepoint. We do not need to rely on every workstation to authenticate users and log activities; we can simply forward authentication and logs on to the chokepoint controller. This allows us to focus security efforts in a central area rather than in each and every workstation.

Many other applications allow for access chokepoints, including some single sign-on and portal applications. Large organizations oftentimes develop a front-end application that secures access for many back-end applications. Applications that create an access chokepoint are very helpful in securing large organizations.

Social Chokepoints

Just as our networks and applications can be directly exposed to attacks from external entities, so can our employees, executives, partners, and customers. It is important to understand that, in the average organization, employees are given a great deal of information that is useful to a hacker. If every employee is in direct contact with everyone else in the world, then there is a great potential for a social engineering attack to perform. No doubt, one employee will prove to be the weak link within the social chain and disclose sensitive information to an attacker.

Creating a social chokepoint can be accomplished in many ways. In extreme cases, employees are not allowed to directly contact the outside world during business hours. This approach, however, is not applicable to many organizations. A good solution for many organizations has been to create virtual chokepoints for specified types of information. For example, employees can be trained that passwords and other sensitive information can only be discussed with a very specific group or department in a very specific context. Some form of predefined verification process must occur before such information is disclosed. Meanwhile, employees will be informed about confidential information, and that such information will never be solicited via email, outside phone calls, Web browsing prompts, or other unsafe contexts. Such techniques can be used to guard other information, such as employee names, phone numbers, physical security measures, access points, as well as passwords and other technical security measures.

Consolidating Chokepoints

At first glance, we may conclude that all access should be consolidated though a single chokepoint. Indeed, for some organizations, this is the best choice, but certainly not for all. When allowing access though a chokepoint, we are essentially opening a hole and potentially a vulnerability in our defenses. If, for example, we make both the Internet and trusted partners filter though the same chokepoints, we may experience some undesirable results. An untrusted entity, for example, could try to gain access by masquerading as a trusted partner, or by simply attacking the partner and attacking our organization from there. A chokepoint that controls 100 access points will be very difficult to properly secure.

For small organizations with few network connections, consolidating all access though a single chokepoint is probably the best option. However, for larger organizations, it may be desirable to separate access between multiple chokepoints, keeping higher risk enforcement policies away from more trusted ones.

A Note on Singe Points of Failure

One inherent problem with chokepoints is the tendency to introduce a single point of failure into the environment. If a component running a chokepoint service were to fail, the effects would be far more dramatic than if a component controlling a single access point failed. As such, it is important to increase the availability measures taken in relation to the number of access points consolidated. If, for example, we forced the Internet, our partners, and all dial-up traffic though a single chokepoint, we would most likely desire to add a level of redundancy by introducing a redundant chokepoint.

Applying the Chokepoint Concept

Here are some simple steps to take when contemplating chokepoints:

1. Identify all access points to a particular resource or related set of resources.
2. Consolidate all such access points though a single security object.
3. Enforce tight controls, monitoring, and redundancy on that security object.
4. Establish a policy for future access points, stating that they must be filtered through an approved chokepoint.
5. Continue to test and scan for new access points that do not filter through a chokepoint.

LAYERING SECURITY

When looking at security architecture, it is important to recognize that no single device is without flaws. *Every significant application, server, router, and firewall on the market harbors some vulnerabilities.* Additionally, all devices have a good chance of being misconfigured, unmonitored, and improperly maintained. On their own, each object will eventually become the weak link that allows a hacker into the network. This understanding is what leads to the expression: "Nothing can be 100% secure."

If nothing can be 100% secure, then it would certainly not be wise to trust any one device with all security. The firewall, for example, should not be the only thing guarding a perimeter network. Always consider the fact that a security device will have some flaw in it that will ultimately be an exposure to attack.

Basic Security Layering

Rather than focusing on any specific device or application as an all-in-one security solution, we must look at security in layers. If one device succumbs to an attack, another device should be there to save the organization from exposure. In most situations, we should consider at least three layers of security (see Table 5.2):

- *Internal layer*—The internal layer consists of controls that are applied directly to protected objects. If an attacker penetrates the outer layers, he or she should still not have complete access to internal resources. examples of this type of control include a host-based IDS on a server and a locked cabinet inside a computer room.
- *Middle layer*—The middle layer consists of the primary security devices, such as firewalls and the front door to the server room. This is the main line of defense against outside intruders.

- *External layer*—This consists of controls that protect the middle layer and help to protect us in the event that the middle layer fails. Example external layer devices include a screening router that protects the firewall and a gate outside a building.

Table 5.2   Examples of The Three Layers of Security

Scenario	External Layer	Middle Layer	Internal Layer
Perimeter network	Screening router	Firewall/IDS	Server-based controls
Physical security	External gate	Front door	Internal locked cabinet

Layering Network Security

It is common to practice layered security within networks. Perhaps a hacker cannot gain access to internal systems because he or she is stopped by a firewall (the middle layer), but the firewall itself can be vulnerable to attack. Thus, we also implement measures to protect the firewall from attack, and to maintain security even if the firewall is compromised. Rather than just placing a lock on the castle gate, it is best to build a moat to protect the castle and the lock itself. A thief is far less likely to pick the lock if he or she must first swim a moat filled with hungry alligators. Similarly, we can force the thief to pass through multiple locks and multiple moats before access is granted. Once he or she passes the front gate, the thief will find that the treasure room also has a lock on it.

We will look at this concept more in the section titled, *Perimeter Defenses* in Chapter 11, *The Rules in Practice*. For now, consider the following tips for layering network security:

- Start by having a firewall separating internal and external networks (middle layer). Enhance this by placing other security mechanisms, such as an IDS on the network between the firewall and Internet.
- Program an external router to limit access to the firewall and internal systems (external layer). The router should perform some minor sanity checking to catch any obvious attacks.
- Terminate all remote access services outside the firewall. Many dial-up and VPN vendors place security directly on remote access devices themselves, and recommend placing them in direct contact with the internal network. Doing so removes the essential middle layer and is a bad security practice. Make sure that such devices have security enabled, but are placed outside the firewall.

- Enforce strong internal security controls (internal layer). Make sure that if someone breaks through the perimeter and attacks the network, there are additional defenses. Controls should be placed on individual systems, services, and devices.

Layering Systems Security

When possible, systems and devices should have some form of layered security. There are many resource control options within most operating systems and applications, making layered security possible. An intruder may be able to attack an operating system, for example, but critical resources are still controlled by the application. Even better, if we follow our practice of zoning, we can separate critical data from externally accessible services. By doing so, we can apply security on the both front-end and back-end systems:

- Apply front-end controls, preferably ones that are centralized for multiple applications (like chokepoints). These controls should be the primary line of defense, protecting background data and services.

- Apply security that protects the front-end. For example, provide a network filter to limit Internet Protocol (IP) ranges and ports to help protect the front-end from being attacked.

- Apply security directly to back-end data and services. This includes direct controls for protecting the DB, filesystems, and operating system.

Layering Physical Security

Physical security should always be constructed in layers; the more controls that can be layered, the better the ability to control and monitor access. This can include simple layers, such as a locked front door, a locked server room door, or a locked cabinet within the server room; or, this can be complex, with stationed security guards, cameras, and other forms of access control in each area. The following guidelines will help in establishing physical security through layering:

- Protect your sensitive equipment and resources via strong centralized controls. Try to consolidate such controls by limiting the physical areas where equipment is stored. Locking doors, alarm systems, and cameras should be considered in this main area.

- Use physical protection that prevents unauthorized users from even trying to gain access to critical equipment areas. Hallways outside of sensitive rooms should be restricted to authorized personnel. If possible, cameras and other security measures should be placed in areas that lead to entranceways. At a minimum, staff should be trained to question any unknown person who is near an entry point to a sensitive area.

- Controls should be placed on sensitive objects within protected rooms as well. Critical servers and devices should be locked in cabinets. Someone gaining unauthorized access to a room, or even someone with authorized access, should not necessarily have access to all objects within the room.

Applying the Concept of Layered Security

The following steps will help when contemplating layered security within your own environment:

1. Take any object and apply as much security directly on the object as is reasonably possible.
2. Consider the access points to the object and apply as much security between the subjects and the object as is reasonably possible.
3. Consider all the object's dependencies, including operating systems, third-party services, etc., and apply security to each. This should be performed for both the object itself and any security mechanisms protecting the object.
4. Make sure the object itself and anything guarding the object are monitored and generate access logs. If one object is compromised, secured logs should exist elsewhere on a secured device.
5. NEVER consider an object safe simply because another object is protecting it. NEVER forgo directly applying security on the object assuming no one will ever be able to attack it.

WORKING IN STILLNESS

In information security, we must always be "listening" for our enemies. When someone steps across a security boundary, a log should be generated and an alarm should go off, spurring us into action. Such logs and alerts are vital elements to our overall security practices. Just like in the physical world, however, *it is impossible to "hear" the enemy if there is excessive surrounding noise to confuse us*. We will not notice the hacker tripping over a security checkpoint when our logs are full of millions of unimportant activities.

I have seen many organizations make a considerable investment in devices that alert them about anything and everything going on within their environment. Sadly, such security measures create excessive "noise," resulting in thousands of logs and alerts that need to be searched. Meanwhile, the hacker quietly slips in and out of the treasure room, his or her footsteps hidden in the chaos.

In security we listen; but for there to be noise, there must first be stillness. Security strategists from all ages have used silence as a key tool of defense. So much of security relies on the ability to detect enemies as they attempt to enter the castle. Thus, before we learn to combat our foes, we must first learn how to create silence within the environment.

Creating Stillness

Creating stillness requires a level of silence at every location where a security check takes place. This involves the art of alert filtering, making sure we only hear that which is suspicious. When a new security device is put in place, a new operating system is installed, or a new application is created, it must go through a "noise-tuning process." The tuning process should include some post-installation tweaks and adjustments, one of which should be log reduction to provide filtering. Here are some simple guidelines for tuning an object:

Five Steps for Tuning Silence

1. Study the logging and alerting features of an object. Every device and application works a little differently and weighs security events in its

own unique way. It is important to understand the classifications and severities of different events, as well as the actions that trigger them.

2. Initially set the logging and alerting mechanisms to be sensitive, thus generating a substantial number of logs and alerts. Let this run for a few days and note the types of alarms and logs that are naturally generated within the environment by "normal activities." You will most likely see many types of traffic that the security devices will consider "suspicious," even though they are harmless.

3. Adjust the settings and apply filters to remove common acceptable events. It is important to be as specific as possible and to not filter out so much that you miss a hacker performing malicious events with similar qualities.

4. Once "normal" events are operating silently, other abnormal events should begin to show up. These events may not be malicious, but they may not be authorized. Commonly logged activities include devices with misconfigured network settings, pointing them outside the local network, and broadcast services like print servers. In cases where traffic is unauthorized but not malicious, it is important to stop the event from happening at the source, rather than filtering the logs and allowing the action to continue. When possible, go to each device and make changes to stop unauthorized activities.

5. Once all "normal" activities are filtered and abnormal activities are stopped, we are ready to start monitoring. It is important to document any filters that were put in place to ignore "normal activities." Others should know what is not being monitored in case there is ever a security issue related to such an activity.

Once all the common events are removed from the environment, we will be much more likely to notice strange events that may indicate an attack. Having finished the tuning process, it will become a part of our daily effort, applying proper filters as new log-generating activities occur.

Tiered Silence

While it is important to maintain silence at security checkpoints, it is also important to maintain a thorough and accurate record of the events taking place. Many of the events filtered out of the logs could potentially play an important role in a future investigation; do we really want to erase them? When filtering events from logs, it is best to not simply discard them, but rather to store them in an unfiltered archive, separate from normal viewable logs. In this case, logging is set to record

Unfiltered Logs in Firewall X
Log generated by misconfigured printer server
Log generated by normal user activity
Log generated by misconfigured router
Log generated by normal server activities
Log generated by harmless Internet request
Log generated by hacker
Log generated by normal user activity
Log generated by harmless Internet request
Log generated by misconfigured router
Log generated by misconfigured printer server

Filtered Logs in Firewall X
Log generated by harmless Internet request
Log generated by hacker
Log generated by harmless Internet request

Figure 5.9 Basic log filtering.

many types of events that could potentially be of importance in the future. Only the logs that are the most significant, however, are held in the monitoring system; the rest are sent to an archive server. This way, we can filter out all the extra noise, but still have events on record in case we ever need to go back and do a detailed investigation. At a minimum, this should be performed with critical applications and servers, IDSs, and firewalls.

Original Unfiltered Logs Stored in Archive
Log generated by misconfigured printer server
Log generated by normal user activity
Log generated by misconfigured router
Log generated by normal server activities
Log generated by harmless Internet request
Log generated by hacker
Log generated by normal user activity
Log generated by harmless Internet request
Log generated by misconfigured router
Log generated by misconfigured printer server

Filtered Logs in Active Log Viewer
Log generated by harmless Internet request
Log generated by hacker
Log generated by harmless Internet request

Figure 5.10 Filtering with log preservation.

Striking a Balance

There is a delicate balance that must be struck when creating silence within an environment. If enough of the noise is not filtered out, an attacker's steps could be lost in a sea of extraneous logs and false alarms. If too much is filtered, the alerts will never show a hacker's presence. Here are some good higher practices to follow:

1. Watch for common events in logging and alerting systems and determine the cause of them. Who is doing what, where, when, and why?

2. Design a filter for such events, being as specific as is practical. Often, including extra conditions like the time of day for "normal activities" is important in your filters.

3. Before applying them, filters should be presented to management or others within the security group. Follow the *Rule of Change* (see Chapter 4) since configuring devices to intentionally ignore security events is a very important action. No one should perform such actions alone.

UNDERSTANDING RELATIONAL SECURITY

Information security involves numerous chains and relationships. It is rare to have a security situation handed to us in a nice little box, isolated from the rest of the world. Any given object will almost always have a series of relationships with other networks, applications, events, etc., which will prove to be of great significance to our security considerations. The security of any object is dependent on the security of its related objects, and if we fail to see these relationships, we will be unable to properly address security. I call this *relational security*.

A server, for example, may be considered safe because it is not connected to the Internet. It is, however, accessible by the administrator's home computer through a dial-up session. The administrator's system itself is connected to the Internet through a DSL connection. Thus, by following this chain of relationships, the server is actually connected to the Internet (see Figure 5.11).

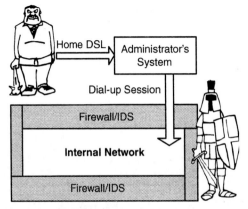

Figure 5.11 *Security Relationships.*

Following such chains can point out where systems and networks that are considered to be safe are, in reality, vulnerable. Such relationships are commonly exploited by hackers and eventually lead to the compromise of many organizations. Here we will take a look at some of the most frequent problematic chains, including:

- Vulnerability inheritance
- Chained values and risks
- Chained trusts

Vulnerability Inheritance

Probably the most vital and yet most neglected security relationship is that of vulnerability inheritance. The level of vulnerability within any object should be considered in relation to the vulnerability of its related objects. A file share between a secure system and a vulnerable system greatly diminishes the security of the secure system. If the secure system is accessible in any way from the vulnerable system, then, to some degree, it will inherit those vulnerabilities. This is especially true when considering chained paths of entry and chained trusts.

Chained Paths of Entry

Everything in this world is connected in some way or another. We could, for example, draw a physical path between any two locations and any two objects. A castle treasury exists on the same physical ground as the thief desiring access to it. The two are connected by the air, by the earth, by the empty space between them, and by their common relation with the guards and night janitors. In security, we work to recognize and remove or defend such relationships.

In the Information Age, most computers and devices are connected to each other. If any computer is connected to a network or phone line, then we could literally follow a path of wires leading from the inside of my laptop to the inside of that computer. Even if some systems are not connected, we could draw a logical map connecting my laptop to another computer, and then from there to an unconnected computer via exchanged CDs and floppy disks.

Good hackers are continually thinking in terms of such chains. They take an object and think of everything that it is connected to: the Internet, the local network, the phone system, employees, a floppy disk, a printer port, anything. Given so many possible connections, a hacker will simply evaluate the easiest and quickest method of gaining access. Most often, a hacker does not even have to look for such relationships since they simply stumble onto them while exploring an environment.

> Modern worms are great at exploiting simple paths of entry. A Web server on the Internet is infected through an infected home user's client. Another client accessing that Web server is infected through the Web browser application when accessing a Web page. A partner is infected though an infected email sent from that client. The partner's boss's PC is infected via an open file share to the partner. The partner's boss's home system is infected by copying some files onto a floppy and taking them home. Then, the boss logs on to the Internet and it starts all over again.

The basic point is that a distinct relationship exists between the majority of computers in the world, including systems that are not even connected to the Internet. Consider all theses common paths of entry that chain systems together:

- Direct or dial-up Internet connection
- Email, instant messaging, and other forms of networked communications
- Partner and vendor network connections
- Modems, remote access, and VPN connections
- Removable media like floppy disks, CDs, DVDs, and zip disks
- Employees that work with multiple systems
- New computers and equipment configured outside the local environment

Any object that has one of these possible paths (which just about every computer system does) is accessible indirectly by all of them. And such chains are not limited to systems or networks. Applications commonly consist of modules that are chained together, some directly accessible and some hidden in code. Many hackers spend a great deal of time exploiting a common application module and then search for all the applications that have integrated that module.

With this concept in mind, it is important to expand our scope of entry points beyond those that are obvious. A firewalled Internet connection does little if home VPN users do not have adequate protection on their PCs. When considering the security of an environment, or any situation, it is a good idea to draw a map of all significant and likely chained access points. Never consider any system safe simply because it does not connect directly to the Internet.

Chained Privileges

When a subject is granted access to an object, that object now shares some degree of risk with the subject. The risk, however, goes far beyond the trust extended to that individual or system. To determine what level of risk we are really dealing with, we must look at the chain of access behind the scenes. Consideration should not only be given to the subject to which we are granting access, but also to the other subjects that have access to that subject. If X grants access to Y, and Y is accessible by Z, then X is somewhat accessible by Z as well.

We could, for example, trust John with access to our treasure chamber and give him the only key. John, however, is accessible by a great many people. His wife will have access to the key if she so desires it, as well as his children and his best friend. John could get mugged on his way into work and thus a mugger would have access. When we give John access, we are giving some degree of access to all of these people.

Similarly, an application that creates and runs an administrator-level process on a server has complete access to the system. This might be considered acceptable because the process is running for a benefit. However, by granting such a high level of privilege to the process, we have also granted privilege to everything with access to that process. When a hacker determines how to access the process through an exploit, he or she may be able to operate with administrative privileges.

Chained access is a big problem within modern organizations, especially with more and more ways to conveniently access systems. Home-based VPN connections are giant issues for corporations because the home system is also accessible by the employee's children, family, friends, and is most often connected to the Internet. Such relationships must be considered whenever making a security decision.

Chained Values and Risks

Relationships are also important to consider when thinking in terms of values and risks. I will not spend a great deal of time discussing this here; we have a whole section on risk coming up. However, when determining where risks exist and what degree of risk is within each object, we must think in terms of relationships. A simple example would be a server room. When determining the degree in which we need to protect the server room and what risk this server room's loss would pose to us, we obviously need to think beyond the value of the room's construction. The room itself may hold minor value to us; whereas the room has many related objects that could suffer should the roof fall in. The room may have servers, routers, WAN links, and people within it; all of these come into consideration when we think to secure the room. This is true for all of objects, as we will see later.

Chaining Trusts

"Trust" is one of those words that should instantly make one think of vulnerabilities and exposure. Of course, we must extend some level of trust to the world around us or nothing will ever get accomplished. It is also true that many day-to-day activities can be handled much easier when we are able to trust someone or something. With every degree of trust, however, there is a degree of exposure that must be considered. Unfortunately, such exposures are often hidden in what I like to call a chain of trust.

> When receiving a file through an email from an old friend, there is little concern that he or she would desire to infect our system with a virus, or send us malicious code of any kind. The immediate response is to run the executable he/she sent without question because we trust that individual to not have any motivation to try and attack our system. It is not, however, the trust of that friend with which we must concern ourselves. The fact is that when we trust our friend with this file, we also trust a great many other people with whom we have no formal relationship. We trust, for example, the person who sent him/her that file in the first place to not have put a virus on it. We are also trusting all the applications that our friend has executed since he or she installed the system, because any one of them could have infected this file with a virus. Thus, we are trusting a great many people, applications, and events that could potentially lead us to installing a virus on our system.

Trust in Networking

Most organizations have a lack of concern when attaching their own networks to the networks of trusted partners and vendors. The security concerns of the Internet seem far too obvious, while the concerns of hooking up the network of a local supplier are minimal. Similar to the file sent by the old friend, however, the trust extends far beyond our partner. Any given partner will probably have other connections into other networks as well. They may, for example, have a connection to the Internet, in addition to connections to other partners, customers, and vendors. Are we willing to trust all of these connections as well? Before any foreign networks are connected, it is important to think about the potential chains involved. As a general rule, no external entities should share connections with a local organization unless filtered through a security device.

Many years ago, I was working with a client in the research industry who connected a network to a trusted vendor. This connection had no firewall, only very basic router filtering. After performing an audit, it was discovered that this vendor had similar connections to every major competitor of my client. On top of that, this vendor had an Internet connection without firewall protection! Thus, my client was unknowingly connected to the Internet and all their major competitors without even using a firewall.

UNDERSTANDING SECRETLESS SECURITY

In everyday life, basic security often relies on some form of secrecy. If you have $1,000 in cash under your bed, you are reasonably safe as long as no one knows it is there. Likewise, if you have all your money in a safe and the combination is 35-21-02-31, you can be pretty sure that it will still be there when you wake up tomorrow morning as long as the number remains secret. These security solutions are all based on secrecy, a concept that makes up the most basic form of security possible. If no one knows about it, or no one knows how to gain access to it, then it is reasonably secure. The only problem is that secrets are difficult to keep.

Relying on secrets for security has several weaknesses. For example, secrets have a tendency to leak out. If you talk in your sleep or if you unlock your safe in front of a window, your secret can be easily compromised. Secrets can also be guessed. A thief may look under your bed while in your house, or he/she may steal your safe and spend hours guessing the correct combination. The basic point is that *secrets are very hard to keep secret*. If you magnify this problem by a few thousand end-users and several administrators, then you will probably be spending more time securing your secrets than securing your valuables.

Secretless Security

The best security solutions are those that rely as little as possible on secrecy for protection. Our strongest forms of protection come from devices and applications that the entire world could know about, and yet would still remain secure. We should never assume that systems will remain secure simply because no one knows where they sit or what their addresses are. Likewise, we should never base security on the idea that a hacker would have to know a great many things about an environment to be able to break in. It should always be assumed that all secrets are going to be discovered. Let's take a look at some classic examples where secretless security is commonly applied.

Open Encryption Algorithms

Many older forms of encryption relied on secrecy for protecting information. For example, the writer of an encrypted message would scramble up the words, and the reader would reverse the process to decode the message. If, however, someone knew how the words were scrambled, they could also unscramble them and thus, would have access to the information.

Most modern encryption is based on secretless algorithms. The computation that is used to scramble and unscramble a message can be known to everyone in the world and yet the encrypted information remains safe. The algorithm is published for the world to see, giving everyone an opportunity to find a flaw and break it. Bad algorithms are broken in a manner of weeks, while good algorithms remain secure.

The weakness of any encryption algorithm exists in its key. The key is the small component that is only known by people with permission to decrypt the information. Therefore, the focus of encryption is mostly concerned with protecting the key.

Open Security Applications

A security application is at its best when the code for the application can be seen by everyone, and yet the application still remains secure. Applications that base their security on a secret provide a very weak level of protection in comparison. As has been proven time and again, the secret will eventually be discovered and the security will be rendered useless. Good security applications never base their security on secrets. I will discuss this more in the section titled *Open Source vs. Closed Source Security* in Chapter 10, *Modern Considerations*.

Secretless Authorization

Secretless authorization has been an emerging trend in information security over the past several years. With the dismal failure of secret-based solutions like passwords in protecting large enterprises, many organizations have implemented alternate approaches. Advanced authentication no longer bases its decision on something you know, but also on something you have or something you are. It is much easier, for example, to fake someone's password at an authentication prompt than it is to fake their eye pattern during a retinal scan. I will discuss this further in the section titled, *Handling Authentication* in Chapter 11.

The Necessary Evil of Passwords

Passwords are the most common form of security based on secrecy. Unfortunately, passwords are everywhere, including at the very start and end of an encryption process. Keeping a large number of passwords secret is extremely difficult if not impossible for large organizations. A high percentage of hacker attacks begin with the use of a stolen or guessed password, making these things one of the biggest problems in modern security. Chapter 11 will discuss the password problem in detail; for now, we will address it as yet another area where security based on secrecy fails. It is important to recognize the incredible weakness inherent in secrecy-based security mechanisms such as passwords. Organizations that must rely on passwords for security should go to great lengths to secure them from unauthorized access.

ZDNet published a good article on the secret password epidemic called "Psst... I Know Your Password"; you can find it at: http://zdnet.com.com/2100-1105-920092.html

DIVIDING RESPONSIBILITIES

A primary rule for doing business is to never put all your eggs in one basket. Never have all your investments in one industry; never rely on a single individual for performing critical processes; and never, *never* assign all security responsibilities to one employee, one system, or one process. And, if you are a security professional, make sure you are never the one with all the responsibilities and power.

Two things about us humans: We are very curious and we are very good at deception. Earlier I talked about "The Rule of Trust," which ties very closely to this concept of division. Since we should never fully trust anyone with our security, we must make sure that everyone is subjected to the same degree of security checking. This includes our security professionals, our managers, and our consultants. These individuals should have to request access, be required to authenticate, and have their actions restricted and logged just like everyone else. Anyone who is not restricted by such measures is a security threat to our environment, even if "he's/she's the nicest person in the world." A common mistake organizations make is to put complete power into the hands of their best employees. If Jane is the smartest woman in the world and can fix any problem in a matter of seconds, we have a tendency to give her access to everything and monitor nothing that she does. This, however, presents an all too fatal hole in our security model and will often lead to major security problems.

During one consulting engagement, I was brought in because the head UNIX administrator was starting to cause problems. Apparently, he did not receive the raise he desired and began to act strangely and make threats. Unfortunately, this individual had access to everything UNIX-based and was also the employee enforcing and checking security. Before anything could be done, the individual erased the entire DB storing client data gathered over thousands of hours. Much of the information was time-sensitive and could not be recovered.

Separating responsibilities does not stop with personnel, however. This concept applies just as strongly to placing all our faith in one security application, or one security device. If Server X is the only thing protecting our entire company, performing filtering, content management, intrusion detection, and authentication, and running our VPN and logging, we have a security issue. No system is perfect, and no security device is unbreakable. At a minimum, we should always have something monitoring and protecting the security of our main security devices.

Practicing Division of Responsibilities

Dividing responsibilities requires that we follow some standard management practices:

- **Maintain redundant staff**—Even if you are not budgeted for two people trained in a specific area, make sure that there is a designated back-up employee who can take over another security employee's primary responsibilities.

- **Monitor everyone equally**—Ensure that any security measure applied to the organization is either universally enforced or has some equivalent security measure applied to the administrators and security staff. If the security staff monitors everyone's access, make sure you have someone else in charge of monitoring them. This does not mean you have to have a duplicate guru in every area of practice, just someone who is capable of keeping an eye on the other employees. Always follow the Rule of Trust, especially with more powerful staff members.

- **Enforce security rules on everyone equally**—Everyone should be made aware of the rules and the fact that no one is an exception. In many organizations where Administrator X was found knee-deep in sensitive information, it is all too easy to give the excuse that administrator privileges were needed for various reasons. If, however, there are standard security measures to get through, then he/she is unlikely to bypass the required clearance. If such clearance is bypassed, then at least there is an indication and evidence that something is going on.

• **Always follow layered security practices (discussed earlier)**—If the firewall fails, what then? Will everyone be allowed into the network? Will we even know? Every security device should have some small external component assisting in security. Firewalls, for instance, should be behind screening routers. Even if the firewall was compromised, the router would still only allow specific traffic through. The firewall, as with all security components, should be reporting logs back to a central logging server that is separate from the firewall itself. This logging server should be able to tell when a system has been compromised, and should be capable of monitoring the important security devices.

FAILING SECURELY

You may have noticed that most of the examples of security issues I provided in this chapter involved some devices or applications that failed in one way or another. Hackers commonly use exploits that cause services to fail due to unexpected events. Most exploits are simple scripts that cause services to crash and open security holes. The worst examples are services that run as administrator and, when successfully attacked, give up control and allow the attacker to become the administrator.

Many times, the failure of an application, networking service, or operating system can be performed gracefully. When dealing with critical DB servers, for example, failures usually trigger events that attempt to leave the data in a usable state. Similarly, a firewall that detects a failure will oftentimes shut down access services to avoid allowing unauthorized access from outside entities. This is what is called *failing securely.*

Everything is subject to failure no matter how robust or expensive it is. Such failures often lead to lost productivity and potential security issues. As such, potential failure scenarios should be considered before any new implementation. When programming an application, failures should be made to lock down security. When a network architecture is designed, failures should not result in bypassing security as is commonly done. If a power outage occurs, services, applications, and devices should apply security during the reboot process. Consider failures in all devices and services, walk through the contingency plan, and consider the security implications therein. This is especially essential for major failure plans like disaster recovery policies.

I have had many clients implement an expensive firewall and intrusion detection architecture to protect their Internet connections and remote vendors. Knowing that a router or firewall may fail, however, they implement an inexpensive ISDN or DSL connection to act as a backup. This backup hooks directly into the network, bypassing the firewall and security. Many attacks are designed to disable a firewall or network devices, wait for an unsecure failover to take place, and then take advantage of the unlimited access.

6 Making Security Decisions

HEADS OR TAILS...

USING THE RULES TO MAKE A DECISION

So here we are! Thus far in this book, I have provided the essential components for contemplating security in just about any given situation. With this information coursing through our minds, we now possess the tools required for making a wide variety of strong and effective security decisions. By reflecting on the rules, virtues, and other concepts we have discussed, security issues and their solutions should start becoming easier to identify and resolve. At this point, it is useful to present a formulaic process through which we can use these tools. This section will be a quick guide in how to utilize the information given thus far for recognizing, understanding, and dealing with security issues.

Notes on Policy

One of the great functions of a security policy is to simplify the process of making everyday decisions. The following techniques will lead us through a logical path, starting from a clean slate, gathering and weighing the details, and making an informed security decision. Once such a decision has been made, the efforts to make this decision can be simplified for the future by writing the end results into a policy. After making a security decision, writing it down in a globally applicable format will ensure that we will not have to go through the entire decision process again in the near future. Written policies also have the advantage that they tend to put more weight behind a decision, making it easier to enforce and more readily accepted by others.

THE DECISION-MAKING PROCESS

The next few pages will guide us through a process that will greatly simplify and enhance our security decisions. Having studied the techniques and theories discussed so far in this book, we will now put them to practical use through the following steps:

- Identify the components of a security issue
- Identify the risks and threats
- Walk through our list of rules, briefly taking each into consideration
- Make the proper decision

Identify the Components

When a decision needs to be made, we must first discover and isolate the various components involved. Doing so will help to ensure that multiple aspects of security are considered. Almost every situation we face consists of several important components bound in some form of relationship. A decision about a router affects all its related WAN connections; a decision about a room affects all the equipment in the room; and a decision about a server affects the software, processes, and users of that server. To see all these components and understand their relationships, it is helpful to write them down in a list such as that shown in Table 6.1:

Table 6.1 Security Decision Example

Objects	Example: A WAN Connection
Direct objects	The WAN link itself
	Data traversing the WAN link
	Entities connected on both sides of the WAN link
Related objects	The routers
	The room that houses the routers and where the WAN link terminates
	The carrier that controls the line

Identify the Risks and Threats

I will discuss risks and threats in much more detail later in this book. For now, I will give simple examples for considering these topics.

Each component considered will have some level of risk and some related threats. Just about everything can have a risk or threat associated with it, but the goal is to identify those that have some significance to the organization. We need to consider each component individually and think of it in relation to the risks and threats involved. We will consider both the risks introduced by a component, as well as the risks the environment poses to that component, as illustrated in Table 6.2.

Filter Through the Rules

Once we have identified the different components and their risks and threats, we need to consider what each rule says about the matter. Would the decision violate one of the fundamental rules? Can we come up with a solution that is effective and follows all the rules? Below I have listed each rule and a series of sample questions to consider for each security situation.

Table 6.2 Component Risks and Threats

Component	Sample Risks and Threats TO A WAN Link	Sample Risks and Threats FROM a WAN Link
WAN	How valuable is this connection to our organization? Do our users rely on its services? Is the data sensitive or valuable?	If the WAN link and its data were compromised, what could happen to the organization? If the WAN link became unavailable, what could happen to the organization?
Room	If the room was compromised, what could happen to the WAN link? If the environment conditions were poor (bad power, heat, etc.), what could happen to our WAN link?	N/A
Router	If the router was compromised, what could happen to the WAN link? If the router failed, what could happen to the WAN link?	If the WAN link was compromised, what could happen to the routers? The routers hold other connections; what might happen to them?
Connected networks	If either entity was compromised, what could happen to the WAN link? If either entity had a networking failure, what could happen to the WAN link?	If the WAN link was compromised, what could happen to the connecting networks? If the WAN link failed, what could happen to the connecting networks?

The Rule of Least Privilege

We should be sure that our decision is made in such a way as to limit all parties and devices to the exact amount of access as is required and nothing more.

- Do all subjects involved have the least amount of access to the object as is required?
- Are all subjects capable of handling the object securely?

- Are we actively enforcing the Rule of Least Privilege and security against unauthorized access?

With the Rule of Least Privilege, it is important to consider access in both directions. Going with the WAN link example, we may consider each question in reverse: Are we allowing only those that require access to access the WAN link? Are we allowing access from entities on the WAN link only to areas that are required?

The Rule of Change

We should ensure that any changes being made are clear, well thought out, and have been coordinated with all affected parties. There should be a formal change process in most security considerations. Some important questions to think about are:

- Are we following a formal process, or at minimum, coordinating with all the parties that could potentially be affected by the change?
- Have all the changing components stood the test of time? Are we in danger of being a guinea pig?
- Are we introducing any completely new objects into the environment? Could a similar solution include technologies, brands, and products already running within the organization?

The Rule of Trust

Most situations, will involve some form of trust. Different subjects warrant different levels of trust that may affect our security decisions. Here are some good considerations to keep in mind:

- Are we treating every subject with some measure of security and caution?
- Are we trusting any entity more than it has proven to be trustworthy?
- Are rules being enforced on every subject involved?
- Is there any subject that is granted special privilege that may reduce our ability to maintain good security?

The Rule of the Weakest Link

In comparison with other security measures, we must always be looking for the weakest link in any new endeavor. Any addition or modification to an environment has the potential of introducing a new vulnerability, risk, or threat. New decisions should reflect the Rule of the Weakest Link and be as secure or more secure than other similar decisions.

- Has the security of any addition or modification been tested and ranked against existing security?
- Are we introducing any vulnerabilities in an area where such vulnerabilities never existed before?
- Are the security measures we are applying in any way weaker than security measures we have applied before?

The Rule of Separation

Following the Rule of Separation, we should look at the issue and determine whether or not we are combining objects or subjects that are better off remaining separate. If our decision has to do with enabling a service, installing a new application, or granting privileges, we should make sure we reflect back on the Rule of Separation to check for inherent weaknesses.

- Are we isolating sensitive or vulnerable components through the practice of zoning?
- Are we combining elements that should be separate, such as services and applications that have different risks and levels of security? If we add together all risks and vulnerabilities from all elements, are we comfortable with going forward?
- Have we divided power in such a way that no one individual or device is fully responsible for security?

The Rule of the Three-Fold Process

Every decision should be thought of in terms of the Rule of the Three-Fold Process. Before implementation has begun, consideration should be given to the tasks that will take place after the project is completed.

- Have we included proper consideration, effort, and funding for all three processes?
  - Implementation
  - Monitoring
  - Maintenance

The Rule of Preventative Action

When relevant, security decisions should focus not only on the specific problem at hand, but also on the source of the security issue. When solving a problem, look beyond the specific instance and contemplate solutions that will help to solve similar situations as well.

- Are we thinking proactively and making decisions that will affect the source of the problem, and not just fixing a symptom of a larger issue?

The Rule of Immediate and Proper Response

Security decisions that are made in reaction to issues, or that relate to the planning of a reaction, should follow the Rule of Immediate and Proper Response.

- Is this decision being considered in accordance with the organization's written policies? If policies or processes are not written, should they be drafted for the future?
- Has the response been well thought out, or could this be a knee-jerk reaction that may cause more damage than good?
- Are actions going to be taken in an adequate time frame as to not lose evidence or allow further damage to be done?

Considering Zones

As we look at a security issue, we must make sure that we create solutions that fall in line with the zoning principles. Most security decisions involve access to some resource by some application, system, or party. Using the Rule of Least Privilege, we must identify exactly what access is required, and using zones, we must isolate the access to protect the resource and other resources. Thinking in zones is, however, a very dynamic process. Having read about zoning in Chapter 5, *Developing a Higher Security Mind*, and understanding each exposure concept, we should be well-equipped to apply it in many different situations. Here we will walk through a few of the most common concepts:

- If an object is being accessed from an external party, is it isolated in a protected DMZ?
- If communications are taking place between trusted and untrusted parties, can we place some form of protected relay in between?

- If an object needs access to sensitive data, can the data be stored, processed on a separate device, and pushed, or do we need to allow for direct access?
- If we compare the solution to the different zoning solutions, are we following the most secure zoning scenario that is reasonably possible?

Layering Security

Any decision made should be thought of in terms of layers. What if a device fails? What if an attack is successful? What will we do then? It is always good to assume that an individual security measure will fail and make sure that other security measures are in place. It is also wise to assume that blending different forms of security will provide a much tighter defense than a single security layer.

- Is all security relying on a single mechanism?
- If security was to fail in any area, are there other means of protection that will continue to limit the potential damage?

Considering the Overall Level of Security

Finally, when considering any decision, we must be aware of the security of the surrounding environment, as well as the ultimate security goal of the organization. In accordance with the Rule of the Weakest Link, it will do us little good to make any one item secure when everything around that item is left completely vulnerable. We should avoid focusing so narrowly on the security decision at hand that we lose sight of how it fits with the rest of our security. We should not build a fortress of one system, when the remaining systems are left open, unless this system is of much higher risk or we are planning to build all other systems up to this level as well.

The Policy Test

A good test of a decision is to think of its outcome in terms of a policy. Would we be comfortable documenting this decision and requiring that the same decision be followed over and over again? Every good security decision should be directly in line with the overall security goals of the organization. We should feel comfortable adding it to our policies and procedures, even if we choose not to. It is important that all security decisions are consistent with previous and future decisions, and we should avoid making too many variations or introducing a weak link. If we are not comfortable making this decision into a permanent policy, we should question the quality of the decision itself.

EXAMPLE DECISION

Here, I have created an example situation where we would need to make a good security decision. I follow the process outlined above, making note of the applicable rules and theories that have gone into the decision-making process. Of course, it is not recommended that every security decision be written down in the following manner. However, when we can train our minds to follow this process, it will be easier to make good, strong, and consistent security decisions for our organizations.

An Example Security Issue

Our organization just announced a new partnership with Big Bob's Billing. Big Bob's is a third-party billing group that will handle all customer financial issues, such as payments, credits, and delinquent accounts. To accomplish this, Big Bob's requires some link into our order tracking system. The work is on a real-time request system; therefore, we cannot simply send them the information. Big Bob's works with other organizations through VPN-encrypted Internet tunnels, and with some customers through direct links like ISDN and frame relay. They will require some form of connection to our DB server and have asked us how we desire to handle it.

Identifying the Components

This decision includes several components, each with its own security issues, risks, and threats. We have identified the components that we have some concerns with in Table 6.3:

Table 6.3   *Identified Components*

Component	Description
Connection	The connection to and from Big Bob's Billing that will allow access into our DB. This includes the connection itself as well as the data traversing the connection.
Order tracking DB	The actual DB and server to which we are allowing access.
Internal network	The network where we will terminate the connection and to which the DB server is connected.

Filtering Through the Security Rules

The following is a sample instance where our organization will follow the previous process to analyze the situation and make a decision:

Table 6.4   The Rule of Least Privilege

Connection	Big Bob's will terminate a connection within our organization. We should take steps to implement some form of connection authentication to ensure Big Bob's is the only organization able to make this connection.
DB server	Big Bob's will need access into the DB, but only for the particular data records that affect them. Big Bob's only needs access to read information; therefore, no write or delete privileges should be granted. We should limit DB access accordingly through whatever means possible. The DB server can enforce authentication and authorization restrictions, but it would be even better to isolate Big Bob's data on a separate server.
Network	To gain access to this data, Big Bob's employees will have to traverse the internal network. Since they only need access to this one server, we should strictly limit access within the network via source, destination, ports, time of day, and any other applicable filters via a firewall and other forms of layered filtering (such as a router and server).

Table 6.5   The Rule of Change

Connection	The connection will be plugged into an existing router. This is a simple process, so we just need to inform the IT group and schedule the change in advance.
DB server	A few minor adjustments will need to take place on the DB server to allow for the access. The changes will be performed off-hours and all steps of the change will be documented and reviewed in advance. All related DB and application developers and administrators will be informed of the change.
Network	Introducing the new network connection will require a simple change in internal routing. This change will be announced to the IT group, scheduled in advance, and documented in change logs.

Table 6.6 The Rule of Trust

Connection	Big Bob's is a foreign entity, ungoverned by our policies; as such, we cannot trust them. We will put security devices in place to strictly control and monitor what subjects have access to what objects.
DB server	We do not trust that Big Bob's will access only the DB server and we will do everything we can to monitor such access and limit it to exactly what is required.
Network	Big Bob's is an untrusted entity and will not be granted any form of access to the internal network beyond the required access.

Table 6.7 The Rule of the Weakest Link

Connection	The connection to Big Bob's will be treated like any other partner or vendor, and does not introduce any significant risk or threat that we do not already have.
DB server	This is the first time we will allow access to the internal DB server from an external party. We need to research any vulnerabilities that we have not considered, since to date we have been using it strictly for internal access. Allowing access into this server may expose vulnerabilities never before considered by the staff.
Network	The internal network does not currently allow anyone access to internal systems within the environment. Allowing Big Bob's employees to traverse the internal network introduces a new weak link for the organization. We should consider pushing the data out to the DMZ to avoid reducing security of the internal network or creating any new exposures.

Table 6.8 The Rule of Separation

Connection	As already decided, the connection will be filtered through a firewall and isolated from other network connections.
DB server	When accessed by Big Bob's client systems, the DB server will be somewhat exposed to the vulnerabilities of those clients. This supports the idea of pushing the data off the DB server and having clients grab the information from somewhere else beside this critical system.

Table 6.8   The Rule of Separation *(Continued)*

Network	The Rule of Separation further supports the idea that the DB should live on a separate DMZ network, isolating any exposures from the sensitive internal network.

Table 6.9   Rule of the Three-Fold Process

Connection	The monitoring and maintenance of the connection itself is taken care of by the telephone company, and we should verify that this is the case. As for the router, it is included with the regular maintenance plan for all the networks. We will develop a process to adequately monitor and maintain any security device put into place.
DB server	We will need to inform the group that monitors the servers of these changes, and may desire to set up scripts to closely monitor the access from Big Bob's. We will continue to maintain the DB's security level by keeping up-to-date with security-related patches and fixes.
Network	The network will be continually monitored for intrusions from Big Bob's and other external entities. Other objects within the network will be updated regularly with security patches.

Table 6.10   The Rule of Preventative Action

Connection	The connection with Big Bob's will be included in regular security audits. All components related to this connection will be inspected.
DB server	The DB server will be continually maintained with any new security updates. It will also be scanned and inspected during audits for any new vulnerabilities.
Network	Controls to protect the internal network from Big Bob's will be reviewed and tested during regular security audits.

Table 6.11 *The Rule of Immediate and Proper Response*

Connection	A simple plan will be drafted stating how to handle a potential intrusion from external networks like Big Bob's. The connection with Big Bob's is not required on a 24×7 basis, so it will be specifically listed as a connection that can be "unplugged" during an incident.
DB server	Plans will be made to revoke external access, including Big Bob's, in the event of an attack against this sensitive server.
Network	Since it was determined that Big Bob's can be disconnected without issue, the network security staff will be informed to do so in the case of a network attack originating from Big Bob's, or related to the DB server.

Identify the Risks and Threats of Each Component

As part of the agreement with Big Bob's Billing, we have no responsibility for the safety of their company through this connection, and we will not go out of our way to protect them any more than our other networked partners. We have recommended that the organization place their end of the connection safely behind their own firewall for protection. For our organization, each component in Table 6.12 has been identified to have risks.

Considering the Zones

To help enforce the Rule of Least Privilege, we will place Big Bob's connection in front of our firewall. However, we not only want to limit Big Bob's access to our networks, but we also want to control the area that will be responding to Big Bob's communication requests. Considering several zoning scenarios, we find that the indirect inbound access scenario best secures the organization and its resources. Rather than allowing connections to go directly into the network, we will instead set up a DMZ with a smaller middle DB server that hosts only the information Big Bob's needs to access. This system will be fed information every couple of hours by the normal DB server. The middle system will not have direct access into the internal network and will not expose us to a relayed attack. We will also not allow this system to directly communicate with external parties, thereby reducing the risk of internally launched exploits.

Table 6.12 Risks Associated with this Connection

Component	Risk from Big Bob's Billing
Direct risk	In three months, this connection will most likely become very valuable since our entire billing system will be switched through to Big Bob's Billing. The work of about 20 local employees and all immediate revenue generated from customer bills will depend on the link. A full-day outage could cost an estimated $10,000 in damages.
	The data transmitted across this line is very sensitive and valuable to others since it includes credit cards and personal information about clients. If it was compromised, it could cause great damage to the organization. The data must also be accurate and free of error to ensure proper billing takes place. The data must also be hidden from the eyes of others.
Room	The connection must be terminated in a room or closet with a router. The line could be made unavailable of exposed due to poor environmental conditions, untrained personnel tripping on cords and pulling wires, or if the termination is "tapped." As such, the room should be secured and protected from these threats.
Network	The line will either directly connect us to Big Bob's Billing at a medium cost or be terminated through the Internet at a very low cost. Traversing the Internet poses much greater threats than a direct connection, and the risk of information being exposed is very high for the organization. Despite the cost savings, the Internet is not considered safe enough for this form of transmission, even with VPN encryption. There is no guarantee that the VPN device will not fail, be misconfigured, or be hacked and expose extremely sensitive data.
	Regardless of how access is granted, the organization is introducing new potential threats into the organization. As with any external connection, there is always the possibility of an exposure to the outside world.

Layering Security

Security in this situation will be layered in the following manner:

- All requests will be performed against the secured middle server, not directly against the internal server.
- The external router that terminates the connection from Big Bob's will have basic access controls to limit traffic, providing an additional layer and protecting the firewall.

- All requests will pass through the firewall and IDS servers, which will filter and log access attempts.
- The DB server's operating system will be hardened to reduce vulnerabilities and increase security.
- The DB application will enforce its own security controls with user authentication and authorization.

Considering Overall Security

The organization recognizes that it is taking on new risks by connecting with Big Bob's network and by allowing Big Bob's access to sensitive information and services. However, we have some level of confidence in Big Bob's reputation and the security of their organization and employee practices. We have put enough security measures in place to make up for many of the new risks. As such, this decision does not lessen security, nor does it require excessive measures or costs to secure our network from this foreign entity.

Putting It All Together

The example process of examining the rules in light of a specific security issue has provided us with all the elements for making a good security decision. We have determined several areas of concern and the security precautions we should take to avoid exposure. Given the information documented above, we could draw the following conclusion:

The connection to Big Bob's Billing introduces several risks that the organization has never been exposed to before. By allowing an external party to connect in such a manner, we are putting the internal network and critical DB server at risk. Sensitive customer information is going to be transmitted to Big Bob's via a network connection, putting this data at the risk of exposure. Also, by relying on an external entity to perform a critical function, there is a high risk if the connection becomes unavailable. This risk, however, can be greatly reduced through the following security precautions:

- **Connection**—The connection should be terminated in a secure location, preferably behind a locked door. Wires and such should be organized to reduce the possibility of accidental damage. The termination point should have security controls that ensure that only Big Bob's has access to make the connection. The changes made on the router terminating this connection should be scheduled in advance, with our change management staff.

- **DB**—The critical DB server has, thus far, only been accessible to the internal community. Allowing Big Bob's access to it introduces several new threats and justifies enhanced security controls. To reduce the amount of exposure, it is desirable to push the information required by Big Bob's onto another server dedicated to Big Bob's and any future partner with similar needs. If this new server was attacked, only the information used by Big Bob's would be exposed, and there would be no need to modify or erase information on the main server.

  The DB information will be read-only to Big Bob's employees and the server will have control such as authentication, authorization, and logging to keep unauthorized users out. This server will only accept updates from the main server on the internal network.

- **Network**—Some form of access must be granted into our organization's network to accommodate Big Bob's. Access from a dedicated connection was decided to be much more appropriate given the highly sensitive nature of the information. In addition, rather than allowing for this partner to traverse the internal network, the data will be pushed to a DMZ. Access to this DMZ will be highly restricted by a firewall and monitored by an IDS. Information will be pushed to this network on a regular basis, and access will be allowed from Big Bob's or from the DMZ into the internal network. It has also been determined that sensitive information needs to be encrypted while in transit. Big Bob's will need to coordinate some form of encryption via the secure sockets layer (SSL), a local VPN, or through the DB itself.

- **Overall**—All components of this connection will be included in regular security audits. Additions will be made to the incident response plan as related to this new connection and access. A connection policy will be drafted to detail all the information discussed above. This policy will be reused for any similar situations in the future.

7 Know Thy Enemy and Know Thyself

UNDERSTANDING THE MODERN HACKER

Security is one of the few fields in technology where the problem and the solution both deal with human beings. We do not simply beat a router to death because its protocols are not functioning. Rather, we deal with other people who, like us, have the capacity to be incredibly cunning and dynamic. So, just as a networking engineer must have an understanding of routers, so must a security engineer have an understanding of hackers.

> Before we begin, let me state that the term "hacker" is not necessarily the correct term for describing a computer criminal. "Hacker" basically refers to an individual who is proficient in a specific subject; someone who knows the ins and outs of a particular technology or topic. Terms like "attackers," "crackers," "freakers," and such are more accurate in describing digital enemies. Since, however, it is now commonplace to use the term "hacker," I will make life easy and continue the misuse of this term.

As a general rule, stereotyping is to be avoided. After all, a hacker is human and has feelings as well. In deference to all the friendly computer criminals I have met and known over the years, the following section is meant as no offense. For the sake of education, however, I will lay down some of the more accurate stereotypes that have emerged over the years for they are quite useful in defining the individuals we see time and again.

Summertime Hacker

The summertime hacker is an average, run-of-the mill "Joe" who has spent a little too much time on the Internet and has read one too many Usenet postings on how to hack the FBI. Few technical people can honestly say they have never considered trying to hack into a computer or network. Search across all the homes and businesses in the world and you will most likely find a high number of L0phtCrack and NMAP installations on the systems of curious individuals. Most employees of an organization will, at some time, attempt to access resources they are not authorized to access.

Motivation

Hackology is a very interesting topic to many people. The summertime hacker is motivated by a general curiosity of the topic, the tools, and of his or her ability to execute them. Many summertime hackers are individuals exploring the world of information security, only without the permission of the groups they are attempting to exploit. Technical employees with extra time on their hands are the most likely to be summertime hackers.

Methods

Hacker tools are available left and right on the Internet. You may have to close a few hundred pornographic Web page advertisements before you actually get to where you are going, but it is quite simple nonetheless. Summertime hackers will use any readily available tool, most often without understanding its purpose or capabilities. These individuals are usually more interested in trying out a new tool than actually causing any damage.

Severity of Threat

Lucky for us, simple hacker tools used by an individual who does not have any particular motivation or hacking skills are a relatively minor threat in an environment that has applied good security practices. After one or two failed attempts, the hacker will have changed focus and become intrigued by something else. In an environment that lacks security, however, these individuals can be far more destructive than even they imagine.

Hacker tools acquired from the Internet are often loaded with back doors and Trojan horses that execute unknown to the hacker. In an environment where an administrator has downloaded Hacker Tool X to his or her workstation, there is a good chance that the tool will make the workstation vulnerable to attack from other hackers. Installing such a tool as an administrator can easily give administrative privileges to hackers all around the world. Thus, the summertime hacker often does much more damage than he or she intends. Additionally, since these individuals rarely spend the time to fully understand the tools they are using, there is a high probability that a tool will be used improperly and potentially cause far more damage than intended.

At one client, an employee trying to perform a simple DoS attack on a coworker's computer actually ran the attack against the entire network. The tool ended up temporarily disabling over 60 computers before he realized his mistake.

Script Kiddies

Generally speaking, script kiddies are bored individuals without girlfriends or boyfriends who can think of nothing better to do on a Saturday night than make people come into work to fix a failing system. Script kiddies can be good company for people awake at 3 a.m. who desire to play video games or debate which Open Source operating system is really the best. However, script kiddies are an incredible nuisance in the security world; this is mostly due to the fact that there are thousands and thousands of these individuals out there running around with dangerous tools and a general desire for chaos.

Script kiddies are usually teenagers and college students that have more of an interest in causing damage than actually learning about technology. The average kiddy preys on unsecured networks, home systems, universities and schools, and anyone they can find on the Internet.

Motivation

Not young enough to be innocent and not talented enough to be truly malicious, script kiddies are normally a mix of the curious and those desiring the sense of power that professional hackers feel. Most kiddies "hack" because it entertains them or makes them feel like they are being active in some particular cause. Often, it gives them a chance to show off their skills in a strange world where they have a chance of actually being admired by other script kiddies. Many also see it as a claim to fame, mostly among other kiddies and kiddie wanna-bes within the hacker community.

Methods

Sometimes, script kiddies will target a specific site; but more often, they will continue to roam from address to address, looking for that one unpatched server or unfiltered network. This process of hacking without a specific target in mind is a large contributor to their ultimate success (quantity, not quality). When a new type of vulnerability is discovered and an exploit is developed, a large number of these hackers will be inspired to try it out on random networks. The more advanced kiddies will use their skills in programming to chain together common exploits developed by skilled hackers. One in several hundreds of kiddies will actually program a good original exploit; in which case, the others will start using it as well.

Severity of Threat

With the exception of worms and viruses, script kiddies are probably responsible for causing most of the damage we see in information security. This is not due to any particular capabilities, but due to the sheer number of kiddies out there and their unfocused interest in doing damage. One of the major threats of the kiddies is that it is quite easy to become one, and thus the world is flooded with them. If you place a computer on an active Internet connection with a personal firewall, you will be lucky to go 15 minutes without at least one probe from a system controlled by a kiddie. If there is an unpatched and accessible device within the environment, eventually a kiddie will find it.

The majority of security measures that organizations put in place are geared to defend against this form of hacker. Firewalls and IDSs are at their best when battling against script kiddies.

Targeting Criminals

The main difference between a script kiddie and a targeting criminal is focus. Often, a targeting criminal will have more resources and a higher level of skill, but it is the focus and determination that end up devastating the target. When the average person hears the word "hacker," this is the type of individual that comes to mind.

Motivation

Most targeting hackers are focused because they have some form of real-world incentive. Frequently, they are looking for profit, attempting to steal valuable information, such as customer information, bank accounts, or credit cards. They may attempt to manipulate such information; for instance, they may try to change grades at a university, or add an extra million to their bank accounts.

Sometimes, these groups and individuals are motivated by the desire to hurt another person or organization. I have seen skilled hackers break into hospitals where family members have died. I have seen members of activist groups hacking into and causing millions of dollars in damages to organizations that are enemies of their cause. Often, enraged customers will attempt to hack into companies that they feel treated them unfairly. And, it is quite common to find an upset former employee using his or her newly discovered free time to exact revenge on the company that terminated him/her.

Methods

Anything goes for the methods used by this form of attacker. Normally, a series of events will take place, including a process of information gathering, exploiting development, and attacking. Such actions are not at all limited to programming and network-based measures, either. Dumpster diving for discarded access information, calling up employees, and visiting the facility usually yield enormous amounts of information. Low-cost methods that only require focus and determination are the tools of the average targeting criminal. This person will normally have all the time in the world to wait, plan, and attack.

Severity of Threat

The good news is that a hacker of this nature is not nearly as common as the script kiddy or summertime hacker. Of course, the larger the organization and the more active it is, the more tempting a target it will become. The bad news is that if a targeting criminal really wants to do some damage, it is extremely difficult to prevent it.

More often than not, someone intelligent enough to be a targeting criminal also has some sense beyond the desire to simply destroy everything in sight. The ultimate level of damage the individual inflicts will end up depending not only on his or her level of skill, but also on his/her level of motivation.

Employees (and Consultants)

Open any book or article on security published in the past five years and they all say the same thing: "Concerning digital security, your employees are the most lethal threat." It's not that employees are innately evil; it's just that they often have access to too many things, and we humans are a very curious species. In any case, employees are indeed a top security concern for most organizations.

Motivation

Motivations exist left and right for employees. Employees are most often summertime hackers and script kiddies operating from the inside of networks. This trait makes them more dangerous. Often, employees hack simply because of the "Could I?" thought. Downloading the latest hacker tool is so much more entertaining than filling out a boring time card. For some employees, it is simply a hacker power trip, having the capability to cause devastation within their own environment.

The far more serious threat comes from those who are motivated by ambition or anger. Such employees are similar to targeting criminals on the outside of the organization, only an employee is scheming, planning, and probing safely from the comfort of the inner keep of the castle. The employee hacker with strong motivation can be an extremely destructive element to any organization.

Methods

The sky is the limit for these individuals. It is not uncommon to find a wide variety of hacker tools installed on employee systems. Nor is it uncommon for an employee to look over the CIO's shoulder while a password is typed. Being on the inside of the organization, the individual will have access to systems on the LAN, file shares, email, and other employees. The advantages employee hackers have are further amplified by the inherent trust that is shared within the organization. If a support engineer wants to use your computer for a second to install some little application, why would you say no?

Employee hackers often plant Trojan horses, remote control applications, sniffers, and keyboard stroke recorders on systems in which they are interested. It does not take a great deal of effort for someone on the inside to learn everything there is to know about the organization through unauthorized information access. Even months and years after an employee has left a company, the tools can still be there, listening.

Severity of Threat

A normal hacker would have to accomplish 20 tasks breaking through an organization's security systems simply to get to the point where an employee already is. On top of this, an employee is there every day and knows far more about the company than an anonymous hacker. It is thus reasonable to say that an employee has far more power to unleash pain on company systems and networks than an outside hacker could ever dream of. There is no limit to the devastation a disgruntled employee can cause to an organization, especially if he or she has no fear of being caught.

True Hackers

If we follow the literal definition of a "hacker" as someone talented and knowledgeable concerning all aspects of a particular subject, and combine that with a streak of malice or a general lack of consideration for others, we get what is called a true hacker. Such hackers are extremely gifted in programming, as well as with knowing how to assemble and disassemble processes. Being at the top of their game, such hackers often crave finding something that will challenge them. They work to develop new worms or viruses, or develop new ways to break encryption patterns or exploit security applications. In any case, these individuals are a big threat to the world of information security and can cause billions of dollars in damage.

Accidental Hackers

Another extremely common type of hacker is the accidental hacker. These hackers are often employees, customers, and partners. They are individuals who are authorized to access systems and resources, but accidentally strike an unexpected key, trip over a cord, or delete a file that causes a device to crash or exposes information to the world. When we think of protective measures, we must think of the occasional mishap from the normal user community as well. Such hackers are often overlooked and can truly devastate an organization without any malicious intent.

The Hacker Community

An inspiring motivation for many hackers is simply to be a participant in the hacker community. There are thousands of Web sites, news lists, and mailing groups dedicated to the hacking and cracking of systems and networks. There are also many thousands of hackers who subscribe to such sites, submitting their ideas, new tools, and long tales of how they single-handedly cracked a federal mainframe or wrote something semi-clever on the front page of a high-profile Web site.

The hacker community also tends to attract some extremely intelligent and talented individuals who, to be quite honest, you would never want as enemies. While on an Internet chat discussion, these individuals tend to be quieter; they may interject comments and opinions on occasion, usually to reprimand the younger hackers for their "ignorant bantering."

The hacker world parallels the security world in many respects. Hackers have their own conferences held all around the globe. Some hackers make a living from selling their tools and techniques to other hackers, or selling books to the general public. All in all, the general hacker community is extremely active compared to many other digital organizations.

Community Wars

When looking into the world of the hacker, one should not be blinded into thinking the war has only two fronts. Hackers do not limit their attacks to professional organizations or remain true to some mystical hacker code of honor. Hackers have their own society, and as with any society, there are battles to be fought.

Hackers are continually attacking other hackers in a struggle for resources, fame, and pride. Many consider it to be a great accomplishment to destroy the site of a fellow hacker. Others may disagree with the political views or motivations behind opposing hacker organizations and thus, launch attacks. Many of these battles result in different hacker groups building up great forces on either side. Thousands of systems around the world launch attacks against other hacker sites without the system owners ever knowing.

> Remember when Yahoo, eBAY, CNN, and other major sites were taken down by thousands of zombie computers around the world? Could you imagine that a single hacker group could coordinate such an effort? Imagine, however, if over a period of years, several groups of hackers fought wars among themselves, building up hundreds of zombie systems and pitting them against other hackers. Now, imagine if all those hackers decided to call a temporary truce and use their combined forces to blast a number of high-profile sites. It becomes very clear how such efforts can take place. Like an arms race, hackers build up to gain arsenals on each side until they have the power to launch a major offensive!

WHERE MODERN VULNERABILITIES EXIST

Security vulnerabilities are everywhere and in everything. Have you ever wondered why there are so many successful hackers breaking into systems? Do we really believe that every 17-year-old that breaks into a nuclear power plant is a super-genius? The fact of the matter is that you can't toss a pebble without striking an object that is vulnerable. The average hacker has only to sip a cup of hot cocoa while a scanning application looks across thousands of organizations for well-known vulnerabilities. The hacker may not even know what the vulnerability is or why it exists, but the newly downloaded scanner is pre-programmed with thousands of wiz-bang gadgets and exploits. Given a few hours, the hacker will find more vulnerable systems than he or she knows what to do with.

What Do I Mean by "Vulnerable?"

When an object is vulnerable, it simply means that the object can be affected in an undesirable way or allow for access to information and services without consent or control. When an exploit like a new buffer overflow attack is combined with a corresponding vulnerability like an unpatched Windows NT server, then "something bad happens." A system without a UPS/battery backup is vulnerable to power outages, just as an unpatched Linux box sitting on the Internet is vulnerable to a multitude of hacker tools.

The most common vulnerabilities are related to **DoS** threats, meaning given a specific set of conditions, a system or service will become unavailable for its normal use. An example would be a network-based overflow attack that stops email services from running, or an unexpected string of variables that causes a Web server to reboot. These incidents result in lost time, lost customers, and lost money.

On the more intense side, a vulnerability can also allow someone to gain access to read, modify, execute, or delete actual data on your system. Penetration attacks involve hackers attempting to gain access to systems, networks, and resources they are not authorized to access.

The Origin of Vulnerabilities

Vulnerabilities can come from anywhere or result from any number of circumstances. There are, however, two factors that seem to account for the majority of vulnerabilities: buggy software and human beings.

- **Buggy software**—The vast majority of vulnerabilities in digital technology originate from flaws in software. If the world's applications and operating systems were built with strong security measures in place, there would be far fewer problems in information security. Most of the security measures put in place, including firewalls and virus checkers, are there to keep hackers from exploiting the vulnerabilities in buggy applications and operating systems.
- **Humans**—Humans are another big source of vulnerability within an organization. Place the treasure in the largest, most elaborately secured treasure room and it will be a human that forgets to lock the front door. Whatever it is on our systems, in our networks, or in our physical areas, the ultimate power of security is in the hands of our employees, customers, and other related humans. Unfortunately, most of these humans do not have the proper training to manage such a large responsibility, thus resulting in numerous vulnerabilities.

Vulnerable Operating Systems

If anyone in your organization is using a workstation or server that is running any version of Windows, UNIX, or MacOS, then you have vulnerabilities; it's that simple. Perhaps these vulnerabilities have not yet been discovered, but every significant operating system is full of features that can be exploited to make the system act in an undesirable manner. The thousands of vulnerabilities we have today existed long before we even knew about them! Vulnerabilities that will be discovered next year are actually in our systems today. It is important to understand that when we hear about a new vulnerability being discovered, the vulnerability is not really "new," just "newly discovered." Someone may have known about it several years before and has been using it to silently sneak into systems around the world.

Writing an operating system requires a large staff of programmers who create millions of lines of code under a tight business-driven deadline. Mainstream operating systems like Windows and Solaris are full of millions of lines of hidden code that the public will most likely never have access to. This code is full of thousands of flaws that are nearly impossible to find, even for the handful of people who have access to view the code.

Windows 2000, for example, has more than 35 million lines of code in it, developed by multiple teams within multiple organizations. It would be quite impossible to make a profit if the staff was expected to fully test every line of code under every possible combination and event. It is also extremely difficult to ensure that the programming staff has not inserted its own intentional back doors into the code. Some organizations are better than others at avoiding vulnerabilities and malicious coding, but in reality, it is the general public who is truly expected to put the software to the ultimate test.

A classic example of this is the notorious "Ping of Death" from the mid-1990s. Most operating system developers programmed network utilities to operate within published IP standards, which included a limit on the size of the data within an IP packet (65535 octets, to be exact). Well, someone stumbled onto the simple fact that if you sent a tiny request called a "ping" to a system and gave it more than 65535 octets, most systems would react strangely. For example, many operating systems locked up, stopped talking on the network, and some even rebooted. Why? Because when the average programmer quickly slaps together a tiny program to respond to such "ping" requests, he or she often doesn't stop to consider teaching the program how to handle events that do not conform to the standards. They don't tell their applications, "Hey, if you get something over 65535, ignore it," and leave the systems to their own decisions. Simple mistakes like this made by programmers around the world are the cause of 99% of all vulnerabilities.

Significance of Operating System Vulnerabilities

The operating system should be viewed as the foundation on which the entire castle is built. If someone tunnels under the walls and takes out a support beam, then the walls will come crumbling down no matter how high they are. Likewise, if someone gains access to the operating system, it will be difficult to prevent him or her from gaining access to the rest of the system and the rest of the network.

One important task in information security is to keep operating systems from being hacked. Remember, an operating system controls the basic functionality of everything that is on a computer. The operating system typically has access to every file, every application, every user, and quite often, the history of all actions. The operating system also has the final say in many security-related decisions. If you can can control the operating system, you control just about every application and piece of data on the device.

Vulnerable Applications

Applications are very similar to operating systems. After all, what is an operating system but a giant application? Application vulnerabilities are very common, and most major applications on the market have vulnerabilities in them. The important difference between these vulnerabilities and operating system vulnerabilities has to do with the significance of the threat, which we will discuss in a moment.

The origin of most application vulnerabilities is somewhat similar to that of operating system vulnerabilities. Multiple programmers, working under a deadline, fail to place precautionary checks, and at the same time, make simple errors in the code. Applications are often written with standard programming languages and precompiled toolsets. A precompiled toolset is a part of the program that someone else developed; the application developer is simply including it in his or her application. For example, to make an application play music, the application programmer normally would not want to go through all the trouble of writing hundreds of lines of code when a standard music function has already been written by someone else. Thus, the programmer will pay a fee and insert someone else's code (which they cannot read) into the application and continue on with life. Sadly, such code often has flaws and vulnerabilities that the programmer is unaware of. Subsequently, the programmer has just introduced vulnerabilities into the application, vulnerabilities that the developer has no chance of ever seeing or fixing.

Significance of Application Vulnerabilities

When considering the significance of an application vulnerability, it is important to think in terms of relational security and avoid focusing on just the application itself. Applications have several significant security relations that extend beyond functionality and services. The application has a relationship with its hosting computer, the network it is on, the data it processes, and the clients that access it.

- **Data relationship**—Most applications have some form of data for which they are directly responsible. Accounting software has corporate figures, email applications have business communications, and a memo system may have a reminder to pick up eggs on the way home. A primary concern in considering application security is this data. If the application has some form of vulnerability that allows access from undesirable parties, then that data is at risk.

- **Operating system relationship**—Every application must have some relationship to the operating system on which it exists. Of course, every operating system and every application work differently, but the operating system must allow the application some control over resources for it to function. Most operating systems grant the application a login, as if the application was a person authenticating into the system. Oftentimes, to simplify administration, applications are designed to run as the administrator or root user of the operating system, and, therefore, have access to many other things within the hosting system (of course, this is in violation of the Rule of Least Privilege). When such applications are compromised, access to the operating system can often be obtained as well.

- **Application clients**—The application also shares its vulnerabilities with the clients that access its services. If the application is available to other users, shared on a network, or otherwise capable of handling requests from external sources, the application must share a relationship with all the clients connecting to it. If a hacker is able to manipulate the application's service, he or she can potentially affect all the clients accessing that service as well. A compromised DNS server may send a client who is accessing a bank account over the Internet to a hacker site disguised as the intended bank; a compromised Web server may go so far as to transmit a virus or worm down to the clients reading its pages.

Vulnerable Networks

Our networks are the series of roads, paths, and tunnels that connect our kingdoms to the rest of the world. Some of these roads are wide, clean, and well-lit, while others are narrow, dark, and cross through the backyards of some very questionable characters. Down these roads come many travelers, seeking information and services. These travelers come from unknown locations and can provide little in the way of identification or proof of intent. The requirements for protecting the castle are multiplied by the number of roads that lead to it.

Where Are the Network Vulnerabilities?

The average network consists of many components. Telecommunication lines connect buildings around the world. Routers work to direct communications to and from the proper parties. Hubs and switches distribute communications across numerous devices. Networks also include the desktops, servers, operating systems, and applications connected to them. Therefore, we must widen our focus a bit when considering where a network can be vulnerable. A vulnerable network is simply a network that can be accessed or manipulated without consent. This means that if any device on a network, including the routers, switches, servers, workstations, or even the wires themselves is compromised, the network itself is compromised. Therefore, the network shares its vulnerabilities with all devices attached to it.

Significance of Network Vulnerabilities

A vulnerability in a network is simply a door through which an attacker can attempt to gain access to communications and devices. Once access is obtained, the hacker can steal information and services, or simply stop them from functioning. The two common concerns with network vulnerabilities have to do with vulnerable access points and communications.

- **Vulnerable access points**—When an attacker has gained access to a network via an internal system, device, or service, the hacker has gained direct access to the other systems and services around it. Perhaps there is only a single vulnerability within the organization that can be seen from the outside, but once that vulnerability has been exploited, the attacker is now on the inside of the network and can see the remaining vulnerabilities and weaknesses. Thus, a compromised object in an internal network can lead to the compromise of other objects within the network.

- **Vulnerable communications**—When a device communicates with any other device, the information and actions exchanged are vulnerable to interception and manipulation. Common networking communication protocols such as the Transmission Control Protocol/Internet Protocol (TCP/IP) were not built around the concept of security, which makes standard channels of communication often vulnerable to attack. With networks, access is obtainable by anyone and everyone in the path of communication.

Network sniffing is a very common method through which hackers can gain amazing results. Through a network, an attacker can listen to email communications, gather passwords, obtain files, and discover many things about an organization. Since sniffing only requires the hacker to listen somewhere in the line of communication, there are many hidden areas where an attacker could passively exist.

Communications are also subject to manipulation. A hacker attempting to gain access to a resource may wait for a valid communication to take place and then take control of that communication. A hacker can also wait for a valid user to access his or her account, record the authentication process, and then replay this authentication process later to gain access (a replay attack).

Special Considerations for Network Communications

Similar to a phone call, when we communicate with various parties on the Internet, through WANs or over direct modem dialing, information is traversing devices over which we have little or no control. Take the case of dialing with a modem between two computers. The data communication between these systems is pushed through miles of wires and several phone switches before being received. This information must be considered vulnerable at every point from where the communication left the first modem and entered the second.

On an Ethernet network, the vulnerability is even more severe. Tapping into a local area network (LAN), WAN, or Internet communication exchange simply requires free hacking tools and a computer or device that exists somewhere in the path of the communication. Send an email from anywhere to anywhere and you can be sure there are several people that have the opportunity to intercept it.

Physical Vulnerabilities

Physical vulnerabilities are often overlooked when an organization considers security. What many people don't realize, however, is that operating systems, applications, and networks all rely on the physical security of the devices themselves. How can we secure data or services if the systems on which they exist are not secure?

Where Are the Physical Vulnerabilities?

Physical vulnerabilities include any physical component of a system or device that could be exploited for an attack. They comprise everything from the keyboard attached to a server to the power plug behind it. To properly operate and maintain a system, there must be some form of physical access to it, and by physically being able to touch a computer, one has a great deal of control over it. A hacker, for example, could bang away on a keyboard trying to gain access, or he or she could simply unplug the machine and cart it off the premises.

Commonly, a system or device can be fully compromised by physically accessing it. Many organizations, for example, do not configure passwords for the physical connection (console) port on routers. This means that in many environments, a hacker could simply walk in with a laptop and plug into a router to perform basic configuration options. Even simpler, a hacker could stroll casually into the average server room and will often find unattended systems that have been logged in as root or administrator. In such cases, the hacker could simply take a few moments to create an account that will give total control of the system, and then leave to perform the rest of the hacking remotely.

Significance of Physical Vulnerabilities

Similar to how operating system vulnerabilities can affect the security of applications, a physical vulnerability can affect the security of everything in the area. A hacker with access to someone's workstation has many options that would otherwise be unavailable. Likewise, an attacker that can physically plug into an internal Ethernet port has the unlimited potential to compromise every system, device, and link connected to that network. When such physical vulnerabilities are allowed to exist, it greatly diminishes the security of every system, device, and network communication within the organization.

Chained Vulnerabilities

Vulnerabilities should not be seen independently, but as an interlinking chain of dependence such as is illustrated in Figure 7.1. Holes in security are most often formed through a series of minor vulnerabilities that, considered individually, appear to have no major effect on an organization's security. However, by chaining two or more of these minor vulnerabilities together, hackers frequently find ways of compromising security. Likewise, major security violations are most often composed of small events, which would independently be considered "normal" and not raise any flags. It is by forming a series of normal events into a malicious chain that many attacks actually occur. Because we make ourselves vulnerable through a series of chains, it would only be logical that hackers could attack us by reverse-engineering such chains. We must be certain to be conscious of the chain of events surrounding any given situation, thus we should widen our focus in accordance with the virtues and rules of security.

It is extremely important for those associated with the security of an organization to be constantly thinking about chains. All too often, a security administrator will open a port on the firewall or make an exception to the security rules simply because it seems like a minor vulnerability. Unfortunately, it is often difficult to comprehend the complete chain of vulnerabilities that are related to everyday actions. This is another reason why it is vital that organizations focus on the rules and higher security principles, and avoid making numerous exceptions. This makes it important to follow the concept of "creating stillness"

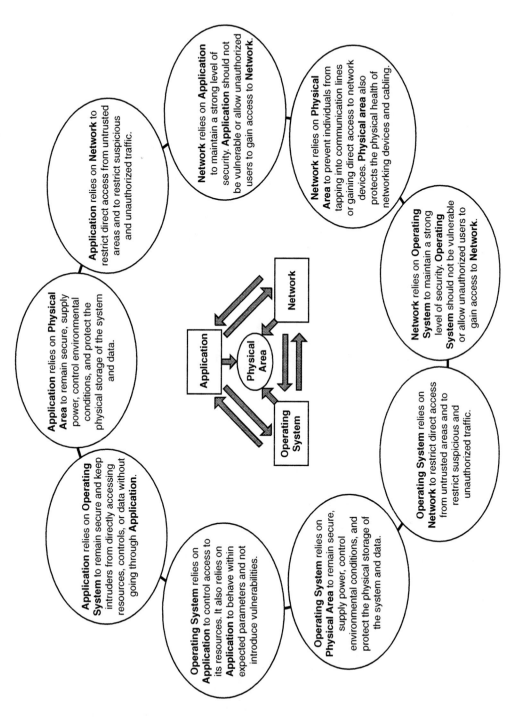

Figure 7.1 Security Dependencies.

139

by having filtered logs for a clear understanding and an unfiltered backup for following seemingly unimportant events (see Chapter 5, *Developing a Higher Security Mind*). Many successful attacks go unnoticed simply because the hacker used a chain of seemingly unimportant events that were never investigated.

MODERN TARGETS

Though every system is fair game for hackers, there are some common targets that warrant special attention. An intelligent hacker will look for the least complicated way of breaking into an organization and he or she will attempt the method of entry that requires the least amount of time, materials, and effort on his/her part. Thus, there are several commonly used entry points that are usually the primary targets of hackers.

DNS Servers

Probably the most common entry points for hackers coming into an organization are DNS servers. Many DNS products have been plagued by hackers since the dawn of networking. It is a good idea to give special attention to DNS servers when considering an organization's security measures and policies.

How They Get In

To start, DNS servers provide a service that is used by just about every networked computer. Internal DNS servers are accessible to everyone on the internal network, while external DNS servers are accessible to everyone on the Internet. DNS servers often bridge requests to both the internal and external networks, and thus have some form of access to both. As a result, DNS servers are highly desirable targets for hackers wishing to compromise an organization.

Many DNS services have been plagued by numerous security holes, and as such, they have been doorways for hackers for many years. A UNIX-based DNS server running BIND is one of the most commonly found services on the Internet. Unfortunately, BIND implementations have had the worst history of security maladies; therefore, BIND has earned a dismal reputation within the security community.

What They Can Do

DNS hacks often compromise the DNS server itself, allowing the hacker to run executables at the DNS server's privilege level. This, of course, opens the possibility for the destruction of the services, and gets the hacker one step closer to the inside of the network. But the real beauty of hacking a DNS server is found when manipulating the function of a DNS server.

The DNS service is ultimately in charge of directing communications by resolving names like "www.somedomain.com" to an IP address like "10.3.2.1." If, for instance, a DNS administrator wanted to redirect everyone in the organization going to www.somedomain.com back to the organization's home page, it would be a simple entry to make. Now, imagine what a hacker could do with this type of access. The hacker could, for example, send everyone going to www.mybank.com to his or her own personal Web server at home. Imagine then that he/she has taken an hour or two to recreate the first page of the intended bank's Web server, just enough to ask for the user's account number and password. Anyone in the organization who goes to access that bank will see the normal page, enter his/her login and password, and be greeted with a simple message saying, "This service is down for the next hour; please try again." Meanwhile, the hacker now has access to the end-user's bank account via the login and password.

Email Servers

Email is often at the heart of communications for modern organizations. Most email server applications incorporate hundreds of extra functions and compatibility options, and sadly, a good share of security flaws to go along with them. What could be more tempting for a hacker than the system that mediates the majority of communications within an organization?

How They Get In

Security holes are commonly found in email systems, oftentimes because of the high degree of functionality attempted by the vendor. In the mid-1990s, Sendmail was one of the most commonly used and extremely vulnerable mail systems. There was a time when, if you were running this lovely service on your UNIX system, you were effectively rolling out the red carpet for the most amateur of hackers.

I wish we could say that times have changed, but today, we are still finding incredible security flaws within the most popular email services. In the past few years, there have been a whole suite of propagating email hacks, primarily targeting Microsoft email servers and client products. Most cause costly outages of email services, some damage systems and corrupt data, and others allow remote access to system resources.

Similar to DNS servers, email servers are usually able to communicate with the outside and inside worlds simultaneously, thus creating a bridge between the two.

However, a far worse vulnerability than a DNS server, an email server must always be able to communicate bi-directionally, receiving messages from one side and passing them to the other. This makes email services likely targets for those wishing to further compromise a network.

What They Can Do

The most common attacks against an email server involve shutting the service down. By forcing an email server or client to create and deliver thousands of fake messages, the services quickly become overloaded and crash. Email systems are also notorious for propagating viruses and redirecting unsolicited spam.

A trend, started in 2000, has been to use automated mail distribution capabilities in combination with unprotected address books to forward malicious applications to millions of people around the world. This has made the email system the greatest propagator of worms and other malicious code to date.

Of course, after an email service has been compromised, there is also a likely chance that the hacker can use the email server to relay attacks to the internal network. Hackers know that an email service will have the ability to communicate with systems on both the outside and inside of a network. Thus, email servers are often used to further penetrate a network.

Web Servers

Web servers are common targets for hackers, which is no surprise since they are often the most visible elements in an organization's presence on the Internet. It is common for a Web server to be widely publicized and widely viewed by the general public. Hackers desiring to make a statement will often target unprotected Web servers to distribute their messages to the world, or to cause great social damage to an organization. In my experience, most organizations greatly underestimate the damage that can be done when a hacker penetrated even the seemingly insignificant of web servers.

How They Get In

The most common Web server vulnerabilities are those that succumb to DoS attacks. For a Web server to operate, it must perform numerous highly diverse functions, displaying graphics, rolling animation, playing sound, and querying information, while all the time keeping track of the state that every session is in. This makes the background architecture of the average Web server much more complicated than a DNS or email server.

The numerous functions that a Web server can perform rely on system calls to small modular applications. Such applications are often written by third parties, and each has its own potential vulnerabilities. Many of these applications come pre-installed with the server, and even when not used, can make a Web service vulnerable. As such, Web servers are notorious for being vulnerable. Just about any unpatched Web server running on a standard installation is vulnerable to some form of attack. In some cases, simply installing sample Web pages introduces vulnerabilities that allow for hackers to execute commands on a system.

What They Can Do

Most commonly, an attacker will simply shut down a service with a DoS attack. This is the most simple, inexpensive, and anonymous method of doing damage. Web servers run so many dynamic modules that finding a vulnerability that will slow or halt the server is usually not difficult.

If an attacker is able to take advantage of the various vulnerability types to execute code on the system, far more damage can be done. Hackers can potentially deface a Web site, often splashing their personal logos on the front page accompanied by various forms of profanity, pornography, or a message stating that the company has been "hacked."

It is easy to lose sight of how powerful Web servers are. The first page of a Web server is normally a representation of the organization itself, and the defacement of it can have a very serious and long-lasting effect on customers, partners, and shareholders. Beyond the negative press a company receives when its front page becomes a posterboard for hackers, imagine the damage when a hacker uses the server to deceive the organization's customers. For example, company stockholders have been sent running to their brokers when a Web site read: "Today we announce our organization's sale to the Acme Corporation of Japan." Many organizations have suffered long-term damage simply because a new system call was installed without applying the proper security patch.

Dial-up Modems

The long-standing bane of the security industry, dial-up modems are a continual headache when trying to ensure the safety of an organization. One of the biggest difficulties in dealing with modem security is that few people outside of security professionals are actually able to see the security threat they pose. Many long political wars have been waged over bloody battlefields while the use of these items has been negotiated.

The simple risk of a modem is that it creates a one-to-one bridge between two computers at any distance, bypassing security chokepoints. Properly controlled through a secured dial-up server, a modem provides no more of a risk than a common Internet connection. The problem is that anyone with an analog phone line can plug a PC or laptop into a jack and call, or answer calls from, anyone. Once a system on a network has a modem plugged in, all the systems are bridged to the rest of the world, bypassing all security measures.

How They Get In

Modems have two states in which they pose a significant security threat to the rest of an organization. Many organizations only work to secure inbound calls, but there is an equal threat from both inbound and outbound modem activity.

- **Outbound calls**—The local Internet connection is down and Jane needs to transfer an email quickly. Rather than waiting for the authorized Internet communications line to be restored, Jane uses the America Online (AOL) account on her laptop to dial up and access her email. While online, Jane's computer is compromised (happens all the time). Until Jane hangs up, her system can now be used as a bridge into the local network. An attacker could also put a back door or Trojan horse on her system, which may grant access after she hangs up and the normal connection is restored.

- **Inbound calls**—Many modems are preconfigured to auto-answer calls for technical support, faxing, and remote access. Additionally, many modems are configured by installed applications to answer incoming calls. A common hacking technique is to use a tool called a war-dialer to search for unprotected systems with modems. A war-dialer is a device or application that automatically places calls to random or sequential phone numbers, searching for an active modem. Chances are that you have been called by a war-dialer several times in your life and never knew it. Basic dialers will simply hang up when a person or answering machine answers; other more sophisticated ones will actually play a voice saying, "Sorry… wrong number," and then hang up. This is to avoid suspicion and getting caught.

  A war-dialer is an excellent method for bypassing security in an organization. An attacker simply learns the analog phone numbers registered to a company, waits until 2:00 a.m., and then begins calling every number in some random pattern. The next morning, the hacker is presented with a list of systems and, quite often, some basic information such as if a login and password were solicited or what application answered a call.

What They Can Do

The capability provided to a hacker who has dialed directly into a device on a network varies greatly depending on how the receiving device is configured. Oftentimes, dial-up is enabled through PCAnywhere or some other form of remote control application, in which case, the hacker would be able to take over a machine completely and use it to infiltrate the rest of the network. Sometimes, dial-up is enabled through remote authentication service (RAS) or some other form of network linking service, which will attach the hacker's computer as if he or she was on the network locally. In either case, the hacker has now bypassed all external defenses and has a nice, warm, comfortable home hidden deep within the network.

MODERN EXPLOITS

An exploit run against a vulnerable object will result in a hacker being able to perform actions without authorization. What exactly a hacker can do really depends on the type of exploit used against our weaknesses. There are several classifications for exploits; we will take a look at the most common and important ones in this section:

- DoS
- Penetration
- Entry-point searching
- Back doors
- Cracking
- Social engineering
- Chained exploits

DoS Exploits

DoS attacks are by far the most commonly practiced exploits. The reason for this is quite simple; they are the easiest and quickest ways to affect an object. Anyone at all can run a successful DoS attack using only a low-end desktop and some easily obtainable hacker tools. It is simply a matter of finding a target and choosing the proper tool, or vice versa.

The Process

The first task when performing a DoS attack is to match a particular vulnerability to a particular device. While attempting to be friendly and easy-to-use, computers and devices have the unfortunate tendency to give out far more information than is desirable (again, in violation of the Rule of Least Privilege). For example, by default, someone across the Internet can often determine the operating system used by an email, DNS, or Web service. To make matters worse, common services often advertise an application's name and revision to anyone opening a connection, so for the hacker, it is simply a matter of:

1. Probing a system for its information, trying to find as many services, applications, and version numbers as possible.
2. Going to one of thousands of hacker sites and searching each service or application for known vulnerabilities. This will usually result in a list of vulnerabilities and exploits that are known to work with such devices, and links to download the tools that perform the DoS attack.
3. Run the application and check to see if the attack was successful.

The Threat

DoS attacks are the easiest to understand in terms of the threat they pose to an organization. By definition, the purpose of a DoS attack is to stop a system or service from functioning properly, thus denying service to all users. To assess the threat a DoS attack poses to an environment, we must be able to calculate the negative impacts of a successful attack at the most critical time using worst-case scenarios. Add in variables like potential data lost and rebuild time and we can quickly assess the damage a DoS attack could do. We will discuss this in more detail in Chapter 8, *Practical Security Assessments*.

It is important to keep the proper frame of mind in light of redundancy and its ability to defend against this common form of attack. When an exploit is run that forces a service to stop responding, a redundant stand-by system may become active to keep the service running. However, by running the same exact exploit again, the hacker can then take out all redundant instances of a system. Thus, redundancy by itself offers little assistance in this situation.

Penetration Exploits (Breaking and Entering)

A penetration attack is where someone attempts to gain access to systems or resources beyond his or her privilege level, thus penetrating or bypassing security. Someone on the Internet trying to gain access to an intranet server is performing a penetration attack, just like an officemate trying to bypass Human Resources security checks to modify his or her hourly rate.

The Process

Penetration attacks range widely in execution and effect. Most often they will follow this pattern:

1. Find a service that is accessible to the hacker, such as a mail server, DNS server, or end-user workstation. These are either services that the attacker is authorized to access as a public user, or services that were installed and are operating unknown to the administrator.
2. Attempt to trick the service into allowing more access than is authorized. Oftentimes, this will involve executing a hacker tool that causes the service to grant file execution or other forms of access to the attacker.
3. Once exploited, use the system as a bridge to the internal network, allowing the hacker to bypass other security measures and further compromise the internal network.

Performing a penetration attack requires slightly more work than the common DoS attack, and it can be more difficult to find a target. Vulnerabilities are, however, discovered every week that allow an attacker to bypass security and execute code, making penetration attacks very common.

The Threat

Successful penetration attacks grant access to those who are not supposed to have it. The level of access granted and what the hacker can do with it are different for each type of vulnerability and exploit. All too often, vulnerabilities lead to the hacker gaining some form of administrative access, at which point, we can consider a system to be in his or her pocket. In the worst-case scenario, once a system has been penetrated, not only is its security compromised, but so is the security of the entire network and all the systems. Hackers will most often make themselves "at home" in a penetrated system, patching up the vulnerabilities so others can't get in using the same exploit, and then laying dormant, passively watching all the traffic passing by, looking for keys, passwords, and other sensitive materials. More on assessing this threat in an environment is included in Chapter 8.

Entry Point Searching

There are two forms of entry point searching commonly experienced: targeted and random. Targeted means that the hacker has chosen an organization specifically and is attempting to find as many entry points as possible from which to attempt an attack. Random entry point searching is when an individual uses a particular medium, such as war-dialer or network scanner, to perform random searches until finding something interesting.

Entry point searches normally precede other attacks. Here, the hacker probes for the "weakest link" within an organization's perimeter. This goal of this process is to find as many entry points as possible and attack each until the hacker is able to contact an internal system.

The Process

When performing a targeted entry point search, the hacker will first perform a study of the environment, much like a professional thief snooping for the one window without an alarm. A hacker will probe systems, make phone calls, and look up public records to find any information of value for determining a perimeter weakness. Through this process, the hacker will usually try to find information such as:

- The IP address ranges assigned to the organization
- The phone numbers assigned to the organization
- Where the organization is located, and the names of the key players
- The name, operating system, address, and services of publicly accessible servers, such as Web, DNS, and email servers

Using this information, the attacker will begin probing for vulnerabilities while trying not to set off any serious alarms. Given a few days, an attacker can usually:

- Scan all the publicly accessible servers for vulnerabilities
- Have a war-dialer call the organization's phone numbers, looking for modems
- Visit the office, or call and talk to individuals within the organization

Performing these steps will frequently yield good results. One system may be unpatched, a modem installed on a router or desktop, or an employee may be perfectly willing to divulge a password given the right story. If, however, none of these entry points works, the attacker can simply move on to the next target and then return in a month or so to find new vulnerabilities, new modems, or new employees willing to give out sensitive information.

The Threat

When a hacker is successful in finding vulnerable entry points into a network, all of the hacker's capabilities become magnified. A hacker attacking from inside a network is the greatest security challenge we will face. Though the entry point search itself will probably yield no damage, it could very well result in the hacker accessing the network from the inside.

Sneak Attacks and Back Doors

Getting an end-user to execute malicious code on his or her system is another commonly practiced form of hacking. The moment we double-click on that little executable file that was sent to us from Russia, we are at the complete and utter mercy of the programmer who created it. Sure, virus checkers and other applications do their part to protect us, but there is no good security measure that will prevent new malicious code execution on a system. This is why executable Trojan horses and other similar back doors are so popular.

The Process

Creating malicious code is quite simple to do and there are many hackers out there doing it. Since common desktop computers are designed to be as user-friendly as possible, they readily accept almost anything a program asks them to do. If a hacker is able to execute, or convince someone else to execute, code on a standard desktop computer, the hacker can grant himself or herself unlimited access and establish a remote connection with his/her own system. In such a situation, firewalls and IDSs are of little help to the penetrated organization.

The Threats

- **Trojan horses**—A Trojan horse is an application that masquerades as something common and harmless to trick the user into trusting it. If, for example, we were to launch a Windows Trojan, the application could overshadow the normal authentication process. Thus, the next time the login and password prompt appears, it is actually a Trojan disguised as a Windows prompt. The information would then be relayed back to the hacker via our own network connection or through an auto-mated email message.

- **Back doors**—Back doors open up hidden holes in a system that allow a hacker to gain access. Sometimes, back doors simply wait to be access-ed by a particular network request, while others will proactively estab-lish an outbound session with the hacker's computer. Once a back door is installed on a computer, the hacker is often able to do as he or she pleases with it.

- **Other malicious code**—There is a lot of code out there that cannot be properly described as a back door, Trojan horse, worm, virus, or other classification. This is code that is intended to be simply entertaining for the hacker or cause damage to a system or network without attempting to break in or capture authentication information or spread itself to oth-ers. Such malicious code could be programmed to simply erase files, format a disk, corrupt an operating system, or take advantage of one of millions of possibilities.

An interesting, yet tragic example of malicious code was an application designed to hide in the background of a computer and, at odd hours of the night, use the modem to make phone calls to various 1-900 num-bers. In any given night, 10–100 phone calls could be made, ranging from $200–$5,000 in charges. It is very likely that the victim would have no clue that there was any issue until the monthly phone bill arrived, with a very large surprise!

Authentication Cracking Attacks

Cracking refers to someone attempting to gain access to a system by determining the proper key or password for access. Here, we are not trying to trick a service into granting us access, we are simply trying to work the combination lock until it clicks into place and we can enter without obstruction.

The Process

Cracking requires that the attacker have access to the authentication mechanism or au-thentication information through which access is granted. For example, if the hacker can go to a Web page and get prompted for a login and password, he or she can then attempt to crack it; if a hacker can gain access to a file with authentication information in it, he/she can attempt to crack it.

Once a connection has been established with a device, whether authorized or unauthorized, a hacker will try to guess the authentication requirement. For example, if a password is required for accessing a Web site, the hacker may instruct his/her computer to continually guess passwords until one is accepted. This is a crude, but simple example of cracking.

Most often, cracking is performed after basic access to a system has already been acquired. Systems hold their passwords and keys inside of files located somewhere within the operating system. Such files are usually stored in some form of one-way encrypted hash that keeps the information somewhat secure from prying eyes. Many utilities focus on gaining access to these password files so that they can be transferred to the hacker's computer. Once there, password files are then cracked using dictionary-guessing utilities (attempting to use all the words in a standard dictionary), brute-force crackers (guessing every possible combination of letter, number, and symbol), or a customized combination of the two. Many crackers also allow a hacker to enter details such as the name of the organization, address, birthday, and other relative information that may be used. Password crackers often substitute basic symbols to find passwords such as "p@ssw0rd." This entire process is performed at amazing speed and the average password can often be guessed quickly by a standard home desktop trying thousands of words per second. Once a password is cracked, the attacker then logs into that account and attempts to gain more access until the files or resources that he or she is after have been obtained.

In my history of performing audits for various organizations, I have had to perform password cracking against many thousands of accounts. I have never entered an organization where I did not find at least one password within the first minute of running a cracker. The vast majority of organizations I have visited host thousands of bad passwords that did not even require a cracking program to uncover.

The Threat

Cracking itself poses no direct threat to an organization. The theft of the data that has been cracked, however, may be of some interest. The most common version of cracking is when someone gains just enough access to a system to be able to download the password file. Once cracked, the password file may yield information that will allow the hacker to gain a higher level of access. Usurping this account will allow the hacker to further penetrate the organization.

The most common account cracking comes from system administrators. By the nature of the account, system administrators with administrative privileges have access to the password file. Thus, administrators only have to download the password file to a disk, take it home, and run a cracker against it for a few hours. One may ask why an administrator who has access to users' files would bother cracking accounts. And while on the subject, why should we even care? There are several reasons:

- **Further compromising the user**—How many users think of one password and use it for everything? The administrator who successfully cracks a user's password may now have access to other systems he or she could not normally get to. Oftentimes, a user will use the same password for his/her computer at work and his/her online bank account! This makes password cracking a very tempting prospect for internal administrators.

- **Deniability**—If an administrator wants to perform an illegal action, he/she would want to do it using an account other than his/her own. This helps to ensure he/she does not get caught. If, however, the administrator simply creates a bogus account or modifies another user's password and takes over the account, there will often be a trail of logs leading back to the administrator. If, however, the administrator logs in using the end-user's password, there will be no way to determine who usurped the account and performed the actions.

Social Engineering

Social engineering is not an attack against technology, but rather an attack against the more human aspects of an organization. In such an exploit, a hacker works to attack what is considered to be the weakest link in most organizations, the employees. This all goes back to the concept of training and how end-user security training is of great importance to information security practices. Social engineering can be performed against everyone, including employees, executives, partners, and customers.

The Process

Social engineering is an ever-creative and changing process. The goal is to extract important information from an organization by either finding someone who does not know the information is important, or by tricking someone into giving it out. The most common form of social engineering seems to be accomplished via email. A hacker generates an account on some anonymous email server and sends an official-looking message to an employee asking for the employee's password or other sensitive information. Quite often, such email messages are forged with the administrator's name, or the name of an executive within the organization. Sometimes, such emails don't ask for the information directly, but rather convince the end-user to download and execute a program that steals the information from the computer.

Other practices include phone calls from people claiming to be performing maintenance or some form of technical support; walk-ins, where someone tours the office looking for important information written on desks, printed in faxes, or otherwise written in the open.

The Threat

The threat of a successful social engineering attack often goes unconsidered within an organization. Most of the time, employees are provided with significant information in relation to the security of the organization. Employees, for example, know passwords, procedures, names, phone numbers, email addresses, important people, important events, key holders, and the positions of alarms. Hackers can often gain a tremendous amount of information from an organization by making a few phone calls and visiting the site. Such information can amplify an attacker's ability to compromise the organization.

Chained Exploits

Earlier in this book, I discussed the concept of thinking in chains and relationships. Unfortunately for us, good hackers follow the same concept when creating exploits. At any given moment, there is a multitude of newly discovered vulnerabilities, each with its own unique method of exploitation, and each with its own impact. Common hackers are limited in the degree to which an exploit can take advantage of a non-critical vulnerability. This creates a difficulty for hackers in determining how they want to damage the specific vulnerabilities they are exploiting. An effective hacker, however, will not limit an attack to a single vulnerability, but rather a chain of vulnerabilities that work together to perform a crippling attack.

The Process

A chained exploit takes advantage of a series of vulnerabilities that exist within an environment. Most companies spend the majority of their time and effort securing their perimeters, especially those connecting to the Internet. A chained exploit is a program or process that is developed to take advantage of one or more front-end vulnerabilities, and then on successful penetration, use a wide variety of exploits that are effective on the internal network. With most organizations, once perimeter security is breached, the entire internal network becomes fair game.

In explaining a chained exploit, it is best to provide an example. Chained exploits can be performed manually in hopes of bypassing the security of a particular location, or through an automated virus or worm as shown in our example:

Example

The NIMDA worm launched in 2000, and other worms that followed a similar path, illustrate how well a chained exploit operates. The NIMDA worm would attempt to breach perimeters through one of two methods: by passing an email infected with NIMDA, or by attaching to browsers that came into contact with an infected Web server. These two exploits took advantage of simple and well-known vulnerabilities that most companies had not bothered to patch, or only patched one and not the other. The trick was simply propagating through perimeters that had not secured themselves.

Once inside, the NIMDA worm had much more room to work. Taking a few picks from a countless number of internal vulnerabilities, NIMDA was programmed to exploit vulnerabilities in Microsoft Outlook, Microsoft file-sharing, and Microsoft Web service products.

The Threat

Chained exploits are a serious threat because they transform seemingly meaningless vulnerabilities into gaping security holes. Complex chained exploits are most often applications, such as worms and viruses, which work to automatically propagate and exploit new systems. Because they are somewhat more difficult and time-consuming to create, the attacker will attempt to target the greatest number of victims as possible. Depending on the nature of the exploit, quite a bit of damage could potentially be done very rapidly across an entire organization.

Chained exploits can be very difficult to protect against since they often take advantage of numerous smaller exploits that may not have made the headlines. Such exploits often combine multiple effects, including DoS, penetration attacking, entry point searching, and authentication cracking. When used in combination, such exploits can turn a series of minor vulnerabilities into a gaping security hole.

NEGLECTING THE RULES: A HACKER'S TALE

I would now like to present two hacking scenarios that occurred in organizations that did not practice the virtues and rules of security. One example is from a professional hacking group that successfully attacked a Fortune 500 company, the other is from a giant organization that fell prey to random script kiddies. These two cases were specifically chosen to illustrate how failure to practice specific rules and virtues, and a general failure to remain security–focused, can lead to disaster.

"Sneak Attack"

This is the story of a hacking group that successfully gained access into the network of a large international organization, which we will refer to as ORG. ORG had a relatively large security practice, including a 24×7 monitored network operations center (NOC), more than 30 centrally managed firewalls, and a structured logging and reporting system at the perimeter defenses. ORG is a very well-known company, and thus has a very high likelihood of being targeted for an attack. Knowing this, the organization made security a somewhat strong focus. ORG's security, however, was narrowly focused on perimeter defenses, with very few attempts to secure the internal networks or systems.

Pre-Attack

In the middle of the week, a series of Internet-based attacks were made against several other corporate giants. This was gaining a lot of news and publicity at the time, and it was thought that ORG would also come under attack. Thus, the Internet firewalls underwent a series of rigid tests to see if the company could withstand similar exploits. For several days and nights, the security devices were tested, adjusted, and retested as the company awaited an attack.

In parallel to this, ORG's employees were reporting strange calls with a very muffled voice saying the same thing, "Oh... sorry... wrong number." This seemed like a very minor occurrence in light of a pending Internet attack, so it was not investigated further.

The Attack

More days went by as ORG waited for an attack to occur, but the hackers seemed to finally end their crusade without ever turning to this organization. It was not until a few days later that an administrator of one of the networks happened to notice that a core router was rebooted without a consent. When looking at the logs, he discovered something very strange: the router was accessed from another router that had been dialed into through a modem. It was discovered that the modem was attached months before for troubleshooting and was never removed. (The modem console on the router was later found to have no password assigned to it.)

Beginning to think this was a security incident, the engineer asked the security team to investigate. Referring back to the router command logs, it was discovered that someone had dialed into this router and proceeded to Telnet into the core router. The hacker then typed a series of commands that would break the router chain, erase the operating system on the core router itself, and perform a shutdown, leaving the entire network in an unusable state until the problem was discovered and the main router rebuilt.

The Effect

By some extreme luck, the hacker made a fatal flaw in the last three commands he or she entered. This router did indeed reboot, but the hacker mistyped the final commands by inserting one incorrect word, thus causing the router to make all changes temporary. After 15 minutes of downtime, the router finished its reboot and came back to its normal state.

Luckily, what happened in this situation was far less damaging than what could have happened. Downtime of the core series routers for this organization would have cost millions in a matter of hours. And, had the attacker's intentions been more than bringing down the network, he or she could have further infiltrated the network and internal systems.

Where Security Failed (Lessons Learned)

Security in this organization failed for many reasons. Here are the correlating virtues and rules that could have prevented the incident:

> *Virtue of Higher Focus*—Security failed because ORG did not maintain a higher focus. So much emphasis was placed on the Internet firewall that no one bothered to look for attached modems or consoles without passwords, or bothered to investigate the automated war-dialer that was calling all the numbers.
>
> *Virtue of Education*—ORG failed to educate the staff on the policy that modems are strictly forbidden. Several modems had been put in place by network engineers who had never read the security policy, nor were they ever educated on the dangers of direct dial-up.

Rule of the Weakest Link—ORG placed so much attention on having strong and secure firewalls, and yet there were several unprotected areas throughout the network. The entire attack never even touched ORG's Internet perimeter, rendering their costly security measures useless. ORG also failed to secure internal routers, believing the internal network to be safe from hackers.

Rule of Preventative Action—No proactive security measures were taken on internal systems. Policies existed that said no modems were allowed within the organization, but no attempts were made to actually enforce this policy or check for existing modems. No security audits ever took place and no penetration testing was ever performed.

"Self-Sabotage"

In this scenario, we have another corporate giant with a very robust and complex global WAN. We shall call this company ORG2. ORG2 had already been the target of multiple attacks, and over the years, had built up a strong perimeter defense with some limited internal defenses as well. In an effort to maintain a robust infrastructure, ORG2 had a matrix of WAN links, which within a few seconds could allow all WAN and Internet traffic to be re-routed through any of its major U.S. hubs. On paper, this very expensive network seemed rather flawless.

Pre-Attack

ORG2 had a large variety of Hewlett-Packard printers in use across its various locations. It became apparent that there were enough printers to warrant some form of central management, but no one was quite sure how to go about it. An employee of the organization decided that this was his opportunity to shine as he began to evaluate different products for print management. In his spare time, he built a UNIX test server and installed a variety of printer management tools.

Meanwhile, a series of network changes were also taking place within the organization. A new communications line was being brought up to a major partner, and a network engineer was working around the clock trying to integrate the two networks. This work was getting a lot of attention, while the printer project was off the radar.

The Attack

In the afternoon on a very busy Wednesday, users started to report a slowdown in their Internet and WAN activities. After about 30 minutes had passed, the entire network began to crawl and no one knew the cause. It was known that the network engineer had been working to bring up the new line, but there was no tracking system in place to see the progress or what actions had taken place on that day. Another 30 minutes passed before the network engineer was tracked down and forced by the CIO to undo all of his work. Routers were rebooted, networks were shut down, and a lot of work was lost, but still the problem persisted.

A little later, the redundant firewalls shut down, and on investigation, a security engineer noticed that the network was being bombarded with what looked like an attack. The firewall's logs were filled up with millions of entries, forcing it to shut down. The redundant firewall failed over, and in a matter of seconds, it also shut down due to the same issue. In a knee-jerk reaction, the company decided to re-route all traffic through its West Coast facility. Twenty minutes later, the network of the secondary facility came to a crawl and the firewalls on their Internet connection shut down.

While working to restore the primary firewalls, a security engineer began to parse the giant log file to see what events caused it to fill up. Looking at it in the calm of the server room, the engineer noticed that the attack was coming from an internal address. He did a lookup and found that the system's IP address was not officially assigned by the corporation. This was brought to the attention of other engineers, managers, and staff, until finally, an employee returning from his lunch break overheard the conversations. Upon returning to his new print management server, he quickly unplugged the network card, which eventually let operations return to normal for the company, after three hours of downtime and chaos.

The Effect

As it turns out, the individual had misinterpreted the configuration option for the printer discovery services of the test server. Thinking he was entering one minute for the group search interval, he actually entered one millisecond. He also failed to specify a proper IP range and had the system discovering all possible addresses (more than four billion in all). This, combined with the power of the system he was working on, let out billions of probing packets destined for all computers on the LAN, WAN, and Internet.

This error resulted in three hours of sporadic downtime, causing great damage to the company. In addition, all the work for the network migration had been reverted to its original state, causing the project to fall behind schedule.

Where Security Failed (Lessons Learned)

It took a combination of several security failures for this incident to occur. These failures, while appearing obvious to someone practicing the virtues and rules of security, were actually not so obvious to this company, which had invested millions in security consulting and security equipment only to find themselves lost in the chaos.

Rule of Least Privilege—Again we find a situation where the Rule of Least Privilege was not practiced, only this time, it manifested in a more physical form. The individual creating the system was in no way qualified to be building or installing a powerful network server on the LAN. He was given the system and began to work with no one ever questioning if he was capable of performing such work.

Rule of Change—ORG2 did not follow the Rule of Change. Too many components of this rule were violated to go into detail on each one, but here is a list of issues related to this rule:

a. The individual attaching the device to the network had given no indication to management, the NOC, or change management personnel that he was going to be performing scans on the internal network. There was no official policy stating he had to do so, and no training in how the corporate process and change management system should work.

b. Likewise, the network engineer had not kept change management up-to-date on his efforts. The new line had been up and stable for days before the attack, but since no one bothered to report this, it seemed like the logical cause of the problem. Though the company had a change management system, it was not practiced by most people and never enforced by management.

c. The print management product implemented was only in its final Beta release with no support and no testing performed. The final release (a few weeks later) fixed the issue and forced the configuration to have a minimum delay well beyond one millisecond. Thus, the company was a guinea pig.

Rule of Immediate and Proper Response—The response from the company to shift networking operating to the West Coast facilities did not come from a written procedure, nor was it well thought out or investigated. Having not fully determined the cause of the problem on the East Coast, the company panicked and forwarded everything, including the problem, to the rest of the network. Rather than helping, this actually amplified the damage done.

The company had no guidelines to follow, nor a proper chain of command to address such issues. Thus, the idea to push all traffic to another location was made by a few people, with little data to explain the anomaly, in the midst of a great panic.

CREATING YOUR OWN SECURITY PROFILE

Security in every organization works somewhat differently. Proper security measures must be determined based on the risks, threats, budgets, and general make up of an organization. The same security measures cannot effectively be applied to different organizations with different values, different risks, and different architectures. It is thus important for any organization desiring security to first develop a security profile.

A security profile defines several of the unique elements within an organization that can help focus security efforts. This is not a risk analysis, nor a vulnerability assessment (both of which are discussed elsewhere in this book); this is simply a guide on how to view ourselves through the eyes of our enemies. The unique security measures that should be applied to an organization should include this information as one of several defining factors.

Unique Hackers

Every organization has its own unique way of attracting hackers. Some organizations can go years without ever being the direct target of an attack, while others cannot last five minutes without attracting someone's attention. By defining who your hackers are and what their capabilities may be, you can better understand how to design a defensive strategy to keep them out.

Unique Targets

There are systems within any organization that are more likely to be struck than others. Combined elements of visibility, functionality, and vulnerability make some devices more likely to catch a hacker's attention. Identifying where such systems exist and why they are potential targets can assist in the placement of security defenses.

Who Are the Hackers?

Earlier in this chapter, we discussed the different categories of hackers, including their unique motives and capabilities. Each form of hacker presents a different type of threat to an environment. Some hackers are quite easy to deal with, while others are seemingly impossible. Knowing the type of hacker that may be drawn to your environment can be key in determining the length to which you will go to secure yourself.

Determining an Organization's Hacker Types

Table 7.1 is a chart of some common elements that will attract the attention of various hackers. This type of worksheet can be very useful in visualizing why an organization would be the target of a hacker and should be used as a guide. Each reader is encouraged to consider the unique elements within his or her environment that may draw the attention of a hacker and list them in the blank rows at the bottom.

Table 7.1   Considerations for a Hacker Profile

Common Hacker Attractions	Summer-time	Script Kiddie	Targeting Criminal	Employee
Is there a dedicated Internet connection?	1	3	1	1
Are there modems attached to some number of desktops, servers, or dial-up concentrators?	–	1	1	–
How many employees and consultants are there?	–	–	–	–
<100	–	–	–	1
>100	1	1	–	2
>500	1	2	1	3
>1,000	2	3	2	4
Is this a well-known type of government or activist organization?	–	1	1	–
Is this an Internet or application service provider?	–	2	1	1
Is this a health care provider or financial business?	–	1	1	1
Is this an organization that is significantly controversial? (Would this organization's function attract attackers?)	–	1	1	–
Is this a Fortune 500 company?	–	2	2	–

Table 7.1   Considerations for a Hacker Profile *(Continued)*

Common Hacker Attractions	Summer-time	Script Kiddie	Targeting Criminal	Employee
Does this organization experience heavy traffic on any of its external services (thousands of hits on a Web server)?	1	1	1	–
Does this organization host a mail server connected to the Internet?	–	1	–	–
Does this organization host a DNS server connected to the Internet?	–	1	–	–
Does this organization perform direct sales over the Internet?	–	1	1	–
Does this organization accept credit card information over the Internet?	–	1	1	1
Total Score				
Score > 3	There is a good possibility you will be attacked by this type of hacker at some point in time.			
Score > 5	Over the course of a year, it is reasonable to assume you will receive multiple attacks from this hacker type.			
Score > 7	It is likely that your organization will be under constant attack from this type of hacker.			

When the scoring has been completed, compare the values derived from the different types of hackers. This should give you a general idea of what kinds of hackers may be attracted to your environment. The higher the number, the more likely an organization is to encounter a specific type of hacker.

What Are the Targets?

Of course, any device within an organization is a potential target for attack. However, some systems, due to their function, content, and location on the network are much more likely to be targeted than others. I previously discussed where common targets exist, how they are commonly attacked, and what damage an individual could do with a successful "hack." We will now use Table 7.2 to help identify which objects are most likely to attract attention.

Determining Most Likely Targets

Take the following points into consideration for each object you wish to evaluate. Objects with higher point values could indicate they are more likely to be targets of an attack.

Table 7.2   Hacker Targets

Common Hacker Attractions	Points
Does this system have a modem and active phone line attached to it?	1
Does this system have access TO and/or FROM the Internet?	2
Does this system provide any network-accessible services?	2
Is this system a DNS, Web, or email (SMTP) server?	2
Does this system have a published entry in a public DNS server?	1
Does this system host customer, partner, or employee information?	1
Is this system an ordering system for purchasing goods or services?	1
Does this system accept credit cards or other forms of online payment?	1
Does this system host any subject matter that would be considered controversial?	1
Does this system receive more than 500 "hits" a day from outside the local network?	1
Total Score	

BECOMING INVISIBLE TO YOUR ENEMIES

As I stated in Chapter 6, *Making Security Decisions*, in the section that discussed secretless security, good security does not keep any secrets and yet remains secure. Once objects have been secured, however, keeping them secret can only help to further protect them. The importance of secretless security is to never rely on a secret to remain secure. Secrecy, however, can be used to enhance security once all other measures are in place. The two main advantages to making us and our objects invisible are:

- To avoid becoming the target of an attack
- To make it much more difficult for an attacker to acquire useful information

Before we are able to conceal ourselves, we must first recognize from whom we are concealing ourselves and what we need to hide. We are already most of the way to our goal since we have defined our common targets and the enemies who are likely to attack them. Now we must work to make our presence hidden from these people. The approach here is to recognize how we will be seen by hackers and how to take preventative measures to avoid them.

What to Hide From

When I talk about hiding from enemies, I am really talking about undermining the tools they use. To hide treasure from a thief, we must place it somewhere where it cannot be physically seen; to hide assets from an electronic thief, we must configure them so they cannot be electronically seen.

What Makes Us Visible?

What gives us away and makes us visible for attack are services and information that we make externally accessible. It is desirable to conceal any and all information that others don't need to know about by following the Rule of Least Privilege. Any information that is not required by others should be concealed. Don't think in terms of what you should hide as much as thinking about what you absolutely need to show.

Becoming Invisible

Like the other topics in this book, becoming invisible is a universal concept that applies to everything within the organization. For any given object that is implemented, the following steps should be taken:

1. Discover what information the object gives out by default. Many devices and applications include network management features to simplify identification, so be especially mindful of these. Common features include Finger, Whois, Banners, SNMP, and a wide variety of discovery services. All such services should be disabled or restricted to allow only that which is necessary or highly useful.

2. Consider all the ways in which the device will be visible to others. Is the object on a network? Is it advertised in some way, or is it sitting in front of an open window? Most systems and devices answer networking requests like Ping, Telnet, and other services by default, so keep an eye out for these.

3. Apply the Rule of Least Privilege on all perimeter devices, including firewalls, routers, hubs, switches, and servers. It does not matter whether or not a service seems harmless. Unless there is a direct need for a

particular service, it should not be allowed. This includes simple services like Ping (echo request and reply).

Here are some techniques to help ensure your networks and systems remain invisible:

- **Limit the methods by which electronic information can be gathered**—Be sure to disable any extra services not running on a system or device. Watch out for common communication services like Ping, SNMP, Telnet, and Finger.

- **Always use network address translation (NAT) for outbound communications**—Whether on the Internet or with your partners and vendors, NAT is a great security tool to use. By talking to an external entity with your own IP address, you give the receiver of the communication, and everyone listening, your internal IP address. This can greatly enhance a hacker's ability to launch an attack.

- **Use NAT for inbound communications whenever possible**—External entities should not know the real internal address of services they are accessing unless absolutely required.

- **Train employees and make policies related to secrecy**—All employees should be trained in an official process by which the local administrators work. Outside of this, all other attempts to gain information should be considered an attack. If an employee receives a call or email requesting information, he or she should check with a manager to make sure it is a legitimate request.

- **Enforce unclassified administration**—The organization should adopt a policy that states no employee, including administrators, will ever request or use another employee's login or password. Nowadays, most applications should be built to hide user account information and not require administrators to know the passwords. Making this a general policy, employees no longer have to think about whether or not to give out a password to a hacker in disguise. This makes it much harder for hackers to solicit passwords from employees.

8 Practical Security Assessments

THE IMPORTANCE OF A SECURITY AUDIT

The importance of understanding and performing a good security audit cannot be overemphasized. Audits are one of the most important tools we have for being proactive in our security measures and keeping up with the enemy. It is vital that an organization be able to discover its own weak links and vulnerabilities before anyone else does.

The importance of a good security audit, however, goes far beyond this. An organization with a security mind must be able to understand and identify risks, controls, and policies. We must have a sense of the organization, its components, what it relies on, and what could cause it harm. The Relational Security Assessment Model will cover this and is a good guide for developing the proper perspective. Even if a security professional has never performed a single formal audit, knowing the concepts behind risk evaluation and control assessment is vital for security development.

UNDERSTANDING RISKS AND THREATS

To ensure that adequate security measures are deployed in the right areas and to the correct degree, and to make sure that we give everything within our environment its proper security focus, we must continually be thinking in terms of risks and threats. If a decision needs to be made about an application, network, or device, it is important to see it in light of the risks it poses. In most situations, security cannot simply be evenly spread throughout an entire organization and still be effective. The server that controls the heartbeat of a sickly person will certainly have more security than the coffee machine down the hall. Security measures must be based on some sort of evaluation processes to ensure that we are neither overprotecting nor underprotecting any given object. I will discuss this formal evaluation process (risk assessment) later in this book, but for now, our focus should be on "thinking" and "seeing" objects in terms of risks and threats.

> This is not to say that we should secure some objects while others are left unsecured. Organizations should have a baseline security policy that mandates every system to have some minimum degree of protection. However, basing degrees of security on a weighted risk level is used to determine where enhanced security controls may be needed, and to focus attention on those objects that are more important to the organization.

What Are Risks and Threats?

Before we begin to discuss how to think in terms of risks and threats, let's get a couple of basic assessment definitions under our belts.

What Is a Risk?

A risk is the potential negative impact a threat can have on an environment. Everytime an organization relies on something (like a server or WAN connection), there is a possibility that the "something" will cease to function or become exposed. Take, for example, a house. If an event could happen that would cause damage to the house and would cost the owner, at most, $1,000 in damages, that house is considered to carry a $1,000 risk multiplied by the actual chance of such an event happening and the effect that the event will have.

What Is a Threat?

A threat is the "bad thing" that could happen to the environment. A fire in a server room is a threat the same as a hacker in a customer DB is a threat. A threat is some event outside of our control that could make our risks into a reality. The house has a $1,000 risk, but it would take a thief breaking into it to actually cause the damage. Thus, the threat is the thief breaking in or any other event that could potentially manifest the risk.

THE TRADITIONAL SECURITY ASSESSMENT MODEL

Assessing risk is normally one of the most difficult tasks in an audit process. There are several official assessment models for determining the risk of each object in light of the threats surrounding it. The two assessment models that are prominent today are based on qualitative and quantitative analysis practices.

Traditional Quantitative Assessment

Think of a quantitative assessment as a process of calculating numeric values for each object being assessed. The goal of a quantitative assessment is to recognize a series of common factors in each object and:

- Derive some dollar amount that represents how much we should spend on protecting it
- Come to a conclusion about which objects are more at risk and which should be addressed first

A normal quantitative assessment follows a process like this (see also Table 8.1):

Step 1 Assign a value to the object.

Step 2 Take the major threats posed against that object and determine the damage that each could do.

Step 3 Calculate the likeliness of each threat occurring on an annual basis.

Step 4 Multiply these factors together to get an annual loss expectancy, or ALE.

Table 8.1   Quantitative Assessment

Object	Value	Threat	Chance per Year	Potential Loss	ALE
Server X	$50,000	Fire	5%	$35,000	$1,750
		Compromised	15%	$22,000	$3,300
		Component failure	25%	$10,000	$2,500
Router X	$30,000	Fire	5%	25,000	–
		–	–	–	–

By using this model, we could look to the ALE figure and determine how much per year we should spend on security for each object. For instance, if we are spending $10,000 a year to secure Server X, then we probably need to rethink our security. Through this quantitative analysis, we can also see the priority of securing Server X vs. securing Router X and other objects.

Traditional Qualitative Assessment

A qualitative approach is very different from a quantitative one in that it works to weigh a series of educated opinions about each object's risks. For each object being assessed, several people gather together who have knowledge of the object and its function within the organization (see also Table 8.2):

- Each person is presented with a list of objects or types of objects.
- Each person is then asked to comment on and rank a series of scenarios and how they could affect the object and the organization.
- The cumulative opinions are then averaged, giving us an overall ranking for the object.

Table 8.2 Assessment for "Server X Being Compromised by a Hacker"

If Server X was compromised by a hacker, how could
this affect the organization (scale of 1–10)?

	Damage to Productivity	Damage to Customers	Likelihood of Threat
John	9	7	5
Jane	3	2	3
Mike	3	3	4
Average	**5**	**4**	**4**

By averaging the scores from each scenario, we can compare different risks within each object. We may also look at the risks of every object within the organization and compare them against each other to create a ranking and priority for dealing with security issues.

Problems with Traditional Models

While these models of assessment give a very formal and repeatable assessment process, they also have drawbacks that make them impractical in many situations:

- Quantitative: It is difficult to reasonably assign a value to an object.
- Quantitative: It is difficult to calculate the chance per year that a threat will occur.
- Quantitative: It takes a great deal of time and resources to perform such an audit with any degree of depth.
- Qualitative: Risk decisions are based primarily on opinion. Opinions could vary widely and thus, render the audit useless. Also, any imbalances, such as people who do not desire to participate or people who give little thought in answering the questions, will invalidate the results.

- Qualitative: Understanding how to interpret the results or what to do with them can be complicated.
- Qualitative: There is a high taxation of employee resources when collecting opinions for each object.
- Both: It is hard to evaluate security relationships with these models.
- Both: Neither of these models scale well to large environments.

THE RELATIONAL SECURITY ASSESSMENT MODEL

I have found over the years that organizations often have a difficult time performing good quantitative or qualitative assessments. Many times, consulting agencies are brought in to perform the assessment process, but the results are overly complex and still not of great use to the average organization. Numerous organizations have stopped performing risk analysis altogether because of these issues. It was with these problems in mind that the Relational Security Assessment Model was created.

What Is the Relational Security Assessment Model?

The Relational Security Assessment Model is a Patent Pending method for performing a risk assessment that combines aspects of both the qualitative and quantitative approaches. The full assessment model as been integrated products like the Relational Security Audit Manager (RSAM) application, which is used by organizations to help automate the security assessment process. Here, however, we will cover a simpler version that removes some of the complexity. Using this relational model, we will define a series of meaningful values and assign those values to different objects. Based on these risks, we will then go a step further and develop a policy dictating how to handle objects of specific risk values. (to see more on the full Relational Security Assessment Model, visit www.relationalsecurity.com).

The Relational Security Assessment Model will break down the assessment process into simple and consistent steps. Within a small organization, this process can be performed without a great deal of effort. Within mid-sized and large organizations, it is recommended to use automated tools like RSAM or to develop your own mechanism for collecting and cross-evaluating the various details we will be discussing here.

Basic Rules for any Risk Assessment

There are a couple of common stumbling blocks I often see when risks and threats are being considered within an organization. The following guidelines are important to keep in mind whenever dealing with such evaluations:

Use a Reasonable Worst-Case Scenario

When considering risks for any particular object, the tendency is to only look at direct damages that could be inflicted and not consider other potential elements. Even though a particular server could be rebuilt in a matter of hours, it would be reasonable to assume it would take a full day given a bad series of circumstances. Consider also that a particular WAN link could go unused about 90% of the time, but it is feasible that disaster could strike during the time at which it is most needed. Taking a reasonable worst-case scenario is the best approach when looking at object risk. If all systems and devices are evaluated based on this worst-case scenario, it will be much easier to compare, contrast, and not be caught off-guard when disaster strikes.

Avoid Tunnel Vision

When performing a risk assessment, it is best to follow formal processes that lead to consistent results. It is also important, however, to stay alert and use common sense. There is no formula in existence that can catch every vulnerability, or fit perfectly in every situation. By keeping our eyes and minds open, we will notice a great deal more about the security of our environment than if we strictly follow the process.

Exclude Existing Security Measures

The process of determining risks and threats is used to determine the proper security controls that should be applied. As such, it is important not to weigh any existing security controls when considering their factors. The goal is to consider risks based on the function of an object and not include any current measures that mitigate such risks. A system on an uninterruptible power supply has the same downtime risk as a system without any power protection.

EXAMPLE

> Take, for example, an organization that has two routers controlling
> the entire network infrastructure. Router A has a redundant device, is
> continually monitored, and has all the latest security updates. Router
> B is not redundant, goes unmonitored, and has no security patches
> applied. Despite the levels of control on each, the natural risks and
> threats for both routers are the same. They are both critical routers,
> and if either went down, it would cause a lot of damage within the
> environment. Both demand equal attention for security.

Use a Consistent Scale with Common Criteria

When considering risks within an environment, it is important to use a constant scale
with similar criteria. Risk evaluations often tend to be inaccurate because organizations apply inconsistent rankings based on circumstances surrounding each object.
Security rankings must, however, be related by some common criteria through which
we base our overall evaluation.

In talking to the directors of Human Resources and Finance, we will see that
both view their systems as absolutely critical. It is obvious to us, however, that one
system is more important to the company than the other. The process of determining
how critical an object is must be based on objective facts. Throughout the entire risk
assessment process, we must use constant factors that can be compared with each other, and that are universally applicable.

EXAMPLE

> Both Human Resources and Finance say that their servers are of high-
> risk value and that any failure would be devastating to their environ-
> ment. This may be true for the individual department, but our assess-
> ment must weigh risks based on the entire organization. To determine
> which server is really of greater risk to the company, we must take
> several constant factors into consideration. Table 8.3 looks at the employ-
> ee effect factors if the main servers are unavailable:

Table 8.3   Example Failure Scenario

System	Non-Objective Evaluation	Objective Evaluation
HR server	Server uptime is critical to us!	1 hour of downtime could cause $1,250 in employee downtime (50 employees require the system to work; average cost/employee is $25/hour)
Finance server	Downtime could not be tolerated at all!	1 hour of downtime could cause $8,000 in employee downtime (400 employees require the system to work; average cost/employee is $20/hour)

Here we can more accurately determine which of the servers is of greater risk to the entire organization. Of course, we will weigh many different factors and ask a variety of risk-related questions. To make the evaluation process as effective as possible, we should try to make our considerations as universally applicable as possible and ask the same types of questions for everything. This will be discussed in the section titled *Risk Factors*.

RELATIONAL SECURITY ASSESSMENT MODEL: RISKS

The Relational Security Assessment Model is composed of several components. Every component is related to a series of other components that all work together to derive a level of risk and a degree of control. While the structure is universal, all components of this process can and should be modified to fit the specifics of the organization being assessed. The basic components of a Relational Security Risk Assessment are:

- Risk levels
- Risk factors

Risk Levels

A risk level is the degree of risk an object represents within an environment. A different set of risk levels could be defined for each organization performing an assessment. The goal of a risk level is to qualify and quantify, on an enterprise-wide scale, a weighted risk value for each object. Table 8.4 shows a common set of risk levels:

Table 8.4   Sample Risk Levels

Risk Level	Description
None	This object and its services are inconsequential to the environment. If the object was compromised or disabled without warning, there would be no noticeable effects.
Low	This object plays some minor role within the environment. If the object was compromised or disabled without warning, there would be minimal effects to the organization.
Medium	This object plays a significant role within the environment. If the object was compromised or disabled without warning, there would be noticeable effects on the organization.
High	This object plays a very important role within the environment. If the object was compromised or disabled without warning, the effects would be quite harmful to the organization.
Extreme	This object is essential to the continued operation of the organization. If the object was compromised or disabled without warning, there could be disastrous effects on the organization.

Important Tips for Defining Risk Levels

- Risk levels should remain universal to the entire organization.
- Risk levels should be quantified with some sample data, such as cost or recovery.
- Only a handful of risk levels should be defined, ideally no more than six.

Within each organization, the interpretation of each level will be somewhat different. Therefore, it is useful to associate some form of real-world data to each risk level. For example, consider the data in Table 8.5.

Risk Factors

It would be a bad practice to simply take each risk level and assign it to a different object without any other consideration. During audit process, it is necessary to talk to end-users, managers, and other employees, polling their insight into the risk of each object. This is similar to the qualitative process, only much simpler, more consistant, and more efficient.

Table 8.5 *Sample Real-World Data for Risk Levels*

Risk Level	Company X	Company Y
Medium	Cost up to $3,000 in repairs, lost productivity, fines, or lawsuits, or the loss of 5–10 customers or a partnership	Cost up to $50,000 in repairs, lost productivity, fines, or lawsuits, or the loss of 100–200 customers
Extreme	Cost up to $10,000 in repairs, lost productivity, fines, or lawsuits, or the loss of 30–50 customers or a partnership	Cost over $500,000 in repairs, lost productivity, fines, or lawsuits, or the loss of 500–1,000 customers or several partnerships

Since risk levels require a high level of understanding, we cannot simply ask individuals, "Is this system high-, medium-, or low-risk?" Doing so would make our results greatly skewed by their opinions, rendering our assessment useless. As such, it is important to interview individuals using basic facts, rather than universal risk levels.

A risk factor is an individual detail about an object in relation to an organization. Each factor has a related risk level that correlates the specific detail to the more universal levels we just developed. Most objects will have several risk factors associated with them.

The goal of defining risk factors is to introduce a method by which we can derive the risk level of any given object though a series of simple facts, not opinions. Rather than asking an administrator to say, "Choose a level of risk for the object," we will present that individual with a group of factors to choose from. Based on the chosen factors, we will then derive the higher risk level.

Table 8.6 contains some example risk factors:

Table 8.6 *Example Risk Factors*

Example Risk Factor	Factor Value	Risk Level
If this object was unavailable for a day, how much employee downtime could result?	0–5 hours	None
	6–10 hours	Low
	11–20 hours	Medium
	21–35 hours	High
	36+ hours	Extreme

Table 8.6 Example Risk Factors *(Continued)*

Example Risk Factor	Factor Value	Risk Level
How many customers use the object in a day (if this object was unavailable for a day, how many customers could be affected)?	0–10	None
	11–30	Low
	31–50	Medium
	51–100	High
	100+	Extreme
Are there any legal, contractual, or social obligations to maintain high availability?	No	None
	Yes	High

Of course, the more variations of risk factors we consider, the more accurate our assessment of the object will be. Organizations will need to determine their own risk factors as related to their defined levels of risk. Table 8.7 contains some other common types of risk factors to consider.

Tips for Creating Risk Factors

Here are some general tips for considering risk factors within your own environment:

- Try to form each risk factor into a simple, non-subjective statement— Remove opinion from the process as much as possible.
- Cover a good range of topics—Choose a wide variety of risk factors, covering the key events that could affect your environment.
- Continually refer to the bigger picture—Put some thought into each risk factor and how it relates to the bigger picture. Make sure each risk factor corresponds to the appropriate risk level.
- Be sure to compare different risk factors to each other—Since each risk factor correlates to a universal risk level, factors with similar levels should make sense. Is losing 40 employee hours (critical) really as important as affecting 60 customers (also critical)?

Deriving Risk Levels from Risk Factors

By using risk factors, it now becomes very easy to assign a consistent and objective risk value to anything within the organization (see Table 8.8). For any given object,

Table 8.7 Common Types of Risk Factors

Example Risk Factor Type	Considerations in Scoring
What would be the effect if the object were defaced or vandalized?	Take into consideration the effects of vandalism on any front-end, if any front-end exists for this device. This is of great importance to any Web server visible to clients, partners, and employees.
What would be the effect if the object's data were erased, corrupted, or modified?	Think about the need, use, and general value of the data on the system. If all data was lost forever, would it have a severe impact on the organization?
What would be the effect if the object's data was stolen?	Consider the effect on the organization if this information was stolen. Does this device relate at all to sensitive financial records, strategic business information, employee records, or any other sensitive information? Are there any legal, contractual, or social obligations for protecting this data? Think of the effects if the data was stolen. Could the company be sued? Are you storing protected health information or customer credit cards on this system?
What is the position of this object within the environment?	Is this system accessible by more than one zone? If so, would it be possible for someone breaking into this system to use it to attack other systems in a more sensitive zone?

begin by choosing all the risk factors that relate to it. Once all related risk factors have been determined, it is simply a matter of choosing the highest risk level of all the related factors. The factor with the highest level of risk represents the greatest level of risk that an object poses to the environment. A system that results in no hours of employee downtime (none) but affects 101 customers (critical) is a critical risk just the same as a router that causes 50 hours of downtime (critical) but affects only 5 customers (none).

Table 8.8 Determining Risk Level

Object	Risk Factor	Overall Risk to Organization
Server X	Would cause 10 hours of employee downtime (low) Could affect 200 customers (critical)	Critical

Table 8.8   Determining Risk Level *(Continued)*

Object	Risk Factor	Overall Risk to Organization
WAN Link Y	Would cause 30 hours of employee downtime (high) Would not affect any customers (none)	High
Application Z	Could cause 10 hours of employee downtime (low) Could affect 40 customers (medium)	Medium

Our Risk Assessment Thus Far

So far, we have performed the first steps of the Relational Security Risk Assessment. We have:

1. Defined universal risk levels for the organization
2. Defined risk factors, each relating to a risk level
3. Assigned risk factors to objects we want to assess
4. Determined the highest risk level assigned to an object

By performing these simple steps, we now have mechanisms by which to assess and compare the risks of individual objects, as shown in Table 8.9. Once the risk levels of our objects are defined, it becomes easier to recognize where risks exist and which objects may not be adequately protected. We can also start seeing correlations between different objects, helping to prioritize which objects are more important to secure first and which require more controls.

Table 8.9   Object-Weighted Risk Levels

Firewall A	Critical
Server X	High
Server Y	High
WAN Link X	High
Server Z	Medium
Wan Link Z	Low

Deriving Relational Risks for Containers

During the audit process, it should become evident that not all objects have direct risks. For example, the risk of a room can only be assessed by looking at the objects that are within the room. Similarly, the risk of a router is completely dependent on the networks it is connecting. These objects are called container objects because their risks completely depend on the risks of the objects contained within them. Since we have already determined the risks of our servers, WANS, and the like, we can use this information to evaluate relational risks (see Table 8.10).

Table 8.10 Determining Container Risk Levels

Container Object	Objects Inside	Overall Risk to Organization
Server Room A	Server X (critical) Server Z (low) Router Y (high)	Critical
Router Y	WAN Link A (high) WAN Link B (none)	High

RELATIONAL SECURITY ASSESSMENT MODEL: CONTROLS

The second part of the Relational Security Risk Assessment delves into the degree to which we want to protect objects. For each object, we need to define a minimum level of protection based on risk level. Objects that are of greater risk will most likely have higher control requirements than objects with no security risk.

Now expanded, the basic components of the Relational Security Risk Assessment are:

- Risk levels (already discussed)
- Risk factors (already discussed)
- Controls
- Control levels
- Risk control policies

Controls

There are various types of controls an organization may standardize on and different types of objects have different types of controls. Servers and routers, for example, provide logging and monitoring controls. A room has entrance controls such as a key-lock or biometric device. As shown in Table 8.11, every object has a series of controls that will help ensure its security:

Table 8.11 *Sample Control Types*

Object Type	Possible Types of Control
Server	Logging, monitoring, authentication, authorization, hardening, drive redundancy
Router	Logging, monitoring, local authentication, remote authentication, hardening
Room	Monitoring, perimeter access control, power protection

Control Levels

For each type of control, there are various degrees in which the control can be executed (see Table 8.12). One version of the control may be more secure than another version. If we take the example of a server room, we can adjust the strength of the control used to protect the room based on its risk level. We could require rooms with

Table 8.12 *Sample Control Levels*

Control Types	Control Levels
Entrance control	Level 0: No access control
	Level 1: Simple key access
	Level 2: Magnetic card access
	Level 3: Biometrics
Monitoring	Level 0: No monitoring
	Level 1: Must pass by staffed desk
	Level 2: Recorded camera
	Level 3: Actively monitored camera

low risk levels to implement a single key-lock, while rooms with higher risk levels implement key-card access or biometrics.

Risk Control Policies

In most organizations, it will not be possible to apply the highest level of control to all objects. We may not have the resources or the budget to place biometrics at every server room door, or to monitor every server on an hourly basis. It thus becomes important to tailor security to place the strongest controls where they are most required. By forming a control policy, we can specify that objects of a certain risk level will require some minimum degree of control to protect them. Through this we can tailor security to maximize resources.

Since we have already worked to define different levels of risks and controls, we simply need to combine the two to form policies. Risk control policies designate the minimal level of control for devices of a specific risk level. The security control for any given object should be at least as high as its risk level dictates, as shown in Table 8.13:

Table 8.13 *Sample Risk Control Policy in the Server Room*

Control Type	Risk Level	Minimum Control Level Required
Entrance control	None	No control
	Low	Standard lock
	Medium	Standard lock
	High	Key-card access
	Critical	Key-card access
Entrance monitoring	None	No monitoring
	Low	No monitoring
	Medium	Must pass by staffed desk
	High	Recorded camera
	Critical	Recorded camera

Scoring an Object

After a risk control policy has been developed, it is easy to score different objects. The score of any object is derived by comparing its required controls to the controls that are actually implemented. Each time an object's control does not meet the minimum policy standard, it is considered a violation. Violations are totaled to give the object a violation score (see Table 8.14). Systems with higher scores are further out of compliance than systems with low or no score.

Table 8.14 Sample Scoring Process

Object	Risk Level	Control	Applied Level	Required Level	Violations
Room A	Low	Access	1: Standard key	1: Standard key	0
		Monitoring	0: None	0: None	0
Room B	Critical	Access	1: Standard key	2: Magnetic card	1
		Monitoring	2: Recorded camera	3: Active camera	1

Scoring an object helps to see which objects are in violation of risk control policies as well as which objects have more violations and need to be given a higher priority. It also allows us to average scores for different facilities or departments and compare them with each other. Scores help to pinpoint trouble areas in the organization and track progress over time.

RELATIONAL SECURITY ASSESSMENT MODEL: TACTICAL AUDIT PROCESS

Performing audits regularly is an essential part of maintaining security within any organization. Audits help to find existing vulnerabilities and proactively stop others from appearing. The more often security audits are performed, the more likely it is that an organization will find its vulnerabilities before a hacker does.

An internal audit can be performed in great depth if so desired. Sometimes, the sheer critical nature of internal systems calls for extremely detailed audits that yield thousands of pages of results, diving into the minute details of every system, physical area, and corporate relationship imaginable. This form of audit, however, is not practical for the majority of today's organizations, as they are quite costly and yield complicated results. For an audit to enhance security within the average organization, it must be practical. By practical, I mean that it must:

- **Be affordable in terms of expenses, time, tools, and expertise**—This includes the time required for individuals to answer questions and otherwise participate in the audit process.
- **Yield accurate and useful information**—Audits should focus on important details, the goal being quality not quantity.
- **Produce easy-to-comprehend results**—Audit results should be understood by everyone, not just the group performing the audit.

The following is a tactical audit process that can be performed in a reasonable period of time, under a reasonable budget, and without consuming numerous resources. In the next section, I will discuss other important audit tasks, but they do not conform so well to a formula. A good assessment includes both the tactical audit process discussed here and the analytical process discussed in the next section.

> When performing a security audit, keep in mind that the audit is a reflection of your policies. During the audit process, work to ensure that objects within the organization conform to security policies. Thus, the quality of the audit should be weighted heavily on the quality of the security policies. If no policies exist, it will be extremely difficult to perform an audit.

Audit Tools

It is recommended that a few tools be acquired when performing a security audit. These tools are used to handle many of the audit's details, leaving the organization to focus on the audit itself. Though an audit could probably be performed without any tools, the following products greatly enhance the results and end up saving a great deal of time and effort.

- **Vulnerability scanning tool**—This tool is used to scan for vulnerabilities within systems and devices. The tool will run against a single device or an entire network and look for thousands of potential security weaknesses. There is a variety of scanning tools available, ranging widely in capability and focus. The most popular professional tool has been ISS's Internet Security Scanner, which has numerous features (www.iss.net/). There are also a great many Open Source tools, one of the most popular being NMAP.

- **Risk analysis tool**—A risk analysis tool is used to collect and process various bits of information about servers, networks, and devices. Such tools are designed to record a great deal of information and draw complex security relationships that are often difficult to correlate manually. These tools will then generate executive and technical reports, making it easier to interpret, share, and archive the results. The risk analysis tool that follows the Relational Security Assessment Model described in this book is the Relational Security Audit Manager (RSAM) from Relational Security Corporation (www.relationalsecurity.com). Other risk analysis tools, including AuditIT, use different risk assessment processes.

- **Assorted hacker tools**—Hacker tools are often nice to use as a supplement to the vulnerability scanning product. Most of these tools are legitimately marketed as a means to audit your own organization rather than break into another. Such tools are easy to obtain and sometimes free of charge. They can be used to perform mock attacks against systems, applications, and services to further determine where vulnerabilities exist. It is important when using such tools to download them from a reputable source and to only use tools that have been tested by other organizations. (There is nothing worse than letting a hacker into your network while performing an audit.) Some important hacker tools include password crackers like L0phtCrack/LC4 (www.atstake.com) and vulnerability scanners like Nessus (www.nessus.org/).

Basic Audit Steps

Again, internal audits can range greatly in complexity of process and depth of results. In my experience, a complicated and extremely detailed audit is of little use to most organizations. The simple steps shown in Table 8.15 have been proven to have the strongest impact on security:

Table 8.15 Steps for a Practical Security Audit

Tactical Audit Tasks	Estimated Time Required
Audit preparation	N/A
Object discovery	N/A
Risk assessment and analysis for servers, WAN links, routers, devices, and rooms	15 minutes/object

Table 8.15 Steps for a Practical Security Audit *(Continued)*

Tactical Audit Tasks	Estimated Time Required
Vulnerability scan on network-accessible objects	5 minutes/server 2 minutes for other objects
Basic hands-on audit of some or all objects	15 minutes/object
Hands-on sampling of desktop security	10 minutes/100 desktops
Physical inspection of rooms and closets	10–20 minutes/area
Compile and score data	N/A
Audit report and review	N/A

Step 1 Audit Preparation

Before beginning the audit process, there are a couple of basic tasks that need to be completed:

1. Acquire audit tools—We already reviewed some audit tools that should be used during the audit process.
2. Define risk levels, risk factors, and auditable controls—Remember, such components should be thought of in terms of the entire organization. The results of the audit process will reflect the decisions made here, so before moving forward, it is important to define each component as described in the section, *The Relational Security Assessment Model.*
3. Schedule technical components—In accordance with the Rule of Change, it is important that administrators and managers be aware of the technical activities being performed. Activities that will be of interest include all network scans, penetration testing, and hands-on analysis.

Step 2 Object Discovery

Before beginning an audit, we need to have an accurate view of what is out there. One major problem I commonly see in audits is that an organization will assume it knows what objects exist and where they are located before the audit process even begins. Often, the weakest links within an organization are objects that no one even knows about. Thus, it is important to start the audit by creating a current list of all objects that are going to be audited.

1. Make a list of all facilities to be included in the audit—For each facility, list important details such as:

   a. Network address ranges

   b. Rooms and closets containing servers or routers

   c. Servers, routers, and other major network devices

   d. Important contacts

2. Attach a network scanner and perform a "discovery scan"—A discovery scan is a network scan that searches a range of network addresses and returns a list of those in use. Normally, a discovery scan will also reveal information concerning the device using the address, such as the name and operating system used. If possible, perform multiple discovery scans at different times of the day and different days of the week to make sure no devices are missed.

3. Review the known devices—Compile a complete list of all devices discovered and have this list reviewed by someone who actively works in the facility. Have that individual add anything missed to the list and then sign the document.

> There are other, more advanced techniques for gathering this information. Techniques such as ARP cache reading, network sniffing, and the like can also be performed, if your organization has the proper expertise. The steps above, however, should catch the majority of objects while using the least number of resources. As the audit proceeds, one of the tasks will be to continually look for devices not previously listed. The goal here is to start with as accurate a view as possible. Objects that are missed should be picked up during the remainder of the audit.

Step 3 Risk Assessment

Now that we have our complete list of objects, we need to come to an understanding of how each major object functions within the environment. Here is where we begin to conduct the audit according to the Relational Risk Assessment Model. During this step, we interview various staff members about each object. Through this process, we assign risk factors to help us determine the risk level each object holds within the organization.

1. Understand each object—For every server, router, WAN link, physical area, and other major object discovered, document information like:

   a. The purpose of the object and its function within the environment

   b. The major applications and services running on the object

   c. The data stored in or transmitted by the object

   d. The types of users with access to the object

2. Discover the risk factors—For each object, interview managers, administrators, and end-users using the list of risk factors created in Step 1. Use this interview information along with the information gathered in the previous step to determine and document the appropriate risk factors for each object.

3. Determine the risk level—Take the highest risk factor for each object and document the related risk level.

4. Inquire about controls—For each object or group of objects, ask the administrators how they were built and what security controls have been put in place. Refer back to the list of controls created in Step 1 if required. Later on, we will compare these controls against the minimum required controls to determine a score.

Step 4 Vulnerability Scanning

Now that we have discovered, verified, and assigned risks to various objects, we can begin performing vulnerability scans using our vulnerability scanning tool. Different scanners have different options, but most include probing policies based on the type of object being scanned. We would not want to scan a router, for example, looking for vulnerabilities associated with a server.

Vulnerability scanners are very powerful tools. They can be extremely helpful, and extremely destructive when used improperly. Here are some key points to consider before performing any type of vulnerability scan:

- Get written permission before scanning any object outside your immediate authority.

- Schedule vulnerability scans in advance and at times when no other network or system changes are occurring.

- Make sure administrators and managers understand that the scanner could potentially have negative effects on sensitive objects.

- Perform the proper scan for each type of object. Scanning a server with a scan intended for desktops could miss a number of vulnerabilities.
- Vulnerability scanners normally come with the ability to perform DoS scans. Make sure you turn this feature off, or coordinate with administrators in the event that the DoS succeeds and the object goes offline.

Step 5 Hands-on Audit

The hands-on portion of the audit is where we go in and actually verify the controls we found in our interviews conducted in Step 3. This portion of the audit has the potential of consuming the most time and resources in the audit process. Different organizations choose to deal with the hands-on audit in different ways. The most accurate approach is to perform hands-on verification of each and every major object. This, however, may not be practical in many situations. As such, I have provided a list of the most common alternate approaches I have seen:

- Perform hands-on auditing on a randomly selected sample of objects
- Perform hands-on auditing for objects of high and critical risk levels
- Perform hands-on auditing for a handful of systems within each department, or under each administrator

During the hands-on audit, we will work to verify the controls discussed during the interview process. Once a control level for each control type is determined, we will document it. Though types of controls will vary for each object, I have included some common controls to audit in Appendix C, *Additional Recommended Audit Practices*.

> In addition to auditing controls, it is a good idea to assess components of security that the security scanner may not have detected. One of the most common actions performed during the hands-on assessment is to extract and crack account passwords. This can be performed easily using a variety of free extraction and cracking tools, like those already discussed.

Step 6 Hands-on Sampling of Desktop Security

As we have discussed, end-users and their desktops play an important role in the overall security of any organization. End-user desktops can have a large influence over the security of an organization. The problem with desktops is that the sheer number of them normally makes it impossible to perform a hands-on audit of each one. There is also the problem that every department will have a slightly different desktop build, thus making auditing a bit tricky.

Of course, our desktops should have already undergone a vulnerability scan, which should have revealed any immediate threats like back doors or open shares. It is, however, important to take a deeper look into desktops to make sure different individuals and groups are conforming to desktop-related security policies. Most often, the best way to perform a desktop audit is to take a random pool of systems within each department and perform a hands-on assessment. It usually becomes obvious if a particular department or facility is enforcing the desktop security policy after sampling five or six of its computers.

When performing a desktop audit, we look for any required controls as well as a wide variety of security issues that may not have been discovered through the network scan. During the hands-on audit, for example, we may look to see if the antivirus software is up-to-date, it there are active modems, or if the computer contains any unauthorized software. Each organization may have its own unique series of issues to look for with desktops. I have included common desktop auditing practices in Appendix C.

Step 7 Physical Inspection

During the physical inspection process, we look at the different areas in which servers, routers, and other important objects are stored. As we have seen, the risk level of an area is going to be determined by the risk level of the objects within that area. Our risk control policies dictate a minimum level of security control for areas based on a certain level of risk. During the physical audit, we inspect these controls and other information about the room, including the environmental conditions, fire control, power controls, and general organization and well being of systems and cables.

When auditing physical areas, it is best to address all areas that contain major objects such as servers, routers, and switches. A server may sit in someone's office, therefore, the office should be inspected. I have included some common physical auditing practices in Appendix C.

Step 8 Compiling and Scoring Data

After performing the object risk and control assessment and reviewing the security of the environment, we have a good amount of data to work with. I discussed previously how to score objects based on their control violations. Scoring our objects will help to determine where risks are and where controls do not meet the standards.

By mapping out where different risk levels exist and where different vulnerabilities and control violations were found, we will begin to see patterns emerge. It will become easier to determine which objects are more critical to the organization as well as which departments, facilities, and administrators have a higher average number of violations. Reviewing this information and these patterns will provide a stronger sense of the security of the organization.

Step 9 Reporting and Review

Now that the tactical audit has been completed, it is time to create reports and review them with the staff. By listing the scores for individual objects, factoring in some statistical averages, and documenting the findings from hands-on auditing, we will have the information needed to create a strong tactical report. Reports should be reviewed with executives and the heads of different departments, as well as the IT staff. Individuals should agree with the findings, or provide a formal dispute, and a plan should be drafted on how issues will be resolved before the next scheduled audit.

It is vital in this step that the reports are clear, concise, and geared toward the target audience. Technical individuals should receive copies of the individual object scores and vulnerability scans, while managers and senior staff should receive statistical figures and summaries. The key here to is to get everyone to read and understand the report so that corrective actions can be taken.

Tactical Audit Schedule

For the tactical audit process to become part of the three-fold process, it will need to be performed regularly. When I say "regularly," this could vary from organization to organization based on size, resources, and general IT practices. Some portions of the audit process should be repeated more often than others to maintain proactive awareness of new vulnerabilities within the environment. The schedule in Table 8.16 should fit the practices of most environments:

Table 8.16 *Sample Audit Schedule*

Audit Task	Schedule
Complete tactical audit and review	Once/year
Review to check on progress	6 months after original review
Follow-up vulnerability scanning on servers and desktops	Once every two or three months

ANALYTICAL AUDIT MEASURES

As much as I would like to say that a single formulaic process could solve all auditing needs, there are other factors that must also be considered. The process discussed in the previous section simplifies 90% of the audit work and gives us accurate, consistent, and measurable results that can be obtained without a great deal of security experience. Some organizations have based their entire audit methodology on this type of process since it provides the greatest impact and requires the fewest security resources. After this process is completed, however, it is important to take a look at the aspects of security beyond the objects. What we need to do is examine at the organization as a whole, in light of the rules of security.

This next part of an audit cannot be placed into any linear formula. I can, however, guide you through some recommended processes and provide key areas for organizations to consider. It is advised that these processes be completed by someone with a good deal of security expertise. Organizations that do not have the proper expertise should look to outside consultants for assistance.

Perimeter Architecture Audit

Before conducting a perimeter audit, be sure you are familiar with the concepts presented in the section titled, *Perimeter Defenses*, in Chapter 11, *Practical Security Assessments*, and the section in Chapter 5, *Developing a Higher Security Mind*, titled *Thinking in Zones*. Examine your perimeter and how access flows to and from all parties. Look at how services are accessed in both directions and determine if the current architecture corresponds to the most secure zoning architecture possible. Also look closely at the rules highlighted in the section titled, *Perimeter Defenses*, to see if your organization's perimeter is adhering to them.

When looking at the perimeter, be sure to test all externally accessible devices for vulnerabilities. This normally will include routers, firewalls, and externally accessible services such as DNS, email, the Web, and others. Run vulnerability scans from an external address and see how much you can access and learn about the environment. Look at the results and think back to the Rule of Least Privilege, comparing what can be seen and accessed to what is really required to be seen and accessed. Also, be sure to examine the rules applied at the firewall and other perimeter security devices to make sure they adhere to the Rule of Least Privilege, that there are no weaknesses, and that they are up-to-date.

It is often helpful when performing a perimeter assessment to run through each rule of security and compare it against your perimeter architecture. Look to each concept to ensure you are creating stillness, working in layers, and following the other concepts of a security mind. It will be quite useful when evaluating the perimeter to look for weaknesses commonly found in other organizations. I have included a list of these weaknesses in Appendix C.

Internal Architecture Security Audit

Before conducing an internal audit, be sure you are familiar with the concepts in the upcoming section titled, *Internal Defenses*, in Chapter 11, as well as the rules of security described in Chapter 4, *The Eight Rules of Security (Components of All Security Decisions)*. The world of internal security can be immense and the higher practices are going to be the best guide. Check on the change management process, emergence response mechanisms, separation of services and responsibilities, and three-fold processes, and always be on the lookout for the weakest link.

We have already performed a tactical assessment and a vulnerability scan of the internal network, which will be of great help. A good approach for taking the internal audit further is to think of yourself as a hacker on the internal network. See what level of access you can obtain, and to what degree you can affect the operations of the internal environment. While you perform such tasks, check to see which attempts for access show up in your logging and monitoring processes. Also, be sure to consider tactics like social engineering.

Again, it is helpful when evaluating internal security to look for weaknesses commonly found in other organizations. I have included a list of these weaknesses in Appendix C.

Auditing Applications

Auditing applications and their implementation within the organization are key components of performing an internal audit. This does not mean that we are auditing the internal structure of an application, or its code. Rather, we are auditing the application's ability to conform to security policies, and whether or not local implementations are in compliance. Application security audits usually come down to three primary checks:

- Compliance with the Rule of Least Privilege—Applications that provide access to services or data should be secured against unauthorized access. Applications should be configured to enforce the Rule of Least Privilege, allowing access to those that require it and can handle it. Where appropriate, applications should include authentication and authorization mechanisms as well as any other applicable means of limiting access. Applications should also have some defensive mechanisms to help enforce this rule. Common mechanisms to check for include:

- Account locking due to excessive violations
- Access violation logging and monitoring
- Password administration:
    - Minimum password lengths
    - Aging passwords
    - Password sanity checking (for simple passwords)
- Compliance with the Rule of the Three-Fold Process—Major applications should be continually maintained to ensure security patches and updates are implemented. Check to see if the vendor is keeping on top of security patches and if administrators are applying them. Applications should also include some form of logging and monitoring capabilities for security-related events. See what forms of logging have been enabled, and how the local staff goes about monitoring them.
- Consideration of zones—Earlier, we discussed several possible zoning scenarios, ranging from the weakest to the strongest level of protection. An application should conform to the most secure zoning scenario possible for its functionality. Frequently, vital applications that are accessible from external entities should store sensitive data on a separate, protected server. Many times, the different zones on applications are definable by the end-user, who chooses where specific data and services should exist. Look to your own implementations of these applications and make sure they reflect the best possible zoning practices.

Auditing Administration

Part of ensuring that security policies are being enforced is to perform an audit of system administration practices within the organization. Administrators, help desk staff, and other IT personnel are commonly charged with the distribution and management of user accounts, as well as the building, maintaining, and monitoring of workstations and servers. With this in mind, it is easy to see how many security practices are left in the hands of these individuals.

To audit administration is to audit the common tasks performed within the organization. An administration audit can include:

- Interviewing administrators to see if their procedures conform to the security policy. This is especially important with the processes of creating new accounts, modifying access privileges, and resetting passwords.

- Checking for system-based password management policies (during the hands-on process).
- Checking for easily cracked passwords and those that do not conform to policy (during the hands-on assessment).
- Checking the process by which administrative logs are monitored and reviewed.
- Checking for unhardened systems and those that are not regularly maintained.

ADDITIONAL AUDIT CONSIDERATIONS

In addition to the audit processes described in this chapter, there are a few other considerations to keep in mind:

Acceptable Risk

Security is always a balance between protection and practicality. Try our hardest to maintain security and there will always be situations where the best measure is simply not practical. This leads to what is called acceptable risk.

Acceptable risk is the acknowledgement that a security issue exists and we are knowingly allowing it to remain. The degree to which the issue remains may be somewhat lessened by practical security measures; however, the measures required to fully remove the risk are not conducive to good business sense.

I see acceptable risks all the time within organizations, usually because the protective measures required would harm productivity almost as much as a successful attack would. There is nothing wrong with an organization accepting a risk as long as the following practices are maintained:

- The risk should be explored to its fullest so that the organization knows exactly what it is risking and the estimated chance of it happening.
- Acceptable risks should always be determined by groups, never by an individual. Major parties that could be affected by the risk should be aware of the issue.
- Any risk deemed to be acceptable should be listed in an "Acceptable Risk Record" that states what the risk is, why the risk is deemed acceptable, and what measures were taken to reduce the risk.

Staffing an Audit

For an audit to be accurate, auditors must be impartial to the results. A security engineer, for example, should never audit his or her own security devices just as an administrator should never audit his/her own servers. Auditors should also not have any outstanding disciplinary problems or grudges against other staff members, since personal feelings tend to skew results. The best security audits are usually those staffed by consultants with no attachment to the environment. While the effort can be directed internally, in most situations it is highly recommended to bring in external resources or contract companies specializing in audits to perform the actual work.

Common Perspective Among the Staff

One vital requirement for an audit is that the entire team must have a common understanding of the organization, its risk levels, and the related risk factors. If any member of the audit team differs in his or her view or method for assigning risk factors, then the entire audit could be unbalanced. One facility, for example, could be given a better score than another simply because the primary auditor differed in opinion from the other auditors. This could potentially cause numerous issues with the audit results and could make the audit lose credibility in the eyes of the audited entities.

It is extremely important to have a basic group training session with all auditors present. During this session, each risk level should be discussed, along with the risk factors and overall audit process. The group should come to a consensus as to what these variables mean and how they will be assigned to different objects. When dealing with a group that has never performed such an audit, it is also a good idea to start by teaming people together for the first couple of interviews and hands-on assessments to make sure they learn and follow similar practices.

9 The Security Staff

BUILDING A SUCCESSFUL SECURITY TEAM

Building a good security team can be difficult for an organization. There are many obstacles out there, even for those organizations that have unlimited recruiting resources. This chapter will discuss the "do's and don't's" of building a strong security empire. Such knowledge is essential for managers, staff, and consultants looking to develop security within an environment.

Determining Whether a Security Staff Is Even Required

The first question we need to answer is whether or not an organization even needs a formal security staff. The security initiatives of some successful organizations have been run solely by an IT director and a good network engineer. A dedicated and specialized security team can be difficult to hire and retain, and some organizations look for months without finding suitable security engineers. A good security team can also be quite costly depending on the level of expertise desired. In general, "You get what you pay for," so it is important to be realistic when budgeting for this type of employee.

As a guide to determine what sort of staffing is required for security within an environment, take the factors listed in Table 9.1 into consideration. Add the corresponding point values to the score for each box that applies to your environment. This should give you a general idea of how to look at security staffing needs.

Table 9.1   Calculating Security Requirements[a]

Question	0 points	1 point	2 points	3 points	5 points
How many workstations does the organization operate?	<75	>75	>200	>500	>1,000
How many servers (Web, email, firewall, etc.) does the organization operate?	<5	>5	>15	>30	>40
Does the organization have a full-time, dedicated Internet connection?	No	Yes	–	–	–

Table 9.1   *Calculating Security Requirements[a] (Continued)*

Question	0 points	1 point	2 points	3 points	5 points
Does the organization allow for external parties (customers, partners, vendors) to connect to any of the servers via the Internet or a WAN?	No	–	Yes	–	–
Does the organization allow for remote dial-in access, wireless communications, or VPNs?	No	Yes	–	–	–
Does the organization host sensitive information, or are servers absolutely critical for the continuity of business?	No	Yes	–	–	–
Does the organization have to conform to legal regulations, or contracts that address security issues?	No	Yes	–	–	–
Total Points					

a.   *Example: If you have 200 computers (2 points) and an Internet connection (1 point), your score would be 3.*

Of course, there are many other factors to weigh in the matter that cannot be represented in a chart or formula. After calculating these primary factors, let Table 9.2 act as a guide to assist in your staffing considerations.

Insight into the Security Engineer Market

Good security engineers have been historically very hard to come by. Oftentimes demanding salaries 20–50% higher than the average networking engineer, security engineers seem to find no shortage of employment opportunities, even in times of economic strife.

Table 9.2 Interpreting the Results

Score	Consideration
0–1	Such a low score would indicate that there is probably no need to have a full- or part-time security engineer. If a major security decision is required, using a temporary consultant may be the best choice. As always, the IT staff should still be security-minded and follow the rules of security. No organization of any size should ever neglect the maintenance of security within their environment.
2–3	This score would indicate the need for an individual or group to be directly tasked with security responsibilities. There is still probably no need for a full-time security engineer, but security must be organized and someone should be in charge of managing and reporting on security measures. Spending a few hours a week with dedicated security focus is recommended.
4–5	This score would indicate that the organization should invest in at least a part-time security engineer, perhaps an individual who has security tasks as half of his/her daily chores. This individual should be formally trained in security with a few years of experience.
6–8	This score suggests that a full-time security engineer should be employed by the company. This individual should be formally trained and have several years of experience.
9+	A score this high suggests the need for multiple security engineers, or a security team. Quite often, the successful scaling approach includes having a single security expert and one or more mentors who perform the daily security chores while developing security skills.

At the beginning of this book, we looked at several factors that separate security from other practices in IT. In short, security is global, high-pressure, extremely dynamic, and is a relatively new practice compared to system and network engineering. The combination of these factors means a shortage of good security engineers. Many would-be security professionals shy away from the more intense factors that surround the occupation, while others simply dislike the human aspects (considering that their primary goal in becoming an engineer was to remove themselves from the human element anyway).

What does all of this mean to us? Simply that security is a different field than others we have had to deal with in the past. When we hire a security engineer, we must hire someone who knows technology, is highly creative, and is capable of interacting with other humans, a difficult combination of skills. Organizations that are able to quickly hire engineers without a good compensation package are either extremely lucky, or are not receiving the quality they need.

What Is a Security Professional?

Security professionals come in all shapes and sizes and can fit just about anywhere in an organization chart. Some high-level security-minded professionals have little use for deep and dirty technical knowledge, while the security-minded firewall-jockey has little need to know the ins and outs of performing a financial risk and impact analysis. There is, however, a middle area that a normal "good security engineer" will fall into, a central base of skills that most non-specialized security professionals should possess.

Overview of Skills and Knowledge

Almost every component that makes up an IT infrastructure has some relationship to security. This includes, but is certainly not limited to, all servers, desktops, applications, operating systems, networking equipment, communication protocols, and physical security. Thus, an individual's security skill set must often span many different technologies. An effective security engineer is going to have to know or learn, to some degree, about most of the technologies deployed within the environment.

The Security Mind (Rules and Virtues)

Before we talk about the nitty-gritty security fundamentals, we must first concern ourselves with the most important aspect of a good security professional: It is important to look beyond the specific technologies an individual knows and ascertain his/her security knowledge and ability to grasp the concept of security as a whole. Just about anyone can configure a firewall, but most people could not begin to tell you how to use it effectively.

This is a very important concept to remember since it is quite common to be deceived by technical know-how. Many people who are in the security market, or who desire to become security professionals, are simply interested in the technology of security. During an interview, it is quite easy to be impressed when someone knows how many bits a network overflow attack should consist of, but such knowledge does not warrant placing someone in charge of information security. Detailed technical knowledge is an extremely useful tool in security, but it is useless unless it is guided by an understanding of the virtues and rules of security.

Operating System Skills

One of the key functions of a security professional is to protect systems from being compromised. Knowledge of how to protect a server or workstation is essential to the average security professional's career. To secure a computer, it is useful to have a strong knowledge of the underlying operating system. A good security professional should have an understanding of the following operating systems (of course, this will vary depending on the environment):

- **Windows**—Microsoft Windows is a fairly simple operating system to understand. The way in which security is implemented and managed, however, can get very complicated on the Windows NT, 2000, and XP platforms. Many of the security features within the operating system are hidden from sight to avoid confusing end-users. While pretty much anyone can quickly figure out how a Windows-based server operates, it is recommended that all security professionals spend some time gaining knowledge of how the underlying security architecture works. This is true for both individual systems and enterprise distributions.

- **UNIX (especially Solaris)**—More complex than Windows for the average user, knowledge of UNIX is almost a requirement for security professionals in a UNIX-based organization. The speed and robustness of UNIX has made it a standard for high-end applications, and its ability to be "tweaked" has made it a favorite for security programmers and hackers alike. Unlike desktop applications, security applications have a tendency to appear first in UNIX, then in Windows. The underlying infrastructure of UNIX has many more security "details" to worry about and it can be much more complicated to implement security. Ultimately, however, UNIX can arguably achieve more security than Windows and, as such, is essential to the security professional's skill set.

- **Linux**—One of the biggest pushes for the Linux operating system has been from the security world. As the leader in publicly accepted Open Source operating systems, Linux has the potential to be secured tighter than most other operating systems. Many high-end applications have been designed to run on Linux-based servers, and they are becoming more common each year. Though Linux is very similar to other forms of UNIX, it does have its own set of unique security components. Knowledge of Linux is a valuable tool for any security professional.

Networking

All security professionals should have a good knowledge of how modern networks function. Many aspects of security and hacking rely on the use and manipulation of networks, networking devices, and networked systems. TCP/IP is just about the only protocol to discuss as related to security, since most other protocols are becoming less and less common to find. Security professionals should understand how networks function and how devices communicate over a LAN, WAN, and over the Internet. A strong knowledge of all the common communication protocols like Telnet, SMTP, File Transfer Protocol (FTP), HTTP, DNS, and ICMP is certainly a plus.

Security Technologies

Security technologies, like firewalls and IDSs, are often what organizations consider to be the primary skills of a security professional. While there are other, more important factors, a security professional should indeed know a good deal about firewalls, network intrusion detection, host intrusion detection, system security (operating system hardening), VPNs, and general encryption. It is also important to know a bit about various security-related topics like packet filtering, proxying, zoning, structures for logging, and reporting. The individual should also be well-versed in the art of penetration and vulnerability testing (as discussed below).

Hacking Technologies

A security professional must have at least some knowledge of how hackers work and operate. Though it is a bad idea to hire anyone who enjoys hacking in his or her spare time (discussed later), it is important for the individual to know the concepts, tools, and technologies of hackers. This should include penetration testing, vulnerability scanning, sniffing, and malicious coding. Knowledge of hacker exploit tools, such as viruses, worms, back doors, and Trojan horses is essential.

It is important for a security professional to be able to recognize an attack when it occurs, whether it is on a network, in a system, or from someone calling randomly through an organization asking for passwords. Most defenses are designed to report interesting activities, but we must still be able to recognize an attack from small pieces of information.

Programming

Though certainly not a requirement, some programming knowledge is extremely useful in security (especially when dealing with Linux, Solaris, or other forms of UNIX-based security). Working knowledge of Perl or some other common scripting language is a big asset to anyone in security.

Written Policies

Policies and procedures (discussed later) are the only hope any organization has for maintaining long-term security efforts. Being able to recognize where policies need to exist and writing them down or doctoring up someone else's policies are vital skills for anyone practicing security; more so is knowing where and when a policy needs to be created, and being willing to do the work. Be wary of anyone continually suggesting new security measures and never talking about a policy or procedure.

About Hiring Hackers

One glorified concept that certainly justifies a paragraph or two in this book is the idea of hiring hackers for the security staff. The temptation is very prevalent to do so, and has been further inspired by movies, the media, and the simple logic that a hacker should know better than anyone how to keep systems from being "hacked."

I have been interviewing security engineers for private organizations and consulting firms for many years now. One of the key elements of my security interview process is to inquire as to whether or not the interviewee was ever a hacker. The question, of course, is usually phrased somewhat cleverly, so as to inspire a tale of some great hacking feat. If an interviewee receives a checkmark in my interview box marked "Potential Hacker," the interview notes are trashed and we move to the next candidate.

In this book, I discuss the difficulty of dealing with employees who have hacker tendencies, and point out how difficult it can be to find and stop such individuals. Take this concept up a few thousand notches when considering hiring a "potential hacker."

There are, of course, a few exceptions, but I emphasize the word "few." Being in charge of, or on a team that is in charge of, information security is somewhat of a power trip. It inspires great pride in most, even if it is just being in charge of security for the local drugstore. For an engineer sitting at a desk with numerous icons of all the latest hacker tools strewn across his or her desktop, the temptation to use them is incredible. For the person in charge of information security, there is often nothing but conscience preventing him or her from completely taking over the IT infrastructure. Now, imagine giving such power to a hacker.

We must, to some degree, inherently trust our security engineers. It could almost be included in the job description: "Must be trusted with the keys to the kingdom." Finding someone we can trust, who can go through the daily turmoil and political battles of work, and whom we could even potentially fire without having a destructive worm released through the infrastructure, is very difficult indeed. If we start to look at hackers to fill these positions, we are asking for a nightmare.

STORY OF AN EMPLOYED HACKER

To quickly share an experience, there was one exception that was made to the "no hiring a hacker rule." A very young and extremely bright individual asking for a moderate salary and with the gleam of potential in his eye was hired as a security consultant. It was known that this individual had been a hacker, but he seemed to be on a straight path and it was too great an opportunity to pass up. Employment lasted approximately eight months with this individual, who would occasionally hint at the hacker life he lived when at home.

The sheer potential of an intelligent hacker employed within the company was enough to cause sleepless nights for those in charge of him. Every time this individual would ask for a raise, every time he made a formal complaint, and every time he asked for special privileges, it was in the minds of all the managers that, "We really don't want to upset this guy." Even when it came time to terminate the individual (for unrelated reasons), the company had to spend countless hours checking and double-checking the systems accessible to this individual for a potential threat. Throughout the entire history of his employment and termination, the individual never made a single (known) attempt to hack the employing company. But even years after, the possibility exists that this individual could have left a hidden remote control application or time bomb within the company or its clients.

Moral of the story: If an organization does decide to hire someone who is potentially a hacker, it is very important to think through the whole lifecycle of employment, all the problems, headaches, and worries it could cause, and only then determine if it is worth it.

Training Security Personnel from Within

Training employees within the organization is highly recommended for many reasons. Total cost of ownership of the employee is normally much lower when he or she is trained; it keeps his/her skills sharp and keeps him/her satisfied in the job; and, training is often the only chance an organization has of acquiring a good security engineer.

Some forms of security training are heavily priced. Taking advantage of the lack of security engineers, training organizations and technology vendors have seen fit to add a nice 50–100% to the bill for a security class. Sadly, the quality of such training is usually no higher than normal technical classes. Paying 50% more for training does not increase the potential of creating a good security engineer. This being said, I highly recommend the idea of training internal staff on security, but offer the following suggestions:

1. Choose very carefully whom you send to training. You want to pick employees who will be attentive and who will retain and apply what they have learned. Also, security classes are very similar to hacking classes, and you don't want to send a disgruntled employee to learn "Hacking 101."

2. Normally, it is more valuable to train in classes that are more global than ones that are product-specific. Unless required, don't take the "Brand-X Firewall" class when you would get more from the "Firewalls for Everyone" class and reading the Brand-X firewall manual.

3. Security conferences are usually a great way to get a good mix of technology, theory, and design. I highly recommend attending conferences like "SysAdmin, Audit, Network, Security" (SANS), where there are numerous short sessions, which can be followed up with independent study.

4. Complement the training class with independent study. Security is a very large field and it is extremely dynamic. A class is valuable for introductions and for some subjects that require hands-on experience. But reading books, magazines, and online articles can provide more information than a class.

Hacker Training

After reading the previous section concerning the problems with "hiring a hacker," one may get the sense that an organization should have nothing to do with hacker knowledge. This is not the case, as knowledge of hacking is essential for anyone to be able to secure an environment. It is highly encouraged that security professionals spend a good amount of time reading through hacker Web sites, catching up on the latest "How to Hack a...." articles, and even downloading and experimenting with hacker tools. All of this, however, should be done within the following guidelines:

1. Company policy should dictate that anyone visiting hacker Web sites, downloading hacker tools, or participating in any way within the hacker community must first get approval from a manager or executive. A hacker tool acquired without permission should be considered a security violation.

2. Whenever a hacker Web site is visited, a file is downloaded, or a tool is experimented with, it should be done on a system and network completely separate from the main company network. Doing this through a separate Internet connection, through a modem, or from a separate leg on the firewall is highly recommended if possible.

3. For anyone using a security tool, including common sniffers, it is recommended that written permission from the CIO is obtained and the letter is then safely locked away. There have been incidents where confidential information was exposed to a security professional without intention, and that individual was terminated or prosecuted for the act.

Interviewing a Security Professional

Conducting security interviews is rarely simple. This does not mean, however, that we have to leave the hiring process up to "luck," or trial and error. I have included the following key points to consider when looking to hire a security professional:

Assess the Ability to Think Out of the Box

Good security requires an individual to think of things that may seem a bit far out, or perhaps deal in abstract logic. When all of a sudden an email system begins forwarding all messages through another server before reaching their destination, the individual has to be able to recognize that something may be wrong and then figure out why anyone would want to do that. A useful tactic to use in an interview is to catch the candidates off guard and force them to think on their feet. Out of the box questions like "Why would you attack a candy maching to the Internet" or "In what ways is an online transaction more secure than actualy going to the store?" Such questions are asked when the actual answer doesn't matter as much as the thought process followed.

Assess the Ability to Follow a Process

Practicing security often involves following logical processes to derive a conclusion about a particular situation. It is very common for a security engineer to be told, "I think someone broke into our system," and then asked to perform an assessment. The process followed does not have to be long or complicated, but it absolutely must be methodical and repeatable. Thus, in an interview, it can be very helpful to give someone a scenario with little information and ask how the candidate would handle it. For example, tell the individual that someone comes to him/her in a panic saying that the email server has been hacked and is now not working. Then ask how he/she would go about handling the situation.

Asking questions like these, we are looking for some clear and logical way of getting to the bottom of the situation. Our ideal candidate will follow a simple process that informs management, deals with the immediate situation, and then performs a logical analysis while documenting every step. A key phrase to listen for is: "Follow the corporate policy and procedure in the matter." Also, consideration should be taken to preserve evidence, but at the same time, the immediate unavailable system must be taken care of. Primarily, we are looking to see if an individual is even aware of such considerations, and secondarily if he/she is able to incorporate them into a procedure.

Use a Group to Ask Technical Questions

Sometimes, it can be hard to ask direct security questions when there are no security experts within the organization. Though by no means should we expect a candidate to be an expert in every field of technology, he/she should be able to answer questions about operating systems, networking, and a few other key technologies. If there is no one in the environment comfortable asking tough security questions, round out the interview with questions from other practices. Ensure the candidate knows the fundamentals of each area and then ask him/her to expound on the security implications of each. If the candidate is good, everyone in the room may learn something. In this scenario, it is important to take good notes to verify any complicated security information later.

Certifications and Other Tall Tales

Certifications are a great concept, and it would be wonderful if they actually worked. To be certified in something should reflect an experienced understanding of the subject. It should measure knowledge that has been practiced, that can be applied practically, and that will be retained for a long period of time. If this was the case, then an employer would be able to look at a list of acronyms next to a person's name and feel confident that the individual is proficient in those subjects.

Sadly, the vast majority of security certifications in today's market simply indicate that an individual was able to memorize a series of facts before writing them all down on paper. The candidate could shortly after forget the information, usually because he/she never really understood it in the first place. This is a hard lesson learned through several years of hiring and terminating certified technology professionals.

I myself have several certifications to my name, as do the majority of my colleagues. Such paperwork is quite useful to have since most organizations do not have the expertise to proper assess security skills and must therefore refer to the symbols next to a candidate's name. Sadly, I know of no good security professionals who place any value on the processes they went through to acquire their certifications.

> Over the years, the majority of professionals I have hired have had no security certifications at all. After some thought and study in the matter, I realized that to accurately certify someone as knowledgeable in a subject would be very difficult and would not allow for profit to be made. Since having people certify and recertify at $100, $300, and $500 a shot is incredible revenue for these training organizations, the idealistic goal of a having a truly useful certification is very hard to achieve. A true, unbiased certification cannot be used to grow an organization or make a profit.

Using a Screening Company

Screening companies are becoming more common for organizations interested in hiring security engineers. A screening company will ask a candidate security questions on behalf of an organization and then provide a score that indicates the candidate's level of comprehension. These organizations are good time-savers, but they have many drawbacks. The individuals performing the interviews are normally just technical enough to ask the questions and understand the answers. Since security requires more creativity than fact-retaining, a good security interview can't be confined to stock questions. If, however, the local staff consists of no security experts, these organizations may provide good value.

BRINGING IN SECURITY CONSULTANTS

Security consulting is a business that boomed beyond all expectations just before the turn of the century. The ever-increasing plague of hackers, worms, and viruses, the growing fear factor in the average organization, and a general lack of security expertise opened the market wide for information security consultants around the world. Basically, anyone who had ever touched a firewall or read about encryption could be gainfully employed in information security as a consultant.

Today, just about every consulting organization has an information security practice and a plethora of security offerings for customers. Security consultants bring in a high rate, equivalent to that of high-end networking, storage area consulting, and other premium consulting services. Such rates are normally well worth the investment when dealing with an experienced security consulting team. Unfortunately, along with the great demand for security services also came an enormous push to develop security offerings within consulting organizations that were not necessarily ready for them. This has resulted in a great mix of quality among the different security services performed by consulting companies.

Dispelling the Consulting Myth

One of the greatest things about hiring a consultant or consulting organization to secure an environment is that we get a nice, warm, fuzzy feeling that the matter is in the hands of experts. Many organizations choose to offload their most difficult or sensitive tasks to an outside organization, believing the organization to have a higher level of expertise than the local staff. Unfortunately, this is not what they always get.

Most consulting organizations, just like any other profitable entity, are run by the sales department. As such, the quality of the consulting services received can often be determined by the practices of the sales engineers. As with any organization, consulting companies have varying degrees of talent within their staff. In general, the most talented consultants will be continually busy and put on the most profitable projects, while the less talented consultants will be more readily available for newer projects. It then only makes sense for the sales engineer to provide the most available resource, commonly the less talented consultant, for the project at hand. In an ideal world, a good sales engineer will be able to tell if an individual is capable of handling a project and will make a sale based on this understanding. Sadly, the majority of sales engineers out there are not able to, or choose not to, follow such a process. It is thus up to the receiving organization to determine whether or not the consultant(s) it is hiring has the proper expertise. This creates a paradox, since assessing talent requires that you have talent with which to perform the assessment.

Purchasing Consulting Services

The main point here is that there should be no illusions when purchasing consulting services from a consulting organization. If individual consultants are going to be brought in for specific projects, be sure to perform a personal interview and make your own assessment of each individual's abilities. This interview should be performed alone, with no other representatives from the consulting company present.

Even more practical is to **purchase packaged services** from consulting organizations, rather than individuals. With a packaged services product, like a security assessment or a specific form of device implementation, there is a great deal of value coming from the consulting organization itself, not just the individual engineers. Organizations that perform the same services over and over tend to get extremely accurate and efficient. Thus, with these types of services, a client is more likely to get the proper engineers to fill the proper positions.

There are, of course, always expectations with this idea. The world is full of many talented and honest independent security consultants. The best approach to bringing in outside consultants is to establish a relationship through a series of smaller projects. Then, when a degree of trust has been established, it is much more practical to rely on the consultant for making major decisions.

Do We Need Consultants?

The real question here is, do we really need to bring in a consulting company to do a security project? If an organization is pondering whether the local staff can handle it or consultants need to be brought in, here are some common considerations:

- Does the local staff have experience in this area?—Most security projects should be performed by someone with experience in the area of security. We have already discussed many ways in which good security practices differ from good technology practices, and someone who can technically install a firewall is not always the best choice for implementing perimeter security.

- Does the organization trust the local staff to perform the project?— There are a variety of reasons not to trust local staff to perform some security operations. Most organizations, for example, should use external entities to perform security audits. The idea here is that a local administrator may not be quite so honest when reporting security issues with his or her own workstation, servers, and networks, or those of his friendly coworkers. Similarly, we may not trust local staff to implement security measures that will affect their own activities, such as restricting access to Web sites or increasing the monitoring of employee activities.

- Can the service desired be purchased in a package?—Packaged service offerings performed by a consulting organization can often be of benefit to us. A consulting company that centers its practices around a handful of packaged services will have already gone through the process of discovering errors, tuning procedures, and otherwise perfecting the service. This usually means that the consulting organization can perform the process much faster, more efficiently, and at a lower cost than if you were to staff the project locally.

OUTSOURCING SECURITY MAINTENANCE

With the growing demand for security services and the high costs associated with hiring a local security staff, many organizations look for alternate methods of managing security. This has opened the market for managed security services wherein clients can pay an external organization to monitor and react to various security issues. Managed services are a great way to provide certain types of services, such as off-hour monitoring of local security devices and running continual penetration scans and attack simulations. Hackers usually attack at odd hours of the night, when security staff are not present. With managed services, however, a staff shared among many clients can be utilized 24×7, rather than hiring a local staff to perform the same functions.

Limitations of Managed Services

At first glance, bringing in a managed services company may seem like the solution to all security problems. Indeed, managed security services can remove much of the work involved in maintaining security. However, remember that a managed service provider (MSP) can only offload certain aspects of security. There are far too many pieces of security to consider any external organization to have "ownership." Security as a whole must be managed from within an organization and seen in all aspects of its operations. Paying an MSP to monitor Internet connections or manage intrusion detection may be helpful, but it does not relieve us of security issues.

Beware of Free Managed Security

As the demand for managed services began to grow, many Internet service providers (ISPs) realized they could attract more customers by managing the security of their customers' Internet connections. Most ISPs offer firewall filtering, intrusion detection, and incident reporting at a minimal fee to their clients. This has led many organizations to forgo implementing their own local perimeter defenses and rely on their ISPs. I highly discourage organizations with more than a few computers from accepting this as their only security solution. Looking back to the discussion on trust, we must fully trust the ISP's equipment, staff, and policies to protect our organization. An ISP's primary focus, however, is not on the firewall or its management, but rather on the networking aspects of the business. As such, it is rare to find an ISP that will give adequate attention to protecting a company of any size. Heavy caution is recommended for any organization outsourcing its perimeter defenses.

A couple years ago, I performed an audit within a giant New York City-based organization. This company had elected to have its ISP manage the Internet firewall for all connections, including a network with hundreds of servers and thousands of workstations. During the audit, I contacted the ISP to inquire about its security policies and how this service was managed. After several days of trying to hunt down a technician, I finally learned that the firewall was Checkpoint 3.51, which had been outdated for more than five years. The system the firewall was running on had never been hardened, and the individual monitoring it knew as little about security as my beloved grandmothers.

Properly Using Managed Security Services

Managed security services are a great resource, when used properly. The best use for managed services is when an organization requires 24×7 monitoring for security events and does not have the staff to handle it. Another good use for such services is to enhance security maintenance, since the staff can spend a lot of time searching for new vulnerabilities, new exploits, and new patches on behalf of their clients. This is a great service if an organization is unable to have a security expert on staff. Before any MSP is used, the following issues should be considered:

- Does the organization have local security devices for the managed service provider (MSP) to manage?—It is usually not a good idea to hook up to an external party's firewall. Firewalls are often shared, and without a local device, there is no chance to directly interact with the device or check up on the service provider.

- Can the MSP be trusted?—Only use MSPs from large companies with good reputations. Choosing the wrong provider can be a horrible experience.

- Does the MSP have security experts on staff at all hours?—MSPs sometimes have a security expert on staff for part of the day and then college interns with no experience as the night-time staff. Make sure there is someone with security expertise on staff at all required hours.

- How often does the MSP research new vulnerabilities, exploits, and fixes?—An MSP should check for newly discovered exploits at least one or two times a day.

- How often will they update your systems?—There should be some form of service level agreement (SLA) that states when your systems will be updated or that your organization will be informed within x hours after a new exploit has been discovered.

- Will the MSP provide reports on potential violations?—Security should never be left solely in the hands of the MSP. Make sure you receive regular reports that you can review and question.

- Will the organization have access to security policies and configurations?—Again, never put 100% trust in your MSP. Make sure you have access to policies and configurations.

- What sort of liability does the MSP accept if a break-in occurs?—MSPs should be insured in case a break-in occurs and it is shown to be because of the MSP's negligence.

- How does the MSP prevent its own staff from hacking into client systems?—Managing security for another organization yields a lot of temptation for the local staff. Many hacks occur from such providers each year. Make sure the MSP has measures to control its own staff, and that reports concerning the MSP's access events into your systems are available upon request.

10 Modern Considerations

USING STANDARD DEFENSES

Most of what the average organization hears about modern security products comes from what they are told by product vendors, partners of vendors, and certified product users. This oftentimes does not provide the clearest understanding of the various security technologies on the market. Most advertisements for security products include some form of disclaimer stating: "This product alone does not guarantee complete security," but they never give the details as to why this is the case.

It is important before implementing any security solution to understand a defense's shortcomings so that we are prepared to handle them. This is not intended in any way to discourage the use of security countermeasures, for without them, it would be very difficult to protect any organization. Rather, the purpose of this chapter is to point out the common misconceptions that can lead to tragic security flaws within an organization. The weaknesses found in each type of security technology do not negate the need for such products, but simply reinforce the need for layering security practices.

The Reality of Firewalls

A network firewall is an application or device that sits on the chokepoint between two or more networks. Each network has most likely been defined as a zone with different security needs and the firewall is used to enforce the access policies between them. An object wishing to communicate to a network within a different zone must first have its communication inspected and approved by the firewall. The firewall does this by comparing the communication against a series of predefined rules. In short, a firewall is one place where we enforce the Rule of Least Privilege between two or more zones.

Packet Filtering or Proxying?

The two most common methods used by firewalls are packet filtering and proxying. Most modern firewalls can no longer simply be classified as packet filtering or proxying since they combine some aspects of both. It is rare to find a firewall that does not have both of these capabilities. However, most firewalls will focus on one approach and use the other to extend compatibility and enhance security features.

- **Packet filtering**—Packet filtering refers to a process that takes place at the network or session layer of communication. This means that the firewall will pick up each communication packet and make a security decision based on network information like:
  - Who is the packet from?
  - Where is the packet going?

- What does the firewall think it is doing?
- Other simple information

Most packet filtering firewalls are now considered stateful, which means that they no longer look at a single packet, but rather keep a short history of previous transactions and make more intelligent decisions based on this past information. Packet filtering is the fastest, simplest, and more flexible of the two firewall types.

- **Proxying**—Proxying refers to a process that takes place higher up in the communication layers. This means that the firewall can make security decisions based on inspecting the actual context of a communication rather than simply evaluating a series of communication packets. Using the proxy method, a firewall receives a communication, processes it as if it was the recipient, and then relays it to the real recipient. The firewall then receives a reply back from the real system, processes it, and passes it on to the originating system.

  As you may recall from the zoning discussion, this is a more secure way of handling communications since it creates a stronger separation between sender and receiver. If an attack occurs, it will be against the firewall, which is designed specifically to handle it. Proxies, unfortunately, consume a lot of processing power and memory to provide this level of protection. Proxies are not as fast or as flexible as packet filters.

- **Hybrids**—Looking at the advantages and disadvantages of packet filtering and proxying, it is easy to see why firewall manufacturers choose to embrace both methods within their products. Packet filtering firewalls, for example, normally have proxies for important services such as email and DNS. Proxying firewalls normally include packet filtering to speed up specific rules, or provide compatibility when a transaction does not function with proxy services. This is called a hybrid firewall, and it is the most common form of firewall found on the market.

The Problem with Firewalls

Unfortunately, having a computer guarding a network or system is similar to hiring the most inexperienced, uncreative, and unintelligent guard to protect the front door of the treasure room. We hand this thug a giant book of rules and have him look at every situation to find the corresponding instances. Most of these rules are common and thus are known to our enemies as well. This means that an enemy has only to stand in front of the guard and try to act on different loopholes in the rulebook. The guard does not understand that the enemy is trying to deceive him; he will simply follow the book until the rules eventually break and allow the enemy in.

Many times, I hear security professionals state that, "A firewall is not a solution by itself," but they cannot explain why this is the case. In reality, a firewall is not a solution in itself because there are too many limitations to the concept behind firewalls. Take, for instance, the following issues:

- Firewalls are not creative and cannot make sense of original human actions.
- Firewalls deal strictly with pattern recognition. Such patterns are also known to our enemies.
- Firewalls are computers themselves and are prone to errors, flaws, and vulnerabilities.
- Firewalls have limited memory capacity and can only recognize a series of events that happen quickly in succession.
- Firewalls are configured by humans and are subject to human error.

In reality, the only firewall that could be considered 99% secure is the firewall that allows no communications to take place on either side of the network, and even this is not 100% secure since the firewall itself could potentially be compromised.

Using Firewalls Securely

As we will discuss in the next chapter, firewalls are a vital element in guarding our network perimeters. A well configured firewall is a great ally in our efforts to keep the enemies on the outside of our castle walls. A common security failure in most organizations, however, is to put too much faith in their firewalls or to treat their firewall as a one-time effort. It is vital when dealing with firewalls to think with a security mind. Here are some good pointers for securely using firewalls:

- Always layer security on all sides of the firewall device. It must be assumed the firewall has vulnerabilities or has been misconfigured. Screen routers, IDSs, and internal defenses should all work to enhance security beyond the firewall.
- Firewalls are complex devices. Be sure the firewall is implemented and maintained by someone who is very familiar with the product.
- Firewalls are useless if they are not maintained. It is important to apply patch fixes to the software and operating system, as well as to perform regular inspections of the configuration and rule set.
- Firewalls return a great deal of information via logs and alerts. Since a firewall is incapable of "thinking" it is important that such information be reviewed and analyzed by a human being on a regular basis.

Intrusion Detection Systems

An IDS is a device that sits on a network or system and attempts to monitor for hacker activities. An IDS sits quietly and passively, watching for attacks, and sends out alarms when it notices suspicious patterns. Normally, there will be numerous IDS sensors watching different networks or systems, all of which are controlled by and report back to a central console and DB.

Signature Recognition or Statistical Sampling?

Similar to firewalls, there are two main ways in which IDSs operate. IDS products can base their decisions on signature recognition, statistical sampling, or some combination of the two.

- **Signature recognition**—In signature recognition, the IDS device will passively monitor its target network or server and watch for specific patterns (signatures) that it has been preprogrammed to recognize. Signatures are created by the manufacturer or end-users and simply tell the IDS what series of events correspond to a known attack. Many email viruses, for example, have a specific message in their subject header and an IDS could be programmed to look for such emails.
- **Statistical sampling**—IDS products that perform statistical sampling embrace a more behavior-based attack recognition method. With such an IDS, activity samples are taken over time to develop a baseline for

"normal activities." Once that baseline is established, the IDS will sit and watch for any "abnormal activities." This method of monitoring allows for a much wider variety of issues to be discovered, but usually results in a significantly higher number of false-positives.

The Problem with IDSs

An IDS is similar to an annoying person who finds numerous problems but never does anything about them. IDS sensors will sit quietly, and once an attack happens, will say, "You just got hit by a bomb; you probably should have prepared for this." Basically, the whole job of an IDS is to sit there and say, "Hmmm... Hate it when that happens!" Of course, knowing when we have been attacked, or more importantly, when we are being attacked, is a great advantage in security. It is important, however, to remember that IDSs are reactionary by nature and do not provide security by themselves.

There are a few IDS products that allow for active measures to be taken when a suspected attack is taking place. Most vendors, however, recommend that such features be turned off and to rely on the firewall for decision-making. This is due to the high number of false-positives the average IDS generates, and the potential for blocking legitimate traffic.

The main problems with IDS products are:

- The average IDS creates a high number of false-positives, making it difficult to work in stillness.
- IDS measures are only reactionary and don't really serve to protect networks.
- Network-based IDS products often have trouble keeping up with high-speed networks. This is normally handled by secretly dropping random packets, which may cause an attack to be missed.
- Host-based IDS products introduce a new complexity into servers, increasing the number of processes, communications, and patches required. All this increases the likeliness of a system failure or new vulnerability.
- IDS devices are often configured with two network connections, one attached to the untrusted network and one attached to the trusted network. This creates a bridge around the firewall, and if a hacker exposes a vulnerability or misconfiguration, the trusted network could be directly exposed to an attack.

On top of this, we still have the same problems that we have with firewalls:

- IDSs are not creative and cannot make sense of most human actions.
- Most IDSs deal strictly with pattern recognition. Patterns are known to both our enemies and us.
- IDSs are computers themselves and are prone to errors, flaws, and vulnerabilities.
- IDSs in general have more memory for recognizing patterns than do firewalls; however, they still have limited memory and can only recognize a series of events that happen in succession.
- IDSs are configured by humans and are subject to human error.

Using IDSs Securely

Similar to a firewall, an IDS should only a small part of a larger security effort. The IDS is a great addition to security, however it is also prone to errors, attacks, and misconfiguration. In addition, IDSs are unable to "think", making it imperative that IDS logs and alerts be actively monitored by a human. The same recommendations we reviewed for firewalls apply to IDSs.

Vulnerability Scanners

Vulnerability scanners are used to discover well-known weaknesses in servers, networks, applications, and other objects within an organization. The most common vulnerability scanners are those that probe for network-based vulnerabilities against standard operating systems and devices. Scanners are commonly used during audits to proactively search for vulnerabilities.

Types of Vulnerability Scanning

There are several types of vulnerability scanning; most products embrace one or more of the following methods:

- **Basic probing**—This is the traditional one-layer scanning process that checks for open communication ports via the network. These scanners look for services and applications with known vulnerabilities by matching a specific request with an expected series of replies. Most often, this is as simple as trying to access Telnet on a system to see if it is enabled and then matching the reply with a series of expected replies that give away system information.

- **Enhanced probing**—Some scanning products include an extra level of probing that yields useful information. When a vulnerability is found, these scanners will exploit it to find more information about the object. For example, if the basic probing process finds an account without a password, then the enhanced probing process can use the discovered access to download the password file or discover more information about the system.

- **DoS simulation**—Some scanners come with the ability to perform a DoS scan. This is really more of an exploit than a scan since the goal is to actually attack an object with a series of DoS exploits and see what happens. This scan provides a much more accurate view of an object's vulnerabilities, but can only be performed with the assumption that the object may become unstable.

The Problem with Vulnerability Scanners

Running a vulnerability scan is similar to hiring an inexperienced and uncreative hacker, giving him or her a laptop, and having him/her follow a huge manual on different attack methods. The hacker is not given any orientation into the environment and is not allowed any interactions outside of his/her local laptop (i.e., he/she can't talk to anyone or even take a look around). On top of all this, the hacker is instructed to only perform attacks halfway, using methods that will not harm the local networks or devices. Thus, the hacker is greatly limited.

The main problem with scanners is that it is impossible to test objects like a hacker would. This can be a good thing since we probably don't want to cripple a network while searching for vulnerabilities. This, however, presents a paradox: To secure objects from exploits, we must exploit the objects! Here are some of the limitations that should be understood when using vulnerability scanners:

- Scanners will only perform "nice" hacks, which does not give an accurate picture of vulnerabilities and potential threats.
- Scanners will only work on devices that are turned on, attached to the network, functioning, and responding to the scanner. If desktops or servers are off during a scan, we will get an inaccurate view of the vulnerabilities. Even worse, if a hacker wants to hide a back door, he or she may program the back door to respond only to his/her system. Thus, the scanner will not detect its presence.

On top of this, we still have the same problems that we have with firewalls and IDSs:

- Scanners are not creative and cannot really simulate a human hacker.
- Scanners deal strictly with pattern recognition. Only previously known vulnerabilities can be discovered.
- Scanners are computers themselves, and they are prone to errors, flaws, and vulnerabilities.
- Scanners are operated by humans and are subject to human error.

Using Vulnerability Scanners Securely

Vulnerability scanners can be a great tool in proactively searching for the weakest links within an organization. Scans should be performed on a regular bases and results should be tracked over time. The following points are essential when using a vulnerability scanner:

- Remember that a scanner can be a powerful tool. Be sure to fully understand the product and all potential negative effects before performing a scan.
- Never assume the scanner will find all vulnerabilities. A scanner is unable to "think" and, as such, is greatly limited in its hacking abilities.
- Scanner products are usually updated regularly. To keep up with modern vulnerabilities and attacks, be sure to update the scanner software often.

OPEN SOURCE VS. CLOSED SOURCE SECURITY

One of the most interesting social achievements in the information industry has been the successful development, deployment, and use of Open Source software. By its nature, Open Source has created a great deal of controversy within the IT industry, as many organizations fight fiercely to defend their commercial products. There is a lot at stake as newer and better Open Source applications appear on the market, and many organizations have a lot to lose in the process.

What Is Open Source?

Though everyone seems to define Open Source somewhat differently, most seem to agree that an Open Source application has *at least* the following properties:

- The application is freely distributable, without having to pay a fee for it.
- The application is available in code format, meaning anyone can view the actual programming source for the application.
- The application can be modified and improved by anyone (though not necessarily distributed in the modified state).

This is not to say that an Open Source application has no owner, or that a programmer must give up rights to the work. Nor does this mean that a developer cannot make a profit off an Open Source product. The owner of the Open Source application, however, gives up the ability to hide the ideas and profit directly from the distribution of the software.

The idea of Open Source may be simple, but its effect is quite profound from both the technical and social aspects. Not since the evolution of the Internet have we seen a concept that has the potential to turn the technical world upside-down. Let's take a quick look into Open Source and how it affects our security practices.

The Problem with Closed Source Applications

When Organization X develops a new software product (a firewall, for example), the entire composition of that product is created within a very restrictive atmosphere. The code of the application is only seen by a handful of core developers who work under high-pressure deadlines to get the software out the door as soon as possible. The test process consists of simulations performed by the developers themselves and Beta-testing users who have no access to "look under the covers." No matter how great the intentions of the organization, no matter how great the budget, and no matter how talented the programmers, developers are severely limited in their ability to discover application errors, potential exploits, and generally improve the functionality and efficiency of the product.

Once the application is completed, the source is locked away, along with all the knowledge used to create it. Thus, there is no way for other developers and organizations to benefit from the lessons learned in the software development process. Every new firewall must be created from scratch, ultimately reliving the mistakes and errors experienced by other firewall developers before. Without access to the source, it becomes extremely difficult to build on the efforts of others, thus greatly restricting the ultimate evolution of a security product.

Finally, new applications almost always incorporate Closed Source application code developed by other organizations. It is rare to find an application programmed completely from scratch because developers rely on pregenerated code from other organizations to save time and effort in their own projects. Thus, a security flaw in a proprietary applet could cause a security flaw in the thousands of other application that were built on that applet by other organizations. This type of situation has caused an extraordinary number of headaches in the world of security. Similar to the previous discussion on trust, application developers must trust all of the pregenerated code integrated in their applications.

The Open Source Dream

The goal of the Open Source concept is similar to the new dream of the Internet: to have a self-sustaining, ever-improving, massive collaboration of effort. In theory, an Open Source application has the greatest potential for achieving perfection from the standpoint of being error-free, tightly secured, and optimally efficient. Open Source development also allows for developers to freely build on the concepts and code of other developers, dramatically increasing the speed at which software development can evolve.

Since Open Source code can be read by anyone, it is subject to the scrutiny of thousands of developers around the world who can pick the code apart. This exposes errors and potential security flaws at a much greater rate than could ever be achieved by a Closed Source application. No development team, regardless of size, talent, or budget, could ever achieve a level of scrutiny as great as that of an Open Source application.

Finally, developers building Open Source code have the ability to review the code before integrating it into their own products. Thus, the developers are able to check the source for errors, security issues, or hidden incompatibilities with their own products before integration.

The Open Source Reality

It is fair to say that Open Source has not yet achieved its ultimate potential. The development of good Open Source operating systems and major Open Source applications and services has opened the door for many changes in technology. Numerous Open Source security applications have sprung up in every genre, including firewalls, penetration testing, and intrusion detection.

Despite all the great Open Source achievements, however, the concept has still not received a welcome among the common user community or the majority of large organizations. Several issues have greatly slowed the reality of Open Source, including:

- Lack of support—One of the biggest problems with most Open Source applications is the general lack of formal technical support. An organization implementing an IPChains firewall, for example, does not have a phone number to call or a technical representative who can come out and fix a network outage. While a great deal of support comes from the Open Source user community, it is very hard to sell this idea within a large corporation where SLAs are highly valued.

- Limited accountability—Developers of Open Source software have no formal accountability that ties them to the quality of their products. If, for example, an Open Source IDS had a major flaw within it, nobody is accountable when that flaw is discovered. Since no one is accountable and no one stands to lose customers or contracts, there is no guarantee that a patch will be generated to fix the problem. This can also limit the developer's motivation to make sure such flaws don't exist in the first place.

- Lack of organization—While Open Source applications can be modified and enhanced by the general user community, there is no inherent ability to organize such efforts within the Open Source model. Each developer has his or her own process for considering modifications from other developers and integrating them into their own products, which can affect the speed of product evolution. Thus, most of the additions and enhancements actually found for Open Source products are available from third-party developer updates that may not be compatible with updates from other parties.

- Lack of Open Source friendliness—The focus of most Open Source products seems to be to make the applications more and more functional, flexible, and have additional capabilities. Most off-the-shelf products, however, are focused on the creation of the graphical user interface (GUI) and tools to make them more user-friendly. Oftentimes, there is no functional difference between the capabilities of an Open Source application and an application that costs tens of thousands of dollars, but the expensive solution is selected because of its friendly presentation.

How Secure Is Open Source?

I previously discussed the concept of secretless security, a topic closely related to the security of Open Source applications. The tendency is to think that a firewall's code should be kept secret so that hackers will not have the opportunity to review it and find its weaknesses. Nothing could be further from the truth as has been proven time and again by the countless vulnerabilities found in Microsoft, Solaris, and other Closed Source operating systems. If a vulnerability exists within an application, it will eventually be discovered; it is only a matter of when it is discovered and who discovers it.

When a new version of Linux is released, a number of vulnerabilities and patches appear within a matter of weeks. This is because the source of the software has come under the scrutiny of thousands of developers around the world. If Linux was Closed Source, these vulnerabilities would most likely not be discovered by a developer reviewing pieces of the code, but rather by thousands of hackers attempting various exploits on it. With Closed Source software, there is a greater chance that the vulnerability will remain unknown until a successful hack occurs.

The Ultimate Potential

Open Source software has a much higher potential for security than Closed Source. If, for example, we wanted to guard national secrets behind a firewall, we could not simply trust the developers of the firewall or the firewall's operating system. Extending that level of trust to a vendor would be extremely risky. At the same time, developing our own Closed Source version would leave us with a product that has not been scrutinized by thousands of developers around the world. Thus, the most reasonable solution would be to use an Open Source product that we ourselves can scrutinize and that has already been scrutinized by the public.

When Should Open Source Security Software be Used?

All this begs the question: When should we use Open Source software? Over the past few years, information security has attracted a great many Open Source solutions. Every off-the-shelf security product has at least a few competing Open Source products with similar capabilities. Organizations implementing security now have the choice to deploy packaged products or Open Source applications within their environments. So, how do we choose which way to go? The considerations in Table 10.1 should help us decide:

Table 10.1 *Considerations Before Implementing Open Source Solutions*

Support Considerations	
How much support does the organization need? Does the operations staff have the expertise and availability to operate without direct support?	Most likely, installation or maintenance support will not be directly available. Most support for Open Source applications is provided through user forums and frequently asked questions (FAQ) pages.

Table 10.1 Considerations Before Implementing Open Source Solutions *(Continued)*

Does the solution have a dedicated Web site and user forum?	Before any Open Source security solution is implemented, an organization should be sure these basic forms of support are available.
Does the Open Source solution provide a complete and comprehensive manual and help system?	Before a security product is implemented, an organization should be extremely familiar with its use. If an error is made in the implementation or maintenance, the organization could be left vulnerable to attack. Unfortunately, many Open Source products do not come with good documentation.
Technical Considerations	
Does the solution provide an easy-to-use interface?	An easy-to-use interface greatly reduces the chance of errors occurring during implementation and maintenance.
Does the solution provide regular updates?	Security products must be constantly updated as new exploits are created. A patch should be released soon after an exploit or vulnerability is discovered.
Has the solution been widely distributed for at least six months?	It is extremely important to avoid being a guinea pig with any security solution. Make sure the product has been widely used for some time before adopting it.
Political Considerations	
Do you need some form of accountability?	Open Source products are not generally associated with any accountability beyond the developer's desire to support the product. There is usually no organization to take legal or political blame for any problems.
Making a Decision	
Given all this information, do the cost savings and other factors justify the use of the Open Source product?	Be sure to include the costs of implementation, support contracts, and maintenance.

WIRELESS NETWORKS

Wireless networking is an extremely useful technology that carries with it numerous security concerns. There have been more failures than successes when it comes to designing secure wireless networking solutions for the average organization. Historically, most wireless products have failed in their implementation of encryption, access authorization, and the general ability to protect networks and communications.

The Security of Wireless

The idea of securing wireless communications is similar to that of securing Internet VPN sessions. Mostly, we rely on various forms of encryption for privacy, and hopefully, strong authentication mechanisms like one-time passwords and digital signatures. A common problem is that organizations tend to treat wireless access the same as if they were plugging directly into a switch when it should actually be treated like a dial-in modem.

The Reality of Wireless Security

Wireless communications pose several major security issues that undermine some fundamental concepts of security. This is not to say that wireless communications should not be used, but it is important to maintain the proper perspective on the risks being taken:

- There is no control as to where wireless communications are being sent— The main advantage we have over hackers trying to listen in on our normal communications is that it is difficult for them to find a place to physically plug into the network without eventually getting caught. With a wireless network, however, hackers can be anywhere within the wireless radius, tapping in, probing, and decrypting without any chance of being caught.
- There is no control as to where access is granted from—This means that a hacker does not have to probe around, searching for a hidden opening, nor does he or she have to scour the Internet and phone lines looking for an access point. The front door to the network is being transmitted invisibly in and around the facility.

Important Misconceptions

When discussing wireless security, I commonly find clients that have similar misconceptions about wireless security. These misconceptions lead many organizations into a false sense of security when working with wireless security products.

Misconception #1: It's difficult to listen in on a wireless transmission, or it takes expensive equipment to do so.—This could not be more wrong. A wireless card can be put into promiscuous mode via software just like a normal network card. This means that a hacker can slap a cheap wireless card into an old laptop and run free software to start listening in on communications.

Misconception #2: People don't just walk around trying to find wireless networks.—There are actually many people who wander around, searching for stray wireless communications. Some travel around in cars with their laptops, others go from office building to office building just checking. Why? Because there are so many unprotected wireless networks out there essentially leaving the door open for hackers. Why would a hacker bother to hack through the Internet or a dial-up connection when the front door is right at his/her feet?

Misconception #3: Wireless products come with high-grade encryption, so they are safe.— Most wireless products offer some degree of encryption, frequency hopping, or other form of access control. However, no one of these controls can protect an organization, and so no one of these controls is infallible (as we have seen over and over again). To top it all off, if an administrator makes a mistake when implementing wireless security, an organization will be completely exposed.

If we really look at it, wireless makes it difficult to work with the Rule of Least Privilege. A person walking down the street does not need to be given an access point into a network, and they should never be presented with one. However, with wireless networking, it is impossible to control who will be presented with a door into the network.

Using Wireless Securely

Am I saying that we should not use wireless communications? Not at all. It is, however, important to use a high degree of caution when implementing wireless networks. It is necessary to classify wireless access points with a higher risk level than most organizations have.

Zoning and the Rule of Least Privilege

A wireless access point should be considered the same as an Internet connection or dial-up service. We have absolutely no control over who is going to be presented a front door, and as such, the wireless access point is outside the perimeter. Regardless of what level of security is implemented on wireless devices, access points should be separated from the internal network. Traffic flowing from the wireless network into the internal network should be regulated by a firewall and conform to the Rule of Least Privilege, similar to other foreign connections (see Figure 10.1). Wireless network users should not be given free reign as they would with a LAN, but rather, they should be limited to accessing required systems and services. When installing a wireless device, look back to the section on zoning and consider the wireless access point with the same caution as you would an Internet or dial-up access point. It is a bad security practice to place a wireless concentrator in the middle of an internal network, even if the device comes with strong security controls.

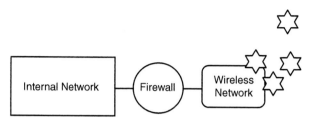

Figure 10.1 Zoning wireless devices.

Layering Security

Security should be layered in the area between the wireless network and the internal network. Most wireless devices come with some form of integrated access control and logging capabilities similar to an external router. These features should be used as the first line of defense, much like a screening router. A firewall can then act as the middle layer of protection. By layering security, we avoid having the network directly exposed, and we ensure that adequate protection is in place if and when a vulnerability is discovered on a wireless device.

Large-Scale Wireless Deployments

Many organizations have chosen to deploy large-scale wireless networks, connecting hundreds of LAN devices as well as buildings and distant WANs. For these organizations, it may be difficult to follow these wireless security practices on each and every network. Placing hundreds of workstations outside the perimeter and limiting access to all of them may not be a viable solution. If the business need for hosting such wireless environments outweighs the major security issues, this is just considered an acceptable risk for the organization. In such cases, it is important for the organization to recognize and document this risk, and to make the major security implications of this decision clear to management and executive staff.

ENCRYPTION

Encryption is the process by which we take information and convert it into a state that can only be read or modified by designated parties. Encryption relies on keys that are used for encrypting and decrypting information. Sometimes, a single key is used (symmetric encryption), and sometimes, multiple keys are used (asymmetric encryption). Encryption has become very popular in modern security practices and it is used for many purposes beyond the ability to hide information. Through the use of encryption, we can enable several security mechanisms, including:

- Information privacy—To keep others from reading data and communications
- Information integrity—To ensure no one changes data and communications without our knowledge
- Non-repudiation—To make it more difficult for parties to refute electronic actions

Encryption is the prevalent means of securing communications and for securing data as it sits on a laptop, workstation, and server. It is also commonly used for performing stronger levels of authentication, and for securing access to Web sites via mechanisms like SSL and HTTPS.

Trusting Encryption

There are many different levels at which encryption can secure information; unfortunately, the actual level of protection offered by different encryption solutions is fairly difficult to derive. For example, we commonly hear about the strength of encryption solutions as related to the length of the keys used. Encryption based on 128-bit keys is considered strong protection, whereas encryption based on 56-bit keys is not. This, however, is an over-simplification in assessing encryption-based security.

The level of security offered by encryption is affected by many factors beyond key length. The quality of the algorithm, the method used to create the key, the range of variations available in key generation, and the mechanism used to protect the key are also extremely important to the safety of encrypted data. If, for example, we use a 128-bit key, but the 128 bits are limited to standard letters and numbers, our key is very weak. Or, if we have the greatest key and algorithm in the world, but the key is protected by a simple secret, like a bad pass phrase, our data is not going to be very secure.

The point here is that the protection of data through the use of encryption involves numerous components, each of which could introduce a flaw or weakness that exposes information. Microsoft's Point-to-Point Tunneling Protocol (PPTP), for example, has been plagued with serious vulnerabilities due to bad choices in the encryption decisions made by the developers. Simply because we choose the 128-bit grade of PPTP encryption does not mean that a hacker can't break it with a few hours of work.

It is very important when we use encryption for protecting sensitive information to perform some research. Many major encryption products and processes have serious flaws that have been documented by security experts. Take some time to search for such issues and make sure you understand the degree to which the encryption product will protect your information. Be sure to choose an algorithm that is not based on secrecy (Open Source), and be sure to only use encryption mechanisms that have been successfully used by others for at least several months.

Managing Keys

The protection of an encrypted piece of data or transaction ultimately comes down to the security of the encryption keys. Keys are normally long and complex, which forces us to store them on our drives, in computer memory, or in hardware devices like smart cards. This introduces a problem since we now have to worry about protecting these keys. Why would a hacker spend time cracking an algorithm when he or she can simply try to obtain keys from a hard drive? Dealing with keys should cause an organization to consider many questions, such as:

- What if someone steals a key and gains access to the data?
- What if someone loses a key and data cannot be accessed?
- What if keys need to be changed, but data is already encrypted with an older key?
- What happens when other objects need to use the keys, such as virus scanners, email servers, and other devices?
- How do we keep track of all the keys within an environment?

These issues have been a big problem when integrating encryption solutions within the average organization. Introducing keys is usually much more difficult than introducing passwords into an environment. To avoid disaster, encryption keys must be managed through a well thought out and tested process. The Rule of the Three-Fold Process should be referenced at all times. Key management usually involves third-party software products from companies like Entrust. This introduces a whole new layer in managing IT as we move into topics like public key infrastructure (PKI). Before embarking on any major encryption initiatives, it is important to understand exactly what the organization is getting into.

Diminishing Security via Encryption

For encryption to work properly, no one should be able to decrypt information outside of the intended recipients. According to the Rule of Least Privilege, this means that no person or device other than the end-user should have the power to decrypt the data. This, however, makes it impossible to perform security checks on encrypted information. There is no way for an email scanner, for example, to check for a virus within an encrypted message. To do this, the email system would have to have the decryption key, which defeats the purpose of encrypting in the first place. All too often, we implement encryption and then make so many minor adjustments that we end up with a very low level of security.

The Rules of Encryption

To implement encryption safely, it is best to understand how it works, to what degree it is protecting the information, and how it relates to the security rules.

Identify the Weakest Link

With encryption, the Rule of the Weakest Link is of great importance. There are many components in the average encryption process, any of which could be the weak link that causes an exposure:

- Encryption algorithms, practices, and products oftentimes have weaknesses. This information can usually be researched on the Internet.
- With any encryption process, focus should be placed on key management. How can the end-users interact with their keys? Can they be exported and saved to a disk? What are the mechanisms in place to protect the keys?
- Keep track of where keys exist and how access can be obtained. Some products like email servers and firewalls offer end-user key storage so that users can monitor encrypted transactions. This can be dangerous, especially if the system hosting the keys is ever compromised.

Rule of Least Privilege

Keys should be treated as extremely sensitive objects and should be guarded through the Rule of Least Privilege. No person or device should be granted access to a key unless it is absolutely required and the key can be properly handled. Products such as email servers and firewalls that offer to store secret keys should be heavily scrutinized, and mechanisms should be put in place to protect such systems from giving unauthorized access to the keys.

Rule of the Three-Fold Process

Encryption is another prime example of where the Rule of the Three-Fold Process must be observed. Large-scale encryption projects are usually complex in design and implementation. Maintenance and monitoring usually end up being even more complex than implementation. Before implementing encryption, thought should be given as to how keys will be created, verified, stored, aged, revoked, and otherwise managed. Providing adequate maintenance for encryption keys is often a major hidden cost for wide-scale deployments.

Secretless Security

Secretless security is of great importance when considering the process of encryption. Most encryption algorithms are based on similar forms of mathematical logic and include unique variations that enhance security. The most popular encryption algorithms like 3DES are Open Source and can be freely downloaded and tested. As such, these algorithms have been scrutinized by good and malicious hackers around the world and have proven their strengths and weaknesses. We can thus be reasonably sure of their ability to protect information.

An encryption algorithm or mechanism that bases its security on secrecy can never be trusted as much as an Open Source algorithm tested by the public. This is an important consideration when determining which products and algorithms to implement.

VIRTUAL PRIVATE NETWORKING

Virtual private networking has been a hot topic for many years now. The ability to have remote employees and home offices connect to a central network via the Internet provides a great cost benefit for an organization. VPN technology has evolved greatly over the past few years, making it easier and less expensive to integrate into the average organization.

The Potential of VPN

Without a doubt, VPN technology has had an incredible impact in the way business is performed today. Through the use of VPNs, many organizations have created encrypted webs, connecting employees, partners, and vendors from around the world. The average VPN product will accomplish this through the following security mechanisms:

- Information privacy—Information privacy is accomplished by encrypting information as it is passed between connected entities. Using whatever encryption algorithm(s) is available in the VPN product, the content of communications will be hidden from the eyes of those listening between VPN end-points.

- Remote and local authentication—When establishing a VPN tunnel, both parties establishing the connection can authenticate to each other. This means that an organization can demand credentials of the client connecting to it, and provide credentials when the client requests it.

- Information integrity—Through the use of various encryption techniques, it is possible to verify the authenticity of information being communicated. This means that the VPN will be able to determine if information has been added, deleted, or modified during the communication process.

The Reality of VPN

The theories and mechanisms behind VPN technology are a great addition to the privacy and protection of communications. Like most things, however, the problem with VPN technology is not in its theories or mechanisms, but in its execution by vendors, administrators, and end-users.

VPNs provide encrypted communications, not secure access points! This is an extremely important difference that organizations implementing VPN technologies should understand. While a VPN session is intended to protect communications from malicious hackers wishing to steal or modify the information, a VPN session does not protect either party in the communications from malicious actions performed by each other. A client infected with a worm, for example, will transmit the worm into the local network just as if it was directly attached; only now, the worm is encrypted while in transit. Also, VPNs only protect data as it is transferred between VPN end-points. This does not include protecting data while it is on the computer itself, or in transit through networks behind the VPN device. A hacker will not need to intercept the data at all if he or she has access to either of the systems sending or receiving the data.

Trusting the Remote Client

There is a high security exposure that comes when an organization treats its VPN as a secure access point. VPNs do not ensure either party's safety during the communication process, and the most common mistake when implementing a VPN is to extend levels of trust to areas where they should not be extended.

A common use for a VPN implementation is to allow an employee to connect to an organization from remote locations, such as his or her home or a hotel. VPN technologies are great at making remote laptops and home PCs appear as if they were sitting right in the office. This, however, is not the case, and it is vital that we always remember it. A system in a remote location is very different from a system on the local network, and the two should be treated with different levels of trust. Recall the Rules of Trust and Separation. When we allow a remote client to connect directly to the internal network via a VPN, the internal network is now inheriting the security vulnerabilities of that remote client. This is horrible for our security when considering the following factors:

- The remote client is not under constant protection by the perimeter security devices.
- The remote client cannot be forced to conform to security policies the way a local system can.
- The remote client is not subject to normal vulnerability scanning and auditing like the local system.
- The remote client is much more likely to have unauthorized applications installed on it.
- The remote client is much more likely to have a virus, Trojan horse, back door, or other malicious application installed on it.
- The remote client is still connected to the Internet while connected to the local network, thus creating a bridge between the two.
- The person using the remote client cannot be physically seen. Thus, this individual could be someone who stole a key, has access to a laptop, or is forcing the employee to operate the client against his or her will! There could even be a family member that uses the laptop when the employee is not home.

The Need for Additional Security

Just as we would never take a system off the Internet and stick it in the middle of our network, neither should we allow a remote system to attach directly to the internal network via a VPN. When a remote client connects to the network, the Rule of Least Privilege should immediately kick in. There is no reason to extend the same level of trust to a remote client as we extend to internal workstations. Therefore, we should provide some forms of security, including access filtering, logging, and monitoring.

Remote VPN clients should only be allowed to access that which is absolutely required and that which they can handle securely. Firewall rules that enforce this concept should be implemented.

VPN Products that Make a Bad Problem Much Worse

To make their products simpler to use and operate independently of external security mechanisms, many VPN vendors include some form of filtering and build logging mechanisms directly into their products. This is a very good feature as it supports the concept of security layering. Many vendors, however, advertise their products as complete solutions and show them functioning independently of the firewall, IDS, and other security products. Installation diagrams show VPN devices being attached in parallel to the firewall, running connections to both sides. This is not a good solution for most organizations. Just as we would not put access lists on a router to avoid buying a firewall, neither should we place security filters on a VPN device to have it bypass perimeter security. A VPN should always terminate outside the firewall. If the VPN device has filters, proxies, and other similar controls, they should be seen as an additional layer of security, not a substitute for perimeter controls.

To make the problem even worse, many firewalls come with integrated VPN options built in, without the ability to enforce any control on such access. The average firewall with built-in VPN capability is designed to make all security decisions at the instance when the communication touches the firewall's network card. Most firewalls do not bother to decrypt a VPN packet before making security decisions, and as such, do not allow for any filtering to be performed. This creates a gaping hole in the firewall and an inability to enforce the Rule of Least Privilege or good logging and monitoring practices.

Worse yet, terminating a VPN inside of a firewall means that transactions will go unmonitored by virus and content scanners. A firewall scanning file transfers for viruses will not be able to scan encrypted communications. Thus, an infected client could very likely infect the organization to which it is attaching.

VPN Client Features to be Avoided

Here are some other horrible VPN features that are important to avoid. Many VPN products allow control of these features during the installation process or at the remote client. Check for these "features" and be sure to disable them if possible:

- Never allow the client system to store the user's password for quicker access.

- Never allow the client system to change the level and form of encryption.
- Never allow the client system to maintain local area and Internet connections while connected to the VPN.

Concerning Remote Control Software

The ultimate criminal with respect to remote access and the Rule of Least Privilege is remote control software, commonly used in conjunction with VPN devices. Applications like PCAnywhere allow for a remote party to access and completely control every aspect of a desktop or server as if the remote party was sitting at that desk. Oftentimes, when a company implements a VPN, they allow for such remote control to take place from the remote client. This type of access, however, makes all filtering and logging useless. When the communications port is opened to allow for remote control of a system, the external party with control now has full access to the object on the internal network. From this object, the remote entity can do anything he or she desires and there is no way for the firewall to filter or log what is taking place.

Securely Using VPNs

Now that I have covered the common security pitfalls of VPNs, let me say that VPNs can be great tools and can be reasonably secure when used properly and with the proper perspective. As always, no packaged solution will be completely secure in itself; they all require some consideration on our part.

Define a Realistic Level of Trust

Clients of a VPN should never be given the same level of trust as an internal device. There is no way that an external system can be secured to the degree that an internal system can be secured. Thus, a VPN client is not as trusted as an internal device, yet is more trusted than a common system on the Internet. Special privileges can be extended to VPN users, but they should be kept within realistic boundaries. Always consider the scenario where a hacker has gained access to the remote system, and then try to minimize the damage he or she can do.

Protect Remote Clients

All remote clients that are going to connect to the VPN should conform to some minimum level of security as dictated by a remote access policy. There are various restrictions we can put on our clients, depending on unique needs. Here are some suggestions:

- Clients must have an approved and updated version of antivirus software installed.

- Clients must use a designated VPN client—Many VPN products can now be accessed by multiple VPN clients via IPSec. Clients vary in their security features, so it is important to designate one or two specific clients that include the desired security controls.

- Clients must terminate all other connections while connected to the VPN—Some VPN clients allow you to block all access to and from the client outside the VPN connection while in an active session. This can help somewhat in reducing the risk of a hacker using the client to bridge into the organization's network.

- Clients must have been hardened according to the organization's desktop hardening procedure—In situations where the client can only connect from a company-owned laptop, the company can perform a hardening procedure on the laptop to secure it before allowing it remote access.

- Clients must not have any unauthorized software installed—Again, for laptops owned by the organization, it is a good idea to restrict the software packages the end-user is allowed to install. This helps to avoid introducing vulnerabilities or malicious applications.

Use VPNs Only When Required

It is difficult to secure anything that gets out of hand. When a VPN system is first put in place, everyone will want to have access. Once news of a new VPN system gets out, people are quick to put their names in to gain access for themselves and their entire departments. From my experience, the majority of people that desire access in the beginning end up never making use of it. This causes problems, since the more accounts there are to maintain, the harder it will be to secure the VPN.

VPN accounts should be handed out sparingly on an individual and as-needed basis. Each user should be required to complete a VPN access request form, stating his or her individual need for VPN access, and including an approval signature from a manager. Gaining access to the VPN should not be extremely difficult, but it should be restrictive enough to reduce frivolous requests.

Create a VPN Agreement

A VPN agreement is a form that every user and entity should complete before obtaining access to the VPN. By signing the form, the end-user agrees to a series of rules for use, which will conform to the organization's security policy. Some specific rules that should be mentioned include:

- Access is granted for the end-user only and cannot be given out to anyone else.
- The user will never be asked for his or her password and is not allowed to reveal it to anyone. A user will never be allowed to copy his/her access key to another system.
- The user's access will be limited strictly to business purposes.
- All user actions while connected to the VPN may be monitored by the organization. This includes actions on the PC the user is connecting with.
- The user agrees to only connect to the VPN using an authorized system.
- The user agrees to maintain the system in accordance with the VPN security rules (like those mentioned above).
- The user has read and agrees to the corporate security policy.

11 The Rules in Practice

PRACTICING THE RULES

Throughout this book, we have looked at the world of information security, its virtues, rules, and concepts. For the last part of the book, it only seems right to talk about this information as it applies to the most common decisions made in information security. Of course, the virtues, rules, and concepts are universal and should be applied in most security practices. As such, this section is more of an example and guide in applying the information within specific topics.

I have selected the following topics since they all require serious attention from security and they apply to most organizations. There are many books that simply focus on one or two of the following topics in more detail. Here we are going to cover some of the essentials of each topic as they relate to the development of the security mind.

- Perimeter defenses
- Internal defenses
- Physical defenses
- Server and device defenses
- Outbound Internet access
- Logging and monitoring
- Authentication

PERIMETER DEFENSES

The primary focus of defense throughout history has been guarding the perimeter. Regulating the flow of access between the outside and inside borders of the home territory has always been an essential component in ensuring one's survival. Today, if an organization has any security at all, it will likely be focused on the perimeter.

Expanding the Perimeter Concept

It must be understood that when I talk about the "perimeter," this does not simply mean "the Internet." Of course, the Internet is an area that we need to be concerned with, but most organizations place far too much attention on the Internet and not enough on the rest of the perimeter. Remember the Rule of the Weakest Link? In most organizations, the Internet has the 20-foot moat and reinforced steel door while the other access points are guarded by poodles and paper blinds. The Rule of the Weakest Link is most often neglected at the perimeter.

In reality, a perimeter point is any location where an external or non-trusted party has some form of access into the internal protected networks. Defining a perimeter means defining exactly how far into the network we will allow the general public, our partners, our clients, and other external entities to wander before they must pass the drawbridge and archers. With the castle, we simple have one or two obvious entry points; but with our modern security infrastructure, we must focus on many more dimensions. Common network perimeter points include:

- Internet connections, including dial-up
- Active modems for inbound or outbound communications
- Partner, vendor, and customer network connections
- Wireless access points
- Other virtual access points such as VPNs and email exchanges

It is important when working with perimeter defenses to have a clear sense of "us" and "them." One of our first perimeter analysis tasks will be to draw out exactly where the perimeter exists and where security controls need to be put into place. Following the Rule of Trust, there can be no wavering or fogginess on this issue. You are trusted, or you are not; you are inside, or you are out; end of story.

Why the Perimeter First?

It is commonly understood that an Internet connection and dial-in access should be guarded by a firewall. The general misconception, however, has been that perimeter defenses are the most important, which is not always the case. While it is generally a good practice to focus first on perimeter defenses, it should be understood that the perimeter defenses are not some magical portal that will keep our castle safe. Far too many organizations have been devastated by attacks that never even touched a perimeter access point. **We do not focus on the perimeter because it is the most important, but rather because the perimeter is the most tangible, easy to focus on, and least costly to secure.**

Perimeter security is where we get the most "bang for our buck." External connections can be funneled through chokepoints, allowing us to have a strong effect on security with a limited set of tools. When dealing with the perimeter, we can lay down a fairly simple structure and justify the costs to nearly any executive. The good guys are inside, the bad guys are outside, so we need to build a drawbridge with a lock. This we can explain, this people can understand, and this we can get funding for. Unfortunately, dealing with internal defenses it not as simple and introduces more complexities. Therefore, we focus first on perimeter defenses.

Defining the Perimeter

Ever sing the song that goes, "This land is your land... this land is my land"? It amazes me how many people are still humming that tune when they are building network perimeters. Oftentimes, there seems to be numerous political desires to share the local network and resources with external parties. The classic line is "In the spirit of cooperation" or "If we can't trust them... ." I have seen many organizations build great perimeter defenses and then proceed to attach vendors and partners via uncontrolled links.

When it comes to the perimeter, its important to create some hard and fast rules. We have already discussed the issue of trust, and trusting another organization with a link into an internal network has a good chance of ending up in disaster. When we look at the perimeter, there needs to be a clear-cut line of what is within each zone. We need to define, in black and white, where and how traffic in and out of the perimeter will be secured:

- Define which assets are yours and which are not—It is important to know where the jurisdiction of the organization ends, whether it is at the router, across the WAN link, or on the server itself.
- Define the logical points where borders meet—Be sure to include all equipment near the middle, and make sure everything has its designated side.
- Determine who and what are on the outside and on the inside—In addition, find anything left in the middle, equally accessible by both.
- Draw perimeter lines with this information and document your policies.

Perimeter Rules

After defining the perimeter, we need to consider what form of security will be placed between networks. Perimeter defenses, despite their simplicity, are very often the point of failure within a security model. The issues involved in separating internal and external networks seem so simple that we leave the design, implementation, and maintenance to a junior engineer who has read a few books on firewalls during his or her coffee breaks.

Even though perimeter security is arguably one of the easiest points for us to focus on, it is important to approach it with a good deal of thought and planning. Every rule and concept addressed in this book has some influence in how we design our perimeter. In particular, the following rules and concepts should be readily observed:

Rule of Least Privilege

Most modern firewalls begin with the Rule of Least Privilege. The standard ruleset for Firewall-1, Cisco's PIX, and other standard products is, "Unless I say it is allowed, deny it." This is a great way to start perimeter defenses; the trick is maintaining this rule as functionality is added. More often than not, the Rule of Least Privilege is the first rule broken when dealing with perimeter defenses. Lets look at why:

- **Simple interface, profound effects**—The simplicity of a firewall saying, "Port X is allowed and Port Y is not," provides many organizations with a false sense of security. Rules in most firewall products are very easy to implement, yet their impact can be quite profound. Since it takes minimal work to open a firewall port, allowing easier access to others, organizations often create far too many openings than are required or more than other parties can be responsible for. It is important that the process of changing firewall rules be taken very seriously, despite simplistic interfaces. Firewall changes should conform to the Rule of Change.

  Simple interfaces can also be deceiving because they hide important components. Most security devices are extremely complicated on the inside, but their complexity is masked behind a simple GUI. It is thus important to fully understand security devices before implementing rules. Often, adding a single rule will make three or four changes to the firewall's policy, some of which may leave us unknowingly vulnerable. The moral of the story: Don't be fooled by easy interfaces such as Checkpoint's Firewall GUI. Firewall implementations and modifications should only be performed by people who have had the proper training.

- **Allowing everything out**—There is a tendency for organizations to deal with security as if it was an inbound traffic-only problem. It would be a great oversimplification to state that, "We don't want anyone on the outside to gain access to the internal network." Unfortunately, some major firewalls promote this idea.

  If we look at the perimeter in terms of what is flowing in, and give little or no consideration to what is flowing out, we are far less secure than we think. A great many attacks occur by opening channels from the internal network and riding back on established connections. Many applications, including Trojan horses, back doors, and even legitimate applications, can create tunnels spawned from internal systems, thereby bypassing an inbound-only ruleset. When dealing with perimeter security, it is vital to review the concept of zoning and enforce the most restrictive zoning rules possible without harming the business. Always think in terms of the Rule of Least Privilege, even when vulnerabilities are not obvious.

Creating a Chokepoint

Creating and consolidating chokepoints are extremely important tasks when dealing with an organization's perimeter. Once the perimeter has been defined, it is best to consolidate as many areas as reasonably possible through one or two chokepoints. Some organizations choose to have many chokepoints guarded by numerous security devices. Keep in mind, however, that the more entry points, the less attention each will get and the more likely we are to find a vulnerability within one of them.

It is important to create a perimeter policy that strictly forbids anyone from making additional perimeter access points. Individuals and departments should be prevented from installing modems, enabling access services, or making any other external connection without going through a designated perimeter chokepoint. Searching for such illegal connections should be part of the regular security audit process.

Layering Defenses

Our castle, of course, will have a deep moat surrounding the keep. High walls will be constructed, blocking access to and visibility of our most vital areas. Archers will line the walls, along with numerous mechanisms to defend against invading forces. And of course, our drawbridge will raise and lower in accordance with the Rule of Least Privilege. Similar to these defenses placed beyond our castle gate, it is best to place external and internal security beyond main firewall and IDS devices.

- Layering the network—Most organizations push external security all the way out to the perimeter routers (also called screening routers). These routers should be configured to block and log any obvious errors and attacks. Common things to block at a perimeter router include:
  - Direct access to the firewall and the perimeter router itself
  - Direct access to internal, non-translated addresses
  - Requests from illegal addresses, or addresses known to belong to the local organization (spoofing)

When dealing with this layer of defense, the controls will not be nearly as granular. Consequently, maintenance on these rules should remain minimal. In addition, external routers should themselves be hardened by turning off nonessential services and protecting their access points.

- Layering devices—Defenses should also be placed inside the firewall. In the next section, I will discuss internal defenses that should be implemented. For now, there should be a special focus on any internal devices that are accessible from outside the perimeter. All accessible devices should, of course, be placed in some form of protective DMZ. In addition, such devices should be hardened and strictly monitored. The firewalls should have their operating systems secured.

Rule of Trust

The chain of trust in perimeter networking is probably the longest trusting chain in the world. If our organization links directly to any other organization, we have no control of who can assess us through them. If an employee of a partner dials into the Internet, that employee basically establishes an unprotected link between our internal computers and the Internet.

Trusting an organization and not placing any security devices between the local network and their network should be avoided, even if the other organization is small, well-known, and even if that organization extends full trust to our organization.

The Rule of Trust states that we should not only examine who we are trusting, but also the contexts in which trust is applicable. We may very well have a saintly company in the Midwest to which we allow special access into our systems, but we must also take into account that the company is traversing the Internet or using dial-up or other unsecure media to gain access to us. This is similar to leaving our door open in a bad neighborhood to allow our trusted friends to enter.

Rule of the Three-Fold Process

When dealing with our perimeter, we must be especially mindful of the Rule of the Three-Fold Process. Since the perimeter is attached to the outside world, security vulnerabilities can be quickly detected by external hackers. Letting security slide at the perimeter can be devastating.

- Maintenance—Perimeter defenses are prime examples of where maintenance must be practiced. The average firewall and IDSs, for example, can only go a short time before some form of update or modification is required. With hundreds of new exploits manifesting every day, we can be sure that hackers will be able to sneak past perimeter devices if they are not properly maintained.

- Logging and monitoring—Another extremely important practice for perimeter defenses is monitoring. Remember that security devices are extremely dumb and are unable to recognize attacks outside of preprogrammed patterns. Security is not extremely complex, but it is made up of an infinite combination of events that could constitute an attack. Many combinations that may be obvious to a watchful administrator may not be obvious to a firewall. A hacker can learn how a perimeter device works and create logical methods to sneak through it. A human, however, is not so easy to fool and has a much greater capacity to understand an attack than any countermeasure. Therefore, all devices at the perimeter should be generating logs of suspicious activities and such logs should be monitored regularly.

The Concept of Thinking in Zones

Though perimeter networks can be as simple as having one inside and one outside zone, most of the time, networks are somewhat more complex. Considering the concept of zoning, we must think carefully of how access is taking place between subjects and objects on each side of the perimeter. Communications that will be allowed to cross through the perimeter should be evaluated against the different levels of exposure as discussed in the section, *Thinking in Zones*, in Chapter 5, *Developing a Higher Security Mind*. Each type of communication that will be allowed to pass through perimeter security devices should facilitate the least amount of exposure as possible. DMZs and relayed services are common security measures found at the perimeter.

The Concept of Working in Stillness

Perimeter devices, especially those connected to the Internet, often have an incredible variety of traffic passed through them. By simply connecting our perimeter to another organization or the Internet, the firewall and IDS will begin finding a wide variety of unauthorized activities.

The average perimeter security device will start by generating hundreds or thousands of logs due to these foreign communications. This renders our valuable logs virtually useless since it becomes nearly impossible to see a real attack among the noise. It is thus very important that we put some effort into tuning the logging of perimeter devices to give us some clarity into the activities hitting these devices. The concept of working in stillness should be applied to all perimeter security devices.

INTERNAL DEFENSES

It is close to impossible to read any security publication without seeing a phrase like, "The majority of successful hackers come from the insides of networks, not the Internet," and this book is no exception to this standard. Protecting internal networks is a very different task than that of protecting the perimeter. With our perimeter, we can define specific chokepoints and consolidate security measures; on an internal network, we are dealing with everything as a whole. There is no firewall that we can filter everyone through, and there is no IDS that will adequately monitor the average internal infrastructure. On top of it all, we have to grant much higher levels of access to internal systems and users than to external customers and vendors. Lucky for us, good internal defenses still conform to the rules of security.

Can it Really be Done?

Certainly, the answer to this question is, "Yes, it can be done." To have a highly secure internal network is achievable and I have seen organizations accomplish this on a minimal budget. Again, the real key to securing an internal network is to focus on the virtues and rules in everything. Security at the perimeter is simply a warm-up; the internal network is where we really get our hands dirty with the concepts of the security mind.

Let's face it: There is no technical solution for securing the inside of a network. Yes, there are thousands of products, each with their own little piece of the internal security pie, but securing an internal network is a prime example of where focusing on the details will cause failure. At least with the Internet, we had a firewall chokepoint, and those who focused purely on the technologies could remain somewhat in control. When we progress to the internal network, however, such methods simply do not work and a great many organizations end up leaving the internal network vulnerable. Securing the internal network requires a much broader vision and the ability to see the rules of security in everything.

The Need for Internal Security

The need for internal security can be seen everywhere, and simply leaving the internal network vulnerable should never be considered. A bank does not just put guards at the front door and let all the money pile up behind the tellers. There are layers and layers of security between the lot where we park our cars and where we touch our first coin. If we choose to launch an attack from the outside, the hallway, the lobby, or from the vault itself, there will be security measures to stop us.

In information security, we need to adopt similar practices. An attack could come from anywhere and under any set of circumstances. A hacker could find a hole in the perimeter defenses, in which case, an attack will surely come from inside. Likewise, a hacking employee, consultant, or anyone to whom we extend a high level of trust will have direct access to the internal network. In these situations, we need to be prepared.

Employee Attacks

Employees within an organization are under constant temptation when it comes to internal access. Even employees without direct motivation often become curious and desire to perform some form of prohibited action. But it is when we have employees with some motivation and some technical abilities that we are really in trouble. I talked about employee hackers at some length in Chapter 7, *Know Thy Enemy and Know Thyself*. Here, I would make an educated guess and say that the average organization with five or more technical employees has probably employed at least one person who has attempted to gain unauthorized access to resources at some point in time.

In general, when someone knows that they are NOT going to get caught, there is a much greater chance that they will perform illegal actions. The temptation to gain unauthorized access to resources within organizations that deploy no internal security is incredible for many employees. Internal security not only applies direct protection, but also keeps honest people honest and greatly reduces the temptation to take unauthorized action.

Successful External Attacks

Eventually, someone will break into the network. Eventually, there will be an unseen entry point opened into the network. Eventually, a worm will crawl through all defenses. Eventually, the perimeter security will fail. What happens next depends completely on the defenses we have deployed internally. A worm that finds its way through external defenses has not yet done any damage. If the worm, once inside the network, finds that all systems are patched, protected, and monitored, we will probably not suffer any damage. This is also the case with hackers who work themselves through a perimeter only to find themselves locked down in a secure environment.

By applying internal defenses, we are essentially layering overall security. When an individual or group manages to penetrate the outer defenses, the amount of damage they can do directly corresponds to the degree of protection deployed on the inside of the network.

Internal Rules

The rules of security are going to be our best allies when working with internal defenses. There are no canned solutions for protecting an internal environment; protection can only come from layering different forms of security measures to comply with the corresponding rules. Every decision about the internal environment should reflect back on the practices already discussed. I have pulled from the following rules because they are often the most useful when securing an internal environment:

Put the Rules in Writing

Earlier in this book, I mentioned that our ability to enforce the rules is highly dependent on the rules being in writing. Proper internal security requires rules to be written and formally accepted by everyone within the organization. The rules should be incorporated into internal security policies and acceptable use policies. Writing internal policies should be performed by policy experts with the guidance of information security staff, or drawn from a good working template. In particular, written rules should commonly include:

- **Policies against gaining unauthorized access**—Using the Rule of Least Privilege, these policies should state how systems and services may be properly used and end by stating that anything not written in the policies is unacceptable. Users should also be directly forbidden from bypassing security mechanisms or establishing unapproved links outside the local network. This should specifically include the use of modems and unauthorized Internet and WAN connections.

- **Policies concerning security administration practices**—These policies enforce strong password and account management practice, the assignment of access privileges, and the monitoring of account activities. These policies should also reflect on the Rule of Least Privilege as well as the Rule of Separation.

- **Policies against unauthorized software**—These policies should provide a list of software authorized for use on desktops and servers, including operating systems, browsers, word processors, and other acceptable applications. The policy should state that software products other than those on the "approved" list are not allowed.

- **Policies against hacker tools and processes**—These policies should expressly forbid the use of hacker tools or any attempts to bypass or compromise security. It is common for employees to download such tools from the Internet or try some form of attack for non-malicious purposes. To maintain security, it is important that the organization be aware of the installation and use of every hacker tool within the environment.

- **Other policies**—There are many other policies that are important to security, especially those concerning how to handle security in specific situations and during disasters. For important security events and for security events that will recur, it is important to establish a standard policy.

Authorized Use Banners

After policies have been established, it is important to create a short summary statement that refers back to the full security policy. This short statement should then be placed in as many locations as possible, including every system and device that allows for a display banner. Common areas where banners should be deployed include:

- Server and workstation authentication prompts
- Telnet, Secure Shell (SSH), FTP, and other remote access service prompts
- VPN and dial-up access points
- Email message footers (usually a variation specific to email)

Rule of Least Privilege

Internal security practices should enforce the Rule of Least Privilege across the entire network. Since we are not dealing with specific chokepoints, the Rule of Least Privilege will need to be placed on individual systems, devices, and applications. These objects should be built and maintained with the idea that access will not be given unless required. Since there are literally hundreds of places where the Rule of Least Privilege should be practiced, it must be a part of our thought process in everything and dealt with through higher security practices. The following is a small set of examples of where the Rule of Least Privilege could be enforced:

- Internal servers and devices should have multiple levels of access defined based on access requirements. For example, someone needing to administer a specific application or set of accounts should not be given full administrator access, but rather an account that limits access to that which is required.
- Access to physical areas should be limited based on an individual's required access. Server rooms, wiring closets, and other critical areas should only be accessible by those who require such access.
- Employees should enforce the Rule of Least Privilege and be instructed not to give out information about internal systems, devices, applications, or procedures to external entities unless there is a verified need for the information.

It cannot be said enough that the Rule of Least Privilege is vital for maintaining proper security practices. The Rule of Least Privilege should be practiced in all aspects of internal security. If access is not required, do not grant it.

Rule of the Three-Fold Process

The Rule of the Three-Fold Process is not limited to specific devices or project implementations; the entire internal network and its security as a whole are subject to this rule as well. Many organizations create internal networks and never provide any form of maintenance or monitoring. The maintenance and monitoring tasks associated with the Rule of the Three-Fold Process are often pushed out to the perimeter, leaving the internal network vulnerable as time passes. Using the Rule of the Three-Fold Process for internal systems and devices has a dramatic effect on the security of an organization.

Internal Auditing • Some of the most powerful security tools available for internal security are the assessment, audit, and penetration testing processes. The goals of such measures are to:

- Understand our risks so that we may apply proper security
- Find vulnerabilities before our enemies do

Of course, performing a full risk assessment or hands-on analysis of each workstation would not be a practical solution. As such, an internal audit must balance effectiveness and practicality. I have already covered one such audit process in Chapter 8, *Practical Security Assessments*.

Internal Monitoring • Internal logging and monitoring are ways we can gain insight as to what is going on within a network. Most modern devices and systems include logging capabilities that can be included in an organization-wide monitoring effort. More specifics on monitoring techniques are included in the later section titled *Logging and Monitoring*. Here, I will simply point out important areas for internal network monitoring:

- Logging from servers and devices—Just about every modern operating system in a server or device comes with some form of logging and monitoring option. Normally, such processes affect the performance of the system and so they are turned off by default. It is important to enable logging on servers and devices and have them report to a central console.
- Mobile IDS logging—While it is often impractical to implement a full IDS within all internal networks, it is common to have one or two IDS sensors that can be rotated in the organization. Packaged IDS appliances

and Open Source IDS applications installed on laptops are ideal for this type of work. Each IDS should sit in place for some predefined period of time, commonly a week or so, after which it can be moved to the next undisclosed network until all networks have been covered. Once complete, the cycle starts all over again. (Note: An IDS used for perimeter intrusion detection should be a dedicated device and should not be rotated. This practice is intended for organizations that can deploy an additional internal IDS within the environment.)

- Host-based IDS logging—A great way to enhance internal logging and monitoring is through host-based IDSs. In this scenario, an agent is installed on each critical server and monitors for suspicious activities. Activities are logged to a central logging server, where they must be monitored regularly. This option can, however, be somewhat expensive.

The Concept of Internal Zoning

Network-based zoning practices should not be thought of as belonging to the perimeter only. Creating a chokepoint and isolating devices in their own zone is a great way to enhance security for other critical services, especially those on the internal network. Devices on the internal network are directly exposed to all other systems on the network, which makes it more difficult to maintain network-based security. Organizations that host critical internal services should consider placing such services behind an internal firewall, helping to layer defenses, separate access, and otherwise protect them from internal hackers.

- Internal DMZ network—For large organizations with large investments in critical servers, it may be worthwhile to create chokepoints and install separate firewalls to guard such systems. For smaller organizations unable to implement such measures, a filtering router or some other such device will still add tremendously to the security of these systems.

- Isolating back-end services—For an organization with a critical DB service accessed only by a designated server, it may be possible to isolate this server on a back-end network without using a firewall. If, for example, an Oracle server is feeding a series of customer tracking systems, we may be able to place the Oracle server on a separate network attached to secondary interface cards on the front-end systems. Of course, such practices are not as effective as implementing a separate firewall. They are, however simple and cost-effective solutions for enhancing internal security.

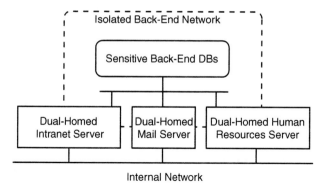

Figure 11.1 Example of internal network zoning.

Rule of Change

Uncoordinated changes within the internal environment often lead to disastrous security issues. With all the potential variables that can lead to vulnerabilities, it is vital that changes be managed in accordance with the Rule of Change. Likewise, it is important to avoid the guinea pig effect and to work with a standard set of applications, tools, and devices.

Rule of Preventative Action

Practicing proactive security in the internal environment requires us to spend time each day researching new security issues. We must prepare ourselves for new worms, viruses, and new types of attacks by keeping up with security news. We must then look back at our own environment and evaluate it for these vulnerabilities and weak links. It is important to stay several steps ahead of hackers by performing vulnerability scans and other checks regularly.

Considering Desktop Management Practices

A great tool for enhancing internal security practices is a desktop management system. Many vendors have developed different types of desktop management products; many include security options that conform to the rules of security. In particular, a desktop management implementation can assist in:

- Rule of Least Privilege—Desktop management platforms often let us lock down workstations so that unauthorized applications cannot be installed.

Many can also lock down certain commands to prevent them from being executed on a desktop.

- Rule of the Three-Fold Process—Many desktop management platforms provide centralized logging for various desktop-related security issues. This can often allow an organization to monitor the security of all desktops from a single location.

- Rule of Preventative Action—Desktop management products often include automated virus and patch updates to help ensure that virus definitions and security patches stay up-to-date on the organization's workstations.

PHYSICAL DEFENSES

Physical defenses are often overlooked in information security practices. Since a physical room is surrounded by four walls, somehow the security of it is not at the forefront of our minds. No one can walk out of the Internet and physically unplug a system, so organizations that are perimeter-focused often never address their physical security vulnerabilities. Physical threats, however, can have the most drastic effect on an organization. Let's take a look at some physical threats and how the rules apply to them:

Casual Damage

One place where I commonly see physical defenses failing is in the causal, everyday damage that occurs in an unsecured physical environment. Tripping over power plugs, dropping devices, overheating components, condensation, and other causal threats cause an incredible amount of damage to organizations every day. I have seen several organizations come to a screeching halt because someone tripped over a power plug, moved the wrong cable, or flipped the wrong breaker.

Physical Attacks

Physical attacks occur when a hacker penetrates physical defenses to attack a server, device, network, or other object. Most physical attacks come from individuals who already have access to the premises, including employees and consultants. The problem with physical attacks is that most security devices fail when a hacker is able to physically access them. Secured routers will often allow administrative privileges by simply interrupting the boot process; servers can often be booted off a removable boot disk to gain access; networks can be accessed by adding or rearranging some of the wires; and, physical objects are subject to theft. With modern components becoming smaller and lighter, physically removing devices from the premises is becoming easier and easier.

A successful physical attack can have immediate and dramatic impacts on an organization. A server that is exploited over the network may take several minutes to bring down; meanwhile, administrators have a chance to discover the attack. A physical attack, however, can immediately affect a device without warning.

Natural Disasters

While events like fires, floods, earthquakes, and the like are more rare, they do have the power to utterly devastate an organization beyond repair. Many companies have been driven out of business when they were caught unprepared in the face of disaster.

Physical Rules

An organization's physical security practices should include each of the eight rules of security. Throughout most of this book, I have addressed the rules in terms of networking and system defenses, though each rule also applies to physical security. It would be a good idea to glance back at the rules and consider each in terms of physical security practices. Here are some of the most important rules and concepts when dealing with physical security defenses:

Rule of Least Privilege

Objects within an organization should be stored in secure areas where the Rule of Least Privilege can be enforced. Access into these areas should only be granted to those who require such access to perform their duties and who are capable of handling such access properly. This includes access to server rooms, wiring closets, utility boxes, and other sensitive areas. Physical security should include some form of access control mechanism such as a key-lock or combination device. The length to which an organization goes to protect an area should relate to the risks of the objects inside (as derived from the risk assessment process). A standard key-lock mechanism will suffice for some areas, whereas magnetic cards or biometrics may be required for others.

Layering Security

Security should start at the entrance to the property and become more and more restrictive as sensitive areas are approached. When applicable, gates and proximity security devices should be installed around the premises, thus creating an external chokepoint. If possible, access into the building should only be granted to those requiring access, for example, employees, customers, and vendors. Access beyond the common area should be limited strictly to employees and those escorted by employees. Finally, access to a server room should be limited to employees with special access privileges. A final layer of defense will often include locking cabinets for protecting groups of servers and devices. An attacker should have to go through several unauthorized areas before gaining access to a sensitive one.

Layering should also be practiced within other forms of defense. Sensitive devices, for example, could be on personal UPSs, even when the entire room in which they reside is on its own alternate power source. When cameras are used, one camera should be watching the hallway or door while a separate camera monitors the internal area.

Rule of Separation

In accordance with the Rule of Separation, objects with different security needs and different physical vulnerabilities should be isolated from others. The simplest example of this is the organization that places the employee copy machine in the same room as sensitive servers and routers. Individuals who enter the room to make copies should not be granted physical access to the sensitive equipment. This also increases general foot traffic and the potential of someone tripping over a wire or causing other forms of casual damage.

When planning or auditing any physical area, be sure to consider the following questions:

- Who are the individuals that will need access to objects within the area?
- What is the highest risk level of the objects within the area?
- Of the people accessing the room, how many need access to the highest risk objects?
- Of the people accessing the room, how many are trusted to be around the highest risk objects?

When we find ourselves in a situation where numerous individuals access a room and have no need to access the higher risk objects within the room, it may be a good indication that some objects should be moved or have their own lockable spaces within the room.

Rule of Preventative Action

It is important for organizations to take a proactive stance when working with physical security. Physical issues tend to occur without warning, and with sudden and merciless results. If we do not install a UPS before a power outage, there is no doubt that our devices will lose power.

- **Put objects in racks**—An object of any importance should be mounted in a rack or some other dedicated container. If objects must be placed on the floor, a table, or a shelf, make sure that the platform is steady, that cables can be properly secured, and that there is adequate ventilation and protection from dust and static. Racks and other containers should be secured to the floor to prevent them from tipping over.
- **Organize and secure cables**—Cables should be organized and labeled. Misplaced cables can have a profound effect on security. During an emergency, a cable may need to be moved, in which case, tracing the cable's end-points will waste precious time or result in the wrong cable being moved. Furthermore, cables should be secured and removed from plain sight. They should preferably be tucked away in the ceiling, under the floor, or alongside a rack to avoid accidental tripping, pulling, or excessive wear and tear.
- **Install fire prevention**—Fires in server rooms are tricky issues since spraying water on electronic components will usually do about as much damage as fire itself. Areas where devices are stored, including server rooms and wiring closets, should incorporate some form of waterless fire protection, preferably incorporated during the original construction of the area. FM-200 extinguishers, for example, should be available in the event of a fire.

Rule of Immediate and Proper Response

Managing proper physical security normally involves a substantial amount of planning. If a fire breaks out, we don't want to be caught running around trying to figure out what to do. Nor do we want to be left wondering who is supposed to respond when the alarm goes off at 2:00 a.m.

Plans for response to physical events need to co-exist with other physical plans, such as evacuation and site recovery. It is important that these plans be made part of a larger incident response plan for the organization. Your organization probably already has a course of action for fires and burglaries; this is the perfect place to add an information security plan. Here are some common plans that should include actions concerning information security response:

- Natural disaster plans such as fire, tornado, earthquake, and flood
- Plans for extended power outages
- Plans for unauthorized access and physical alarm response
- Plans for disaster recovery and relocation

Training Employees

Employees are the greatest allies we can have when physically securing an organization. With proper training, employees are much more likely to witness unauthorized activities than the security staff. It is important that the employees feel confident in their understanding of what is authorized and what is not. The environment should promote the idea of questioning suspicious people and activities. Employees should be inspired to perform such actions, and to not take offense if they themselves are questioned. In general, it is much more difficult to physically infiltrate an area or perform unauthorized physical activities if local employees are properly trained.

DIRECT OBJECT DEFENSES

Having looked into physical, internal, and perimeter defenses, an organization should further layer its security by focusing on individual servers and devices. Since enemies come from everywhere, inside, outside, above, and below, we can never be sure where an attack will originate. This means that we cannot simply rely on the perimeter firewall or a motion alarm system; individual objects within the organization must have their own security applied, thereby layering our security efforts. These security measures may provide for a third line of defense for someone attacking from the Internet, or may even be the first line of defense for someone hacking from an internal network.

Similar to when we looked at perimeter network security, when we look at the security of servers and devices, we must maintain a higher focus. Our security audits have, no doubt, pointed out some specific vulnerabilities within many of our devices, which we must be sure to address. Patching individual vulnerabilities, however, is not the solution to overall security issues. Defending systems and devices is not simply addressing known vulnerabilities, but rather taking all of the rules and applying them to each object within the environment.

Applying the Rules Through Hardening

Vendors have been training us over the years that system security is a process of logging on each morning and having the system automatically install the most recent security fixes. This is a good practice; however, it is still somewhat reactionary since we are taking care of any vulnerability after it is already known to hackers. What if we could deal with a problem before the exploit ever came about? What if we could handle our system security in such a way that most of the next exploits will not affect us?

Dealing with the security of our systems and devices in such a way is possible by applying the concept of layering security and the Rules of Least Privilege, the Three-Fold Process, and Trust. The process of taking a new object and proactively applying these rules and concepts to it is called hardening. Every organization should have a security standard that dictates minimum security practices required for building servers, routers, and other devices. These standard hardening procedures should be applied to objects proactively, meaning before they even touch the network or handle their first transactions. An updated hardening process should be taught to all staff members responsible for installing servers, routers, firewalls, and other critical devices. Systems that have been hardened should be updated with newer hardening practices as they become available.

Rule of Least Privilege

When looking at a server or device, or any services within that server or device, we should be thinking in terms of the Rule of Least Privilege. Though it is not practical to place a firewall in front of every object, it is possible to practice the Rule of Least Privilege within objects themselves.

The problem with security in most operating systems is that they default to being "user-friendly" and, therefore, "unsecure." A Windows 2000 server, for example, will by default provide a NULL share through which other systems on the network can access basic account information. This was implemented to make life easier when applications and administrators needed to access such data. Most people, however, do not require access to this type of information and should not be able to obtain it. There are many similar instances where default features do not conform to the Rule of Least Privilege and manual intervention is required.

The Rule of Least Privilege must also be considered for the services and applications installed on a system or device. Cisco routers, for example, could be running services such as "Small TCP Services." Even though we don't really use this feature, it is simple to enable and can be found running in systems around the world. However, enabling services that have no need to be enabled is in violation of the Rule of Least Privilege. Such services can give away valuable information, or can eventually be vulnerable to a new exploit. Organizations that never enabled such services will not be exposed to their vulnerabilities. The fewer services and applications running on a system, the less vulnerable the system.

The entire hardening process should be based on the Rule of Least Privilege. If there is no need for something to be installed or running, then it should not be installed or running. Even the most simple and harmless of services should be disabled if not required. Such practices greatly reduce the security vulnerabilities and the number of weak links within an organization.

Rule of Change

Objects will undoubtedly change over time. Some organizations add, remove, and modify servers and devices on a daily basis. With each change, however, there is always the chance of reducing the hardening on a system and introducing a new vulnerability. Installing applications, enabling services, even applying patches, could potentially have a negative impact on the security of an object. It is thus important that all changes to systems and devices be fully understood and tested before being implemented. Such changes should also be documented for each system in case a history of changes is ever required.

Rule of the Weakest Link

We have already discussed the weakest link as it applies to objects within the internal network. However, the weakest link also comes into play when considering individual servers and devices. Each object has within it numerous services and applications that can potentially be vulnerable to attack. It is important when considering hardening practices to always be aware of the weakest link. Hardening a system does little good if the hardening process allows for a four-character administrator password. Likewise, disabling 10 services on a UNIX server is of little help when one vulnerable service remains enabled.

Rule of the Three-Fold Process

The hardening process should include the installation or enabling of components that allow the organization to monitor and maintain an object. Servers and routers, for example, should have logging enabled for security-related events. Such logs should be forwarded to a central logging system, where the logs of other similar objects are stored. These logs should be reviewed regularly and critical events should generate notification alerts in real-time.

Systems should also be updated regularly with security fixes to ensure that the security level remains high. There will always be flaws in operating systems, applications, and services that will need to be fixed through vendor patches. Luckily, most vendors isolate security patches from normal patches, allowing us to install them quickly and without too much concern for other changes within the patch.

> Since every patch has the potential of reacting badly, creating a security hole, or causing a failure within the system, many people consider it a good idea to only use patches that relate specifically to the installation in question. For example, if a Telnet patch comes out and Telnet is disabled on a system, then maybe this patch should not be installed.
>
> With security, however, it is a different matter. If a Telnet vulnerability was discovered and our system with Telnet disabled was not patched, we still have vulnerable code inactively sitting on the system. Six months from now, a new administrator may decide to enable Telnet, in which case, he or she will be enabling a vulnerable Telnet service. Imagine also if a hacker is able to gain just enough access to enable the flawed Telnet service so that he/she can further penetrate the system. The Telnet services may also be enabled indirectly when installing a new application or service. If and when Telnet is enabled, we want to make sure it is not a flawed version without the security fix applied. This makes it important to fix all vulnerabilities within an object, or to monitor such activities extremely closely as to not accidentally enable a vulnerable service.

Some Good Hardening Practices

Hardening should be a regular practice for any organization with servers, routers, and other critical devices. There are many good hardening processes published by different security organizations. Hardening processes must remain extremely modular and dynamic to keep up with new techniques and new types of vulnerabilities and exploits. I have included some good resources for finding specific up-to-date hardening information about specific systems and devices in Appendix A, *Tips on Keeping Up-to-Date*. In general, all hardening processes should include the following steps:

- Maintain an active inventory of versions, fixes/service packs, applications, services, etc.
- Download the latest security fixes an organization is comfortable applying, study them, and install them

- Disable all nonessential services and remove all nonessential applications (or if this is a new install, simply don't install them)
- Disable all unnecessary accounts, groups, and access privileges
- Change names (if possible) for commonly known accounts like "Administrator"
- Enable security controls like password filtering, lockout, and aging services
- Enable logging for various security activities and forward logs to a centralized server
- Test security via a vulnerability scanner

OUTBOUND INTERNET ACCESS

The concept of outbound Internet access really relates back to perimeter defenses. However, the protection of such access is so often neglected within the average organization that I felt it warranted its own section in this book. As I mentioned previously, outbound Internet access (when internal employees access the Internet) poses security issues that are often overlooked. There are many inherent dangers in allowing employees to access the Internet that should be taken into consideration when developing Internet security practices.

Applying the Rules of Security to Outbound Internet Access

When allowing employees to access the Internet, some specific rules should be kept in mind. Giving someone Internet access is a powerful action with many potential consequences. By using the following rules, we better manage the security of our Internet users and protect our organization:

Rule of the Three-Fold Process

It is important that any system accessing the Internet be kept up-to-date with the latest security patches. This is especially true for those browsing the Internet with a Web browser. Web browsers are usually full of great features and horrible vulnerabilities. Users that access the Internet must be using properly maintained systems and have had at least some basic Internet security training.

As far as monitoring is concerned, logging outbound Internet access is normally not possible due to the tremendous number of logs that would be generated. It is a good idea to require some form of access authorization before users are allowed to explore the Internet. This way, it will be possible to log systems that attempt to access the Internet without first authenticating. Such logs can point out systems that have back door programs, worms, and other automated applications that attempt to open connections to the Internet without the knowledge or permission of the end-user.

Rule of Least Privilege

Yes, the Rule of Least Privilege even applies to outbound Internet access. Organizations are highly discouraged from allowing all employees to access the Internet freely; such practices make it extremely difficult to enforce outbound access security. I have already discussed issues with attacks riding back on connections initiated from inside an organization and automated applications that establish outbound tunnels. Additionally, the Internet hosts many destructive tools, malicious scripts, viruses, and many sites that attempt to trick employees into giving away valuable information. Given the many dangers in allowing Internet access, the following controls are recommended:

- No employee should have access to the Internet unless required— Allowing an end-user access to the Internet should not be taken lightly. Every individual who is allowed to access the Internet from the internal network adds some level of exposure to the environment. Internet access is a powerful tool, and this should be considered when distributing access accounts. End-users accessing the Internet should also have some degree of training in security awareness.

- Only systems of a non-critical nature should be allowed to access the Internet—By allowing a system to access the Internet, we increase the exposure of that system. As a general rule, critical servers should never be allowed to access the Internet unless required by their function.

- Internet access should be restricted to Web pages with appropriate content—Hacker Web sites provide a variety of tools for the curious employee to download. Such sites oftentimes have malicious coding designed to crash the end-user's system. A content filter is recommended for outbound Internet access and it should be configured to restrict access to hacker Web sites. Though it is impossible to prevent 100% access to such sites, the goal is to limit exposure to the average user.

- Internet access should be monitored—No, this does not mean that we will be up at 5:00 a.m. watching employees check the new Lotto numbers. However, in many situations, it is vital that the organization have the ability to monitor end-user actions on the Internet if ever needed. For an organization to be able to monitor, log, or track employee activities, a policy stating so needs to be signed by each employee.

Outbound Zoning (Proxies)

If we look back to the sample zoning scenarios I provided earlier, we see that there are zoning scenarios designed to address outbound access. Such zones implement a relay system to carry out requests on the end-user's behalf. With Internet access, this usually involves the implementation of a proxy server. Proxy servers are a great way to protect internal systems that need to access external entities like the Internet. Proxies provide protection for the entire session and allow for content filtering, virus scanning, Java script blocking, authentication, access monitoring, and other useful features. Quite often, an organization will implement a packet filtering firewall to stand between the Internet and the internal networks, and it will also implement a basic proxy server that simply forwards requests to the Internet on behalf of the users. This type of solution provides optimal protection when accessing the Internet.

LOGGING AND MONITORING

To maintain the Rule of the Three-Fold Process, logging and monitoring should be implemented in objects all across the environment. This includes objects like servers, routers, and applications, as well as physical areas. Having a firewall go unmonitored is exactly the same as parking a locked car in a dark alley with no one around. Every security device has a weakness, and if an attacker goes unnoticed, the attack will eventually be successful. The unwatched thief will eventually find a way into your car, and the unwatched hacker will eventually find a way into your networks and systems.

What to Log

Earlier we discussed the concept of creating stillness, which should be reviewed for logging purposes. It is extremely important that we log activities that are useful and filter out excessive noise. At the same time, it is important to avoid filtering out so much as to miss a potential attack. Suggestions for how to accomplish this were included in Chapter 5.

Centralizing Logging Efforts

It is nearly impossible to effectively monitor multiple objects if we must continually reference multiple sources for information. A small organization may be able to get away with every system performing its own logging, but for medium and large organizations, it is important to centralize the logs in one or two monitoring devices. By centralizing the logging effort, we will be better able to:

- **Provide a single point of maintenance**—By centralizing our logging efforts we create a single location in which our log maintenance functions are performed. In medium and large environments, checking logs on each individual system is extremely time-intensive, and normally results in systems being skipped and important events being missed. Centralizing log review and administration will be a cost savings for most organizations.

- **Correlate events**—We will rarely find unauthorized activities that affect only one system or device. When good logging practices are followed, hackers will leave a trail of events that will help us to better understand the nature of the attack and the extent of the damage. Centralizing logs from different objects gives us the power to correlate different events and derive a more complete picture. Logs can be grouped by time, similar events, neighboring systems, and in a variety of other ways to track a hacker's steps.

- **Review in real-time**—If we are looking at logs in multiple locations, it will be impossible to monitor all objects at the same time. Thus, while looking at the logs of System X, we cannot see an attack appearing On System Y. Similarly, if an event occurs on both System X and System Y at the same time, we may not be aware of the correlation. Centralizing logs allows us to view events in real-time across the organization.

- **Build archives**—It is important to archive logs for historical records. Archiving logs is very difficult to do if they exist in many different areas. There is a much greater chance that a log will be missed if we must rely on 10 systems backing up their own logs. It will also be hard to retrieve and organize such logs. Centralizing logs allows us to implement consistent and efficient solutions for archiving event information.

- **Provide for disk management**—Log files are notorious for filling up hard drives over long periods of time. If not properly configured, such events can cause a critical system to crash or overwrite important events. By centralizing logging issues, we can remove the local log immediately, thus helping to protect the systems without having to manage individual log files.

There are many methods for centralizing log activity. Most devices are able to send events through SYSLOG, or through an SNMP trap. There are a variety of tools, ranging in price from free to expensive, that will capture logs from different devices, correlate events, and allow for real-time monitoring. Many centralized SYSLOG applications that can retrieve and parse logs from multiple devices are freely available.

There are also numerous commercial products that provide advanced reporting, Web-enabled browsing, and greater control over the presentation of logs. Some of these products specialize in one or two technologies; for example, one may specialize in firewall and IDS devices, while another specializes in operating system events. For large enterprises, purchasing two logging applications usually saves a great deal of time, effort, and cost in keeping track of security events.

Correlating the Logs

When centralizing logging efforts, correlating among different logging devices is crucial. If we receive a log from one device and a completely different log from another device for the same event, we must be able to correlate a relationship between the two. Lucky for us, software developers have been getting better and better about looking at logs from a standard view and correlating logs is not the horrible chore it once was. That being said, there are still crucial areas we must be aware of when centralizing logs.

Classify Similar Levels of Events

Different events are most often given different classifications from different reporting devices. For example, an IDS may report a TCP sweep as a medium-level event, warranting some attention, while it reports a strand of KLENZ as highly important, warranting immediate attention. Such classification systems are designed to provide some consistent method of prioritizing events and to help focus attention on those events that are the most important.

There are two problems with such classifications that we should be aware of as we go forward in the logging and monitoring process:

- The default classification for an event may not correspond to the environment. Something the product reports as "low" may be more critical within the environment, whereas something considered "high" may not be so important.
- Different products have different levels of classification. One product may report a TCP sweep as "high," where another product reports similar activities as "medium" or "low."

It is beneficial to make the centralized logging solution as clear and logical as possible. A high-level event from a firewall should mean the same to the organization as a high-level event from an IDS. A critical event from NT should correspond to a critical event from Solaris. This way, it is much easier to assess threats, filter logs, and search for potential security issues. Many devices permit the administrator to assign a level to each event, and many centralized logging products also provide a virtual representation of events, which allows us to correlate events from different devices.

Synchronizing Time

Running different logging devices off their own internal clock becomes a big issue when dealing with log correlation. Often, it is important to know where an attack started, which device picked it up first, and which events occurred at the same time. Devices that run off their own clock will always get out of sync with each other, causing chaos in the logs. Events occurring right now may appear at the bottom of a report if that device has fallen 30 minutes behind. Similarly, devices on the West Coast may never appear on a screen because they are logged as three hours before East Coast devices.

It is important in log correlation to make sure all logging devices are running off the same clock and in the same time zone (or in a program that compensates for time zone differences). One solution for this is to maintain a Network Time Protocol (NTP) server within the organization. Just about every modern device can synchronize its time with an NTP server, allowing for a consistent view of time across the organization. NTP is normally a low-cost solution that really helps with managing security. NTP services use minimal processing power and come free with many operating systems, networking products, and Open Source packages.

Archiving Logs

It is important to keep a history of logs and to not throw any away. We never think we will use something until an emergency comes along and we need it. When a hacker breaks into a network, he or she may not be discovered for several months, in which case, we will want to have the logs from the last several months on-hand to track activities that occurred since the penetration.

Luckily, logs do not normally take up a great deal of space, especially when compressed. Logs are usually easy to remove from a system and store on a CD or tape backup for future use. Some key points to consider, however, are:

- **Store all logs, even mistakes**—Oftentimes, we are tempted to erase log files, especially when we find that we have been logging more than we need to. However, it is important to maintain all logs if possible. It should be made policy that logs from the centralized system cannot be removed without first reporting, approving, and documenting them.
- **Make archives consistent**—Archives should be consistent with other backups. Log archives should be taken every week, month, or at whatever

interval makes sense. When performing an investigation, logs should be easy to find despite the millions of logs in the archives.

- **Make sure logs are retrievable**—Some log correlation applications require administrators to go through some specific steps before performing an archive. Some applications will not allow for an old log file to be viewed or restored unless it was archived using a specific process.

A NOTE ON THE LEGALITY OF LOG ARCHIVES

Using logs as evidence can be tricky. For some organizations, maintaining logs as legal records is important. In such cases, it is important to maintain the integrity of logs by performing a hash function (like MD5) on each log and storing that value in an encrypted file. Then, all access to the log archives and the encrypted hash needs to be logged to help prove that no one could have tampered with the archives. For a great source on making logs and other electronic evidence legal, see Mandia and Prosise's book, Incident Response.

HANDLING AUTHENTICATION

Authentication is another one of those subjects that easily warrants a book of its own. To enforce the Rule of Least Privilege, we must have some way to uniquely identify subjects that desire access to objects. Authentication is the means by which we determine who a subject is, and authorization is the process of verifying the subject's right to access an object. Authentication and authorization are often the first means, and sometimes the only means by which organizations protect their resources. There are various grades of authentication and many methods of managing an authentication infrastructure. Here, I will cover authentication and authorization as they relate to the rules of security.

Authentication Is Everywhere

Authentication is seen everywhere in information security: at the desktop, through the firewall, in email messages, and even on an employee's ID. Since authentication is so widespread and so closely tied to the Rule of Least Privilege, it should be clear how important good authentication practices are. If authentication practices fail, we lose our ability to enforce the Rule of Least Privilege and will therefore be unable to protect our resources.

Basic Forms of Authentication

There are many forms of authentication, each with its own advantages and disadvantages. Normally, the more protection a form of authentication offers, the most costly and difficult it is to maintain. Since the purpose of authentication is to uniquely identify a person, we must base an authentication process on something unique about that person. This is normally something the person knows, like a password, or something the person has, like a token or unique thumbprint.

Table 11.1 shows some common forms of authentication and considerations for each:

Table 11.1 Common Forms of Authentication

Type of Authentication	Accuracy of Authentication	Manageability of Accounts	Direct Costs to Organization	Acceptance by Users
No authentication	None	None	None	High
Passwords	Very low	Easy–Medium	Very low	Medium
One-time passwords	Medium	Medium	Medium	Low
Tokens and smart cards	High	Medium	High	Medium
Biometric thumb scan	Very high	Difficult	Very high	Medium
Biometric retinal scan	Even higher	Difficult	Very high	Low

Rule of Least Privilege

Authentication is essential to the Rule of Least Privilege. Once we have determined what a user needs to gain access to, we have some way of verifying who the user is. If two people share an account, or someone uses someone else's account through deceptive means, we have lost our ability to enforce the Rule of Least Privilege.

Rule of the Weakest Link

The Rule of the Weakest Link is a common problem when dealing with authentication. A single system can have 100 accounts with strong passwords and one account with a bad password. A hacker is simply going to look for the weakest password, making the total security for the system as bad as the weakest account. Similarly, 100 desktops may require biometric thumbprints to gain access to the domain, while a handful still use passwords; thus, the domain is only as secure as the weakest authentication mechanism.

When dealing with authentication, we must always be searching for the weakest link. Good hackers know that there are always a handful of people and devices that do not follow good password practices and they simple search for such accounts. We can increase security in this area by using proactive security measures:

- Creating good password protection policies
- Enforcing such policies through password filters, aging systems, and other password management controls
- Continually conducting password audits and searching for the weakest passwords

Another good practice is to control sensitive forms of access through higher forms of authentication. For example, a user with administrative privileges is not allowed to reboot a critical server unless he or she has performed a thumbprint authentication. The user can authenticate with a password, which gives him/her some access, but to perform critical functions, a more reliable authentication mechanism is required. This would allow for easier distribution of privileges, but still enforce higher levels of security for critical functions.

Security in Layers

Oftentimes, organizations look to password authentication as the only form of security. We know, however, that basing any practice on a single protective measure is never a good idea. We may, for example, require a user to authenticate to access a particular system. However, since we know this system should never be used from outside the network, we can also check to make sure the user is coming from an internal address. In addition, we know that this system will only be accessed between the hours of 7:00 a.m. and 8:00 p.m., so we tighten the controls even more.

Layering security within authentication is a very good practice. Someone may be able to fake authentication, but by using layering techniques, that person would need to fake it from inside the network during normal business hours as well. This gives the local security team more opportunities to catch the individual and will discourage many hackers.

Secretless Security

As we know, the best security practices are those that do not rely on secrecy to be effective. This is especially true in authentication. Passwords rely on secrecy and are thus one of the worst forms of authentication we can use. Secrets are hard to maintain, continually forgotten, and, oftentimes, given out. Even with training and a great password protection policy, password-based security is extremely unsecure.

Secure forms of authentication are those that are not based on secrets, or that combine secrets with other forms of secretless security. Biometrics and smart cards are prime examples of this form of authentication. Such technologies, however, are still extremely costly, and for the average organization, only practical in situations where high security is required. Common areas that warrant higher forms of authentication security include:

- Remote access via modems or VPNs
- Access to the most critical data centers
- Access to the most critical computers and devices
- Access to the most critical domains and networks

Centralizing Authentication

A helpful suggestion for practicing the rules of security within authentication is to centralize the authentication process as much as possible. The idea behind centralized authentication is to pass a user's credentials off to a centralized system, which returns whether or not the user passed. This pushes the entire process of entering, storing, managing, processing, and removing accounts to the centralized system. By centralizing the authentication process, an organization is better able to control and manage accounts, reducing the number of vulnerabilities and increasing the efficiency of administration. Some common benefits of centralized authentication include the ability to:

- Centrally assign and administer accounts, passwords, and other forms of authentication
- Create a chokepoint and centrally enforce good password protection measures
- Isolate account files and reduce the number of locations where passwords, keys, and other authentication information can be found by hackers
- Centrally audit passwords
- Centrally log account access

There are many methods for centralizing authentication, including several free products. Centralized authentication comes as part of most operating systems, including Windows, Novell, and some forms of UNIX. If multiple Windows systems belong to a domain, for example, the domain controller holds all domain-related account information for the users. With devices such as routers, authentication can be centralized via common protocols such as RADIUS and TACACS. Just about every Cisco device, for example, can pass authentication off to a centralized TACACS+ server. This allows for a single user to have the same login name and password across all routers, dial-up services, and VPNs within the organization.

Single Sign-On Considerations

Expanding on the centralized authentication concept is the idea of single sign-on (SSO). SSO refers to mechanisms that allow users to authenticate with one system, and via internal processes, be automatically authenticated on other systems. This means that the end-user will only need to supply his or her credentials once, and not re-authenticate with every application and device.

SSO solutions can dramatically reduce administrative costs and greatly enhance the end-user experience. SSO technologies are somewhat complex to implement, but more and more products are being made with integrated support. Over the past few years, SSO solutions have been becoming more and more popular.

The Problem with SSO

SSO presents numerous potential security issues for organizations. There are a couple fundamental rules and concepts that can be challenged by some SSO technologies. In particular, the concept of layering security should be considered before adopting any SSO technology.

SSO works to centralize the process of authenticating (and oftentimes authorizing) end-users. When an end-user authenticates to an SSO service, he or she will have automatically authenticated to various devices across the organization via SSO. This means that all authentication security relies on the SSO service. Thus, an individual would only need to fake credentials or obtain access to the SSO service to be authenticated to all devices across the organization. Once an unauthorized session is accepted by the SSO, it will automatically be accepted by other systems that live in complete trust of the SSO service. This greatly reduces the number of security layers we have protecting us.

Properly Handling the Power of Administrator/Root

There are special accounts on most systems that make it difficult to practice the Rule of Least Privilege. In the average system, there is at least one account that has complete and uncontrolled access to read, modify, delete, and execute everything on the system. The existence of such accounts is not in conflict with the Rule of Least Privilege since this level of access is required at times. However, the way in which such accounts are commonly used within organizations does violate the Rule of Least Privilege.

The Inherent Flaw

As we know, it is important to only grant as much access as someone requires and deny anything more. On average, the process of administering a system does not require ultimate and unlimited access. Common administration tasks can be fulfilled without having access to read user files, modify services, or remove critical data. Since, however, there are those rare occasions when a user is locked out of his/her files and the Administrator/Root account is needed to solve this issue, we are presented with the challenge of managing proper administrative privileges. Basically, we have two very large problems: first, the administrators have to be saints; second, the administrators have to be perfect technologists who never make mistakes or accidentally delete things.

The common organization extends far too much trust to their system and device administrators. Organizations screen them, pay them, and then trust that everything will go well. This, however, violates the Rule of Trust and has led to countless disasters for organizations that lose all their data or have everything stolen and sold to their competitors.

The Solution

There is, however, a way to solve these issues while keeping in sync with the Rules of Least Privilege and Trust. It involves special handling procedures for the specially privileged Administrator/Root accounts. We may not be able to fully control what the Administrator/Root accounts have access to, but we can control who has access to the Administrator/Root accounts. The following practices should be followed when dealing with such accounts:

- No superuser account should EVER be used unless absolutely required to perform the task at hand—99% of what the average administrator does can be performed through a power user account, or some account that has access to services, but not sensitive data.
- When a superuser account is required, permission should be granted on a case-by-case basis.
- All activities of the superuser should be logged and reported—These logs should report to a system that is monitored regularly and where the individual does not have the ability to modify or delete data.
- Superuser accounts should be protected by strong authentication security measures—At the very least, a strong password policy should be enforced, but preferably, other mechanisms such as one-time passwords, smart cards, or biometrics should be considered.

A NOTE ON SUPERUSER SERVICES

Services on a system must be granted privileges just like any user. Oftentimes, when we install applications, services grant themselves superuser access. Why? Because vendors know that this will minimize the possibility that their services will be denied some required resource and that we will have to call technical support.

Services running as a superuser are extremely dangerous and should be avoided if at all possible. No one knows what vulnerabilities exist for each service, and when a vulnerability is discovered and exploited, we don't want an attacker to be running around with superuser privileges. Beyond that, who knows what flaws exist in the application and when and where it will choose to erase an entire system. By limiting the privileges of services, we protect ourselves from unexpected or undesirable behaviors.

12 Going Forward

THE FUTURE OF INFORMATION SECURITY

One of the most challenging aspects of security is that it exists in a dimension of time. Security is not the same as it was yesterday, and we can reasonably assume that tomorrow will also be somewhat different. An organization that is extremely safe today can be vulnerable tomorrow, which makes keeping up with security a challenging, yet essential task. Though it is difficult to predict the future, it is possible for us to take a look at modern trends in information security and draw some conclusions as to what tomorrow may hold.

Stopping the Problem at its Source

I previously discussed that the majority of security concerns within the average organization come from vulnerabilities that exist within operating systems, applications, and services. Historically, applications have been written with very poor security, leaving systems vulnerable to attack. This problem has been primarily one of focus. To be competitive, a software development company must focus on what the market wants, which to date has primarily been functionality. The numerous security problems in commercial products such as Microsoft Windows have probably had only a minor impact on the sales of their packages. New products that are extremely secure are put to market all the time, yet we continue to purchase the vulnerable ones. This shows that the world, thus far, has found security issues to be acceptable when compared to products with enhanced features. Products that are less functional and more secure are less attractive than products that are extremely functional and vulnerable. **This attitude, however, is changing.**

Microsoft, for example, notorious for generating buggy code and giant security holes, has begun to take strides by training its staff on producing secure code. Microsoft teams have been working to enhance the security of their products in an attempt to curb the massive tide of vulnerabilities we have seen in recent times. Is this a noble effort? Certainly not. Such companies are simply responding to marketplace demands, and the recent demand happens to focus more on information security. If enhancing the security of a product will result in more sales, then, and only then, will the average software development company make it a top priority.

Lucky for us, the market has begun to focus more and more on security over the past few years, especially since the major exploits in 2000 and 2001 that spurred software development companies into action with their own security efforts. This is a very hopeful sign for those of us in the security industry, and one would hope that it leads to far less vulnerabilities in the future.

Raising the Consciousness

Another great stride in the evolution of information security has been an increased sense of security awareness among the general population. As we have seen, humans have long been big contributors to the vulnerabilities found in most organizations. In recent times, however, people have begun to think, to some degree, about security, and are becoming more aware of their actions. While humans will continue to be a source of security problems for many years to come, we are seeing many good signs that more people are becoming security-focused.

A few years back, security was rarely thought of outside of medium and large companies. Recently, however, it has become evident that security affects everyone, not just banks and corporate giants. With this in mind, the general public has begun to think in terms of security and to protect themselves and their information. Before Jane attaches to the Internet, for example, she activates her personal desktop firewall. A few years ago, Jane would not have even known what a firewall was! This marks a great stride forward in security. After all, **the ultimate evolution of security will come not through technology, but through awareness.**

Technical Developments

The future of security technology is, in my opinion, going to have less of an effect on the average organization than the two topics we just covered. This being said, however, security technologies are continuing to grow stronger, more scalable, and easier to use. A primary focus with new security technologies is to enable the use of security while minimizing the impacts on the environment. Security technology companies understand that, for a security product to be successful, it must be virtually invisible to the end-users. This has led to the development of many technical enhancements that make security somewhat transparent in an organization.

There will, of course, always be stronger encryption algorithms, better enterprise management systems, and a ton of cool toys and gadgets that will compete for space in the security marketplace. Such tools will help to make security much easier and more efficient, allowing us to focus more of our attention on the human security factors. These advancements, however, will have minor impacts compared to the evolution of technical solutions that make security transparent to the end-user.

The Evolution of the Security Mind

To date, security has been a goal unachieved by many organizations. For some, information security appears to be a large, untamable beast that they simply hope will not bite them. As we have seen, though, security is not a monster, but rather a series of interrelated core concepts surrounded by an infinite number of possibilities. By taking our eyes off the infinite possibilities and focusing on the core concepts presented in this book, security becomes a much easier matter to comprehend and deal with. Placing proper focus on daily practices allows organizations to break away from the traditional security nightmares and makes security a natural extension of everyday actions.

When an organization makes decisions using a developed security mind, it separates itself from the struggles and costs commonly associated with information security. In this infinitely dynamic world of IT, practicing such higher principles of security is the only chance we have to defend ourselves against enemies. If organizations continue to embrace new security technologies without developing a higher understanding of security, the enemies will simply be required to develop new and more clever technologies with which to attack us. However, when organizations begin to develop a security mind, they will begin to transcend such common "thrust and parry tactics," and through these efforts, emerge from the war victorious.

Appendix A
Tips on Keeping Up-to-Date

There are two strategies that I recommend for keeping active in the security world and maintaining awareness of new vulnerabilities, exploits, and countermeasures:

- Subscribe to at least two security alert services (free or paid). Such services will normally generate an email when a new threat is discovered. Assign someone to spend 10 minutes a day reading about new issues and determining which ones concern the organization.
- Spend 15 minutes a day reading two security news Web sites, studying those events that could affect the organization.

RESOURCES FOR STAYING INFORMED ABOUT IMPORTANT SECURITY ISSUES

Table A.1 is a list of services to join to receive alerts when new security issues are discovered. Such services can be invaluable for keeping abreast of new vulnerabilities and countermeasures. The URLs in the table are accurate as of the publication of this book.

Table A.1 Security Update Resources

Description	Web Site Address
These are free services for tracking new vulnerabilities, exploits, and countermeasures. Mailings are sent out on a regular basis and as new security issues are discovered.	www.securitytracker.com www.sans.org/sansnews
These are paid subscription services that stay alert to new security issues. These services custom-tailor results to each client. Such services are helpful in maintaining a more accurate and focused view of current security issues.	www.securityfocus.com/corporate/products/vdb www.vigilinx.com/security/vsis.html

RESOURCES FOR FINDING INFORMATION ON NEW VULNERABILITIES, THREATS, AND COUNTERMEASURES

Table A.2 is a list of Web sites to use when looking for information on new and old vulnerabilities and countermeasures. Each site has its own unique spin on security, and each is focused differently. Referencing two or three of these sites daily can be extremely helpful in keeping up-to-date with current security issues.

Table A.2   Security Information, News, and Updates

Description	Web Site Address
These sites are good for researching current threats and exploits, and recommended precautions and countermeasures.	http://www.cert.org/ http://www.incidents.org/ http://www.dshield.org/ http://www.infosecuritymag.com/
This is a searchable online DB of vulnerabilities and exploits. Searches can be performed by name, date, severity, source, and numerous other options.	http://icat.nist.gov
This is a good site for researching statistical information related to information security.	http://www.securitystats.com/
This site has the latest virus and worm-based threats.	http://www.mcafee.com/anti-virus/
This is a good site for free legitimate security tools.	http://www.foundstone.com/knowledge/free_tools.html
These sites are good sources for new vulnerabilities, exploits, and hacker tools.	http://www.insecure.org/index.html http://www.antionline.com/index.php

Table A.2 Security Information, News, and Updates *(Continued)*

Description	Web Site Address
This is a paid subscription service for collaborating and sharing information about vulnerabilities, exploits, and countermeasures.	http://www.wwisac.com
These are good sites for system and device hardening.	http://www.yassp.org/ http://www.sun.com/solutions/blueprints/0100/security.pdf http://bastille-linux.sourceforge.net/ http://www.enteract.com/~robt/Docs/Articles/ip-stack-tuning.html http://www.auscert.org.au/Information/Auscert_info/papers.html http://www.cert.org/security-improvement/index.html http://www.trustedsystems.com/tss_nsa_guide.htm

Appendix B
Ideas for Training

Earlier, I discussed the concept of training end-users in some areas of information security. Security-aware end-users can be some of our greatest allies in the information security war. End-users are always at the frontlines of the fight, and should be given adequate training on how to remain safe and secure.

25-MINUTE BASIC SECURITY AWARENESS CLASS

All users with a networked computer should be required to attend a short seminar on basic security awareness. Table B.1 is an example awareness class that can be easily taught to large and small audiences:

Table B.1   Topics for Basic Security Awarness Class

Recommended Topics to Cover	Estimated Time
Begin by presenting some of the fascinating statistical projections about security: how much damage has been done to the world by hackers, how much organizations are expected to lose, how many hackers are out there, etc. *Here we want to simply get the audience's attention and show how big an issue information security is.*	3 minutes
Discuss how a hacker enters an organization: • Through the Internet connection • Attached modems • Unsecured servers • Unsecured desktops • Installed malicious applications • Walk-in	3 minutes

Here we are looking to apply the security problem to the local facilities and make end-users understand that this is a real threat to the organization.

Table B.1   Topics for Basic Security Awarness Class *(Continued)*

Recommended Topics to Cover	Estimated Time
Discuss how hackers can gain information about an organization: • Through friends employed at the organization • Cold-call and email solicitations • Dumpster-diving • Walking around and looking for written passwords • Probing systems, networks, and sniffing communications	3 minutes
Discuss what hackers can do to an organization: • Take down a system or desktop • Read confidential information and emails • Manipulate information, forge documents, etc.	3 minutes
Discuss how end-users can help in security: • Maintain good password protection • Be sensible about downloading files or receiving attachments or disks • Do not install unauthorized software on a desktop • Remove modems and other external devices • Keep desktop software and operating systems up-to-date • Stay on the lookout for hackers and potential security issues • Question people who sit down at a local computer or who are found wandering through the building unescorted • When in doubt, ask the local security team/expert	10 minutes
Discuss how an end-user should handle an incident: • Give the reporting chain and contact list detailing who to call during a suspected incident • Explain the need for silence until the matter is investigated	3 minutes

30-MINUTE INTERNET SECURITY FOR END–USERS CLASS

It is also a good idea to provide a class on the proper use of the Internet for employees who have Internet access. I have worked in many organizations that have adopted an excellent policy that states: "Any employee needing Internet access must attend an Internet security class (see Table B.2) before such access will be permitted." Having this requirement provides two essential advantages:

- It weeds out many individuals who do not seriously need Internet access.
- It ensures that all Internet users have some knowledge of Internet security practices.

Table B.2   Topics for Internet Security for End-Users Class

Recommended Topics to Cover	Estimated Time
Begin by presenting some fascinating statistical projections about Internet security. Wow them with how incredibly unsecure the Internet really is, and how many hackers are out there waiting for an opportunity to strike. *Here we want to simply get the audience's attention and show how big an issue Internet security is.*	3 minutes
Discuss some of the dangers of the Internet and what a hacker can do: <ul><li>Malicious Web-based scripts</li><li>Unencrypted communications and email</li><li>Malicious downloads, viruses, back doors, Trojan horses</li><li>Browser attacks and reply worms such as NIMDA</li></ul> *Here we are want the end-users to understand how much responsibility they have for the security of the organization. They should understand that their desktops could very well be the weak link that allows a hacker in.*	6 minutes
Discuss good security practices that end-users can follow: <ul><li>Never trust anything or anyone on the Internet</li><li>Never send confidential company information across the Internet or through external email</li><li>Never download or execute Internet-based files</li><li>Never install file-sharing applications or any other unauthorized software</li><li>Never choose to "trust" a Web site unless absolutely sure it is legitimate</li><li>Never share an Internet account with others</li><li>Never access the Internet from an unauthorized system</li><li>When in doubt, ask the local security team/expert</li></ul>	15 minutes

Table B.2 Topics for Internet Security for End-Users Class *(Continued)*

Recommended Topics to Cover	Estimated Time
Review how an end-user should handle an incident: • Give the reporting chain and contact list, including who to call during a suspected incident • Explain the need for silence until the matter is investigated • Explain that all actions across the Internet will be monitored by the organization	3 minutes
End by having each user take a copy of the "Internet Usage Policy." Each user should sign the policy before being granted Internet access.	3 minutes

Appendix C
Additional Recommended Audit Practices

RECOMMENDED DESKTOP/WORKSTATION AUDITING TASKS

Performing desktop audits is an important part of the Rule of the Three-Fold Process. Desktops are simply extensions of servers and networks, and if desktops are vulnerable, so is everything else. When auditing desktops, the goal is to make sure adequate security controls are installed and maintained, and to ensure that end-user desktop policies are being practiced.

In a large environment, it is often impractical to perform a desktop audit of every workstation. A good sampling would be to look at 5–10% of the systems, making sure to get samples from different areas. In smaller environments with around 50 workstations, this number should be increased to around 20%. And in an environment with 20 or less workstations, it is recommended that every workstation be audited.

Here are some common things to look for during a desktop audit:

- Is there antivirus software, are its signatures up-to-date, and is it updated regularly?
- Is there an active modem or other form of external access attached to the system?
- Does the workstation require a login at start-up? Do its passwords comply with local password policies?
- If idle for several minutes, does the workstation lock itself or initiate a password-protected screensaver?
- Does the desktop contain any sensitive or confidential information that should be stored on a secured server?
- Does the desktop have any hacker tools or unauthorized applications installed?

- Is the desktop physically secure? How easy would it be to walk out of the building with it?
- Are there any obvious physical flaws, such as passwords written on the monitor?
- Does a vulnerability scan yield show any vulnerabilities or malicious software?

RECOMMENDED PERIMETER AUDITING TASKS

Perimeter auditing should include the entire perimeter, not simply the organization's Internet connection. Earlier, we defined the perimeter as locations where non-trusted parties have access to internal resources. Common perimeter points include:

- Internet connections, including dial-up
- Active modems for inbound or outbound communications
- Partner, vendor, and customer network connections
- Wireless access points
- VPN access points

The following is a list of recommended tasks for auditing the perimeter:

- **Understand what can be seen from the outside world**—Perform a network scan on the entire address range assigned to your Internet connection. You should not simply scan the addresses you know about, but the entire possible range of addresses assigned to the organization. Here you want to find all the systems that are visible from the outside. During this process, check security devices to see if they are properly reporting your intrusion attempts.
- **Find your direct vulnerabilities**—Perform a vulnerability scan on all externally accessible devices; this includes routers, servers, switches, etc. Scans should not only test the vulnerabilities of systems, but also the effectiveness of monitoring devices in noticing the scans. This should consist of two scans:
    - Scan all devices from within the local network with no firewalls or other security devices between the scanner and the devices.
    - Scan the same devices from the outside network (Internet, dial-up, etc.) with security controls in place between the scanner and the devices.

- **Perform a hands-on audit of all external devices**—During this audit process, make sure systems are properly hardened; check logging, policy settings, password protection, disabled accounts, etc.
- **Audit security device settings**—Log into all perimeter security devices and verify settings and controls.
  - Firewalls—Check each rule and search for any rules that are out-of-date, misconfigured, or not following the Rule of Least Privilege. Make sure the application and operating system are patched with the latest security fixes and that logs are properly administered. Attempt to access systems through the firewall and observe the organization's response.
  - IDS—Check signatures to make sure they are up-to-date and that proper events are being monitored. Simulate attacks to make sure the IDS is properly configured for the network and is reporting properly. Observe the organization's response to the attack simulation (be sure to have permission before taking such action).
- **Check for multiple security layers**—Make sure that external routers enforce some degree of filtering and logging, that the firewall and other security devices are hardened, and that externally accessible devices are properly secured and events are being logged.
- **Perform extended entry point searching**—If possible, download or purchase a war-dialer to call all numbers local to your organization. Some of these tools will simply search for attached modems, while other more advanced products will attempt to further exploit systems that answer.

RECOMMENDED INTERNAL AUDITING TASKS

Internal audits can often leave an organization wondering where to start and where to end. Large internal environments can be quite intimidating at first. That is not to say, however, that internal audits have to be overly complex or crippling to the budget. The main goal of an internal audit should not be to simply find vulnerabilities, but to find the sources of vulnerabilities and take actions to stop them. This usually means internal auditors will spend a good deal of time reviewing internal security policies and auditing how well they are enforced. Here are some good audit tasks to include:

- **Make sure you know what is out there**—Perform a basic network scan of all address ranges used by the environment. Keep an eye out for any unknown servers and routers as well as any suspicious systems, such as unknown laptops or desktops running numerous services. In addition, talk to people in different areas, look at inventory reports, and perform physical searches for unknown systems and devices.

- **Perform a risk assessment process**—We already covered a good assessment process in Chapter 8, *Practical Security Assessments.* This or another risk assessment process should be performed on all internal servers, routers, rooms, and network connection links.

- **Search for technical vulnerabilities**—Perform an internal network-based vulnerability scan against all systems and devices. Be sure to choose the correct policies and to make this a coordinated effort to avoid any unexpected outages or issues.

- **Check if departments and users are conforming to desktop and application policies**—Perform a desktop sampling audit as discussed earlier in this appendix.

RECOMMENDED PHYSICAL AUDITING TASKS

Physical audits are usually the easiest, but the most neglected of the auditing tasks. Here are a couple of essential physical audit tasks every organization should perform:

- **Power conditioning**—One of the most common causes for failure in critical systems is inadequate power conditioning. Policies should dictate that objects of a high enough risk level be attached to an uninterruptible power supply (UPS). All other devices should, at a minimum, be attached to a surge suppressor. Organizations that place numerous critical objects in a single room should also consider purchasing a full-room UPS. Also be sure to look at details like whether or not someone would be alerted if a UPS failed, or if the batteries are large enough to last until a local generator kicks.

- **Environmental conditions**—Another common cause for failure in critical devices is poor environmental conditions such as heat and humidity. Auditors should check to ensure that rooms holding equipment have the proper environment conditioning.

- **Physical access controls**—Auditors should consider the Rule of Least Privilege for physical access. Rooms should have adequate controls to keep unauthorized individuals out. Within the room, critical devices should be locked in cabinets along with access to their power cords and network connections. The level of access control should reflect the highest risk object within the room. A room that stores a non-critical

FTP server may not even need a lock, whereas a room storing cancer research data should require a thumbprint for access.

- **Emergency response equipment**—Electronic-safe fire extinguishers should be located within and near major computer rooms. Fire and intrusion alarms should be in place and tested regularly. Emergency plans for physical issues should be in an easy-to-find location within the room and in a backup location.

- **Monitoring**—The degree to which a room is monitored should reflect the most sensitive object within the room. Auditors should note personnel, guards, and cameras in the area. It is also important to consider how items like door sensors and cameras are monitored by security and how long records and recordings are kept.

- **Cabling and Mounting**—Poor cabling can cause numerous issues with system and device availability. Cables that are unorganized and unlabeled can drastically increase the time required to respond to an event or recover from a disaster. Auditors should check the condition of cables in all areas that hold equipment. In addition, important equipment should be securely mounted in a rack or shelf.

RECOMMENDED CONTROLS FOR RISK CONTROL POLICIES

When auditing an object using the Relational Security Assessment Model, there are many different types of controls that can be checked. Policies should be developed that dictate minimums level of controls for objects of certain risk levels. Table C.1 includes some common controls that should be audited:

Table C.1   *Example Risk Controls Sorted by Object Type*

All Objects	
Local authentication	To gain direct access to the object, what level of authentication is required?
Remote authentication	To gain remote access to the object, what level of authentication is required?
Level of logging	To what degree are the subject's actions logged?
Level of monitoring	To what degree are such logs monitored?

Table C.1   Example Risk Controls Sorted by Object Type *(Continued)*

Internal redundancy	What level of redundancy exists internal to the object (such as a RAID configuration)?
External redundancy	Are there other objects that are fully redundant to this object?
Backup/Recovery control	If the object was destroyed, how much could be recovered and how quickly?
Routers and Other Network Devices	
Level of hardening	To what degree have hardening tasks been performed? Have services been disabled, patches applied, accounts locked down?
Degree of maintenance	How often is this object audited and updated for new vulnerabilities?
Servers	
Antivirus software installed	Is antivirus software installed and running?
Antivirus software updated	Is the antivirus software updated regularly and automatically?
Level of hardening	To what degree have hardening tasks been performed? Have services been disabled, patches applied, accounts locked down?
Degree of maintenance	How often is this object audited and updated for new vulnerabilities?
Physical Areas	
Room construction	Is the room secure enough to store equipment of this risk level?
Degree of disaster prevention	Are there adequate fire controls and other safety precautions?
Environmental conditions	Is the environmental conditioning adequate for a room of this risk level?

Appendix D
Recommended Reading

There are a wide variety of information security books on the market. Many of these books cover a specific technology in information security, while others address enterprise security, general vulnerabilities, and general countermeasures. Most of these books cover the same type of information through different styles of presentation. The following are humble notes on some books that I believe to be extremely useful to information security professionals. Each covers key concepts that, in my opinion, every security professional should understand.

Incident Response, by Kevin Mandia and Chris Prosise

This is a great guide for creating and maintaining good incident response practices. It is extremely thorough and practical for medium and large organizations. This book is about 50% technical.

Secrets and Lies, by Bruce Schneier

This book provides a great explanation of security and its impacts on the business world. It is focused mostly on concepts and historical facts surrounding the world of information security. This book is not technical and could be read by anyone.

Practical UNIX and Internet Security, by Simson Garfinkel and Gene Spafford

This is a great security book focused on networking and system-based security practices. It covers both security theory and hands on implementation for UNIX and the Internet. This book is about 75% technical.

Appendix E
The Hidden Statistics of Information Security

There are many statistical reports concerning information security in the modern world. Most books end with the ever-changing guess that *x* number of systems were hacked and *y* number of dollars were lost as a result. Such information can be extremely useful, but only if seen in the proper perspective. A great source for this type of information can be found at: *www.securitystats.com/*

Rather than giving some statistical samples that will quickly become outdated, it is the goal of this appendix to convey in some small degree how little we, the general public, the government, and even the author, actually know about the real statistics of information security. The goal here is not to instill any amount of fear or doubt, but rather to inform the reader so we may move forward with an awareness of some important facts.

LOOKING UP THE CRIME RATE

When moving an office to a new town, one of the first things on our task list should be to look up the demographic crime statistics for the area. We may not feel comfortable parking the new corporate Lexus in front of the office if 50% of cars in that area get broken into. So, we look up the statistics, discover that the crime rate is quite low, and decide to go ahead and move in.

Now, let's consider our location in the world of networks. If we were to judge the Internet, our extranets, and other networks via the same standards we use to judge a neighborhood's crime rating, people would be much more cautious about taking up residence in cyberspace. Attaching a server to some local ISPs could be compared with building a bank in the worst slum of the most crime-ridden city imaginable.

Sadly, when we are shopping for new rental space on the Internet, we are not provided with the same luxury and convenience of knowing the statistical dangers as we would if we were buying a new home. There is no such thing as a simple, straight-to-the-point document that we can wave in front of the chief executive officer (CEO) as we beg for funding to buy a lock for the front door. Of course, we can't go a day without seeing something related to how Organization X was broken into, but then we hear so few people talking about their own real-world security problems that the whole issue seems overrated. Thus, we have little to no real knowledge of the crime rate in the area.

THE HIDDEN STATISTICS

Sadly, no one knows what the crime rate really is. The best estimates and guesses are based off incomplete data. Every report tells us that the dollar value lost from crimes committed through network and system hacking is horrendous. So, do networks and systems really present such incredible threats to business, or is it simply an overreaction? If there is one thing years of consulting has taught me it's that people do not believe in crime when they cannot see it. Statistical reports have little effect on most executives when they don't see their partners and competitors having security issues. And what is so hard to see? Why do we hear so many statistics about how horrible the electronic crime rate is, and yet hear so few stories from our partners and competitors? Let's walk through an example:

Exploring the "Shhhhh" Statistic

Let's say we are roused at 2:00 a.m. (yes, it always happens at 2:00 a.m.) by a call from the night-shift support desk saying that the main accounting system has been running slowly and sporadically for the past hour. We arrive and conduct an investigation, only to find that someone from a country whose name we can't even pronounce has managed to find his or her way into the system and is currently downloading all customer financial information.

Quickly, we disconnect the system and put up the good, old "Under Construction" page while we phone the CEO and thumb through our Incident Response Plan for the local FBI office. After a brief and interesting discussion with the CEO, our policy book is slowly closed and returned to its dusty shelf, and we find ourselves spending the night alone with the system, performing our own investigation and pretending like nothing happened. In the morning, we get reminded of that wonderful confidentiality paper we signed as a requirement for our employment and are politely asked to not mention this incident to anyone ever again.

More often than not, when a client brings me in for an investigation, the story never leaves the room. Oh, the fascinating stories that will never be told of highly respected organizations experiencing multiple breaches in a day and exposing extremely sensitive data, sometimes openly, to the public! But, the "Shhhhh" mechanism is very powerful, and indeed very necessary. Can we really blame the executive who could easily face his or her own termination or the loss of his/her company if such information made the press?

The world is in a competitive race to become cyber-enabled and to build the most effective e-commerce presence. No organization can afford to have its customers, partners, or investors second-guess the safety of its services and data. Just as we would not expect a customer to buy a new Porsche in a dark alley in the middle of the Bronx, we would certainly not expect a customer to leave a credit card, financial, or medical information with an organization that just announced its third security breach of the year.

In general, the only cyber crimes that get reported are those that have an externally noticeable effect, such as the defacing of a public Web page, the spreading of a worm, or those with such minor impacts that knowledge of the breach would be of little interest. Most often, an organization will only report a breach if:

1. It is an obvious breach that has been seen by the public and covering it up or denying it would cause more bad press than the breach itself.

2. It is to the organization's advantage to announce the breach; for instance, as an excuse for not meeting a deadline, or to distract the media from other events.

3. There is a direct legal obligation to inform customers of the breach. (Even in this situation, many breaches are not reported.)

These three factors apply only to a very small percentage of the security breaches that occur around the world. In light of "good business practices," the millions of security incidents including break-ins, theft, and data manipulation that occur daily go unreported and will continue to go unreported for the foreseeable future. Thus, it is important to remember a very important point: Everything WE would keep secret in our own organization, everyone else would keep secret in THEIR organizations. It does not mean there is no problem; it simply means that we aren't talking about it and it is harder to assess.

Recognizing the "Uh?" Statistic

There is another very important statistic that greatly weakens our security knowledge. I like to call this the "Uh?" statistic. So now it is 3:00 a.m., and our ever-so-vigilant night-shift administrator calls to let us know the system is acting funny again and things are really slow. He wants to reboot the system. He does so and everything returns to normal. When it happens again over the next few nights, the vendor is called and some patches are applied. After a few more incidents, everyone is at a loss, and the system is finally rebuilt from scratch with a new operating system, new patches, and a new copy of the application.

The incidents presented above probably cost the company a few thousand dollars, eight hours of work, and a few hundred upset customers. But it is nice when everything is working again. We just wish we knew what the issue was, if nothing else, to be assured that it will not happen again.

What we never discovered here was that an old login was compromised on this system and seven of its eight processors were being used as a game server for some college student and his/her friends (no laughing matter, this happens all too often). Now, having rebuilt the server, we have no idea it was due to anything but a system failure.

The fact is that intrusions are often difficult to detect. Sadly, many break-ins never get reported because companies never realize they were even compromised before all evidence is destroyed. Many technical issues are not actual issues with systems themselves, rather with the teenager who has used publicly available tools to hide his/her presence in a server. It is quite common to inadvertently destroy all evidence of a breach before anyone even has a chance to discover that an attack happened, thus further obscuring the world's perception of the scope of information security problems.

A CLOSING THOUGHT ON STATISTICS

Again, it was not the intent of this section to invalidate the great benefits of statistical research in information security. Rather it is intended to help the reader view such information with an accurate perception. If anything, information security is a bigger problem than statistics would lead some to believe, and it is important to know this while contemplating security within your own organization.

Index

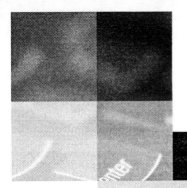